# The Politics of
# Deception:
## TARGET AMERICA

*Karen!
God Bless you!
& your family!
God Bless America!*

### CAPT. JOHN PULSINELLI, USN (RET)

ISBN 978-1-0980-5384-0 (paperback)
ISBN 978-1-0980-5385-7 (hardcover)
ISBN 978-1-0980-5386-4 (digital)

Christian Faith Publishing, Inc.
832 Park Avenue
Meadville, PA 16335
www.christianfaithpublishing.com

Printed in the United States of America

To the memory of my good friends and colleagues Brian J. Kelley (the wrong man) and Richard "Dick" Christian (the magician) and to all my African-American and Hispanic brethren who have been victims of political deception and the slavery of the welfare state for decades and all who fight for the culture of life over the culture of death.

*Finally, be strong in the Lord and power of his might; put on the full armor of God, so that ye may stand against the wiles of the devil and against spiritual wickedness and the rulers of darkness of this world.*
—Ephesians 6:10–12

# CONTENTS

# INTRODUCTION

It's important for those who might pick up and peruse this book to have some appreciation for what has compelled me to write it and to establish my bona fides in addressing the subject of deception and its pervasiveness in both our domestic and international political environments. I am a career intelligence officer with forty-six years' experience as an analyst and intelligence operations specialist. During my career, I have served with the Office of Naval Intelligence (ONI), the Defense Intelligence Agency (DIA), and the Central Intelligence Agency (CIA). My last thirteen years postretirement (March 2003 to April 2016) was spent as an intelligence educator with the CIA teaching and training our officers and those from throughout the intelligence community (IC) in the fundamentals of denial and deception (D&D) and deception planning and analysis. I also taught courses in targeting and warning systems and analysis.

I have been deeply concerned and am more convinced now than ever that the current state of our domestic and international environments, both hostile and polarizing, is not the result of happenstance, but the result of decades of deception, corruption, calculated influence peddling, and espionage to support the infiltration and subversion of our government, educational, and religious institutions. It has only become more apparent since the 2016 presidential election that it has also involved the infiltration and subversion of formerly steadfast federal law enforcement and intelligence agencies, namely, the Federal Bureau of Investigation (FBI), Department of Justice (DOJ), and CIA. The radical Left and so-called Progressives with their militant secularist and socialist ideology and agenda have been and are being aided and abetted by elements of our own and foreign intelligence services. I am convinced that our nation, culture, and society are in peril and currently engaged in a dangerous "uncivil" and "unholy" divisive war. It's not a war of words, or just differences in opinion, but a war between starkly different political ideologies and visions of America's future fueled from within and outside our sovereign national boundaries by the Bolsheviks and Alinsky disciples and revolutionaries of the Left, and elitist career politicians and kleptocrats that threaten the very fabric and future of our great nation and republic.

Leading, aiding, and abetting the ideological battles and war are the establishment career politicians on both sides of the aisle in our Congress, militant secularist bureaucrats, and Progressives in our educational and religious institutions who have nothing but contempt for the American electorate and America and the faith and values upon which this nation was built. The radical Liberals and their domestic and international allies—demons of demagoguery and deception—have seized control of our Congress and are attempting to hijack not only the presidency and our democratic electoral process but also America and her heart and soul, wealth, and freedom. It is a template for revolutionary causes historically in Russia, China, Cuba, and other socialist and communist *failed states* where the radical Left and establishment elites had nothing but contempt for the people and replaced all democratic processes with totalitarian dictatorships. Like him or not, God-fearing President Trump like President Reagan and the American people, the American electorate who chose him in 2016 as the president of this democratic republic, are the only things that stood then and stand now between you, your children, and grandchildren and a life of freedom and prosperity as opposed to a life of economic and social dependence on government programs designed to make and keep you as slaves to the radical elements of the Democratic Party, which they have attempted to achieve since our Civil War and reconstruction.

The demons of demagoguery and deception have seized control of the House of Representatives and are intent on hijacking the presidency and our democratic electoral processes to establish their own version of an authoritarian and "egalitarian" dictatorship for themselves and all elitist bourgeois establishment career politicians. They are all accomplished liars and hypocrites, and deception and deceit is their mantra. We are now at a tipping point politically, socially, and culturally, where every battle, won or lost, by these competing ideologies will determine not only who will win the presidency in 2020 but also whose vision of the future of America will prevail.

"Eternal God whose Mercy is endless and treasury of compassion inexhaustible, look kindly upon us and increase your mercy in us so that in difficult moments, we might not despair nor become despondent but with great confidence we place ourselves in your holy will, which is love and mercy itself" (the Apostle of Divine Mercy, Saint Maria Faustina Kowalska, 1905–1938). Amen.

# CHAPTER I
# An Uncivil War

*So stand fast with your loins girded in truth, clothed with
righteousness as a breastplate, and your feet shod in readiness
with the gospel of peace. In all circumstances, hold faith as a
shield to quench all the flaming arrows of the evil one.
And take the helmet of salvation and the sword
of the spirit, which is the word of God.*
—Ephesians 6:13–16

The battle lines have already been clearly drawn. On the left is the
ideology of the new Democratic "Socialist" Party, which is pushing
its radical left-wing agenda of progressive secularism and now openly
embraces the wiles of socialism and communism. On the right is
the conservative ideology of the Republican Party, the Grand Old
Party (GOP), which is attempting—though lacking the fervor of the
radical Left—to preserve and maintain traditional Judeo-Christian
values and the fundamental principles set forth in our Constitution
and Bill of Rights by our Founding Fathers of limited government,
individualism, and a free market economy.

What Conservatives fail to grasp is that the radical Left *really
does hate them,* they hate America, and they hate our president and
everyone and everything that stands between them and their vision
of what *they* want America to look like. There is no compromise
on their part and no room for negotiations in their minds in the
battles being fought now or those that lie ahead unless it comes on
their terms, and for true Conservatives, that amounts to surrender.

We need to recognize and accept this and wake up to the fact that these left-wing radicals are not interested in reforming the system, but only in destroying it to build their own vision of their kingdom of heaven on earth, which is in itself an illusion, a fantasy, a socialistic nightmare. We can say they're delusional, ignorant, unrealistic, and dismissive but they are not going away. To their disadvantage, Conservatives naively consider these battles and the war against America a metaphor when applied to the politics of the day, while for the radical Left, these battles, the war, and the revolution they support are real. This is why the radical Left is always out to destroy their opponents by demonizing them as racists, sexists, or homophobes and openly engaging in malice, deceit, and hypocrisy, whatever it might take to achieve their objectives. Deception for them is a weapon in a war and revolution to eliminate the enemy and undermine and ultimately dismantle the values, structures, and institutions that sustain our society as it is today. It is also why they pretend to be what they are not, rarely say what they mean, and constantly portray their opponents as the enemies of society, when in fact they are the enemy and hell-bent on destroying America as we know it. The sham kangaroo court impeachment hearings conducted by Speaker Pelosi and the radical left-wing Democrats in the House along with their Bolshevik partisans are shocking examples of their malevolent intentions and reminiscent of the kinds of show trials Stalin and his Bolshevik thugs carried out in the Soviet Union to purge all potential opposition following the Russian Revolution in 1917. Pelosi and her arrogant democratic colleagues' behavior at the president's State of the Union Address on February 4, 2020, was despicable and precisely what you would expect from a bunch of arrogant self-serving contemptable career politicians and losers who didn't get their way in 2016 and know they will lose big in 2020.

Events leading up to the presidential election of 2016 and those since have revealed in a dramatic way that the Alinsky-inspired revolutionaries have already established beachheads in just about every element of our society. Hundreds of Alinsky-inspired and Obama administration-supported community organizations are operating across America. The fact is that they have been actively engaged in subverting American institutions in the shadows for decades and are now more actively and boldly engaged in plain sight with the support of domestic and foreign intelligence services, globalists, and their political vanguard—Alinsky disciples Hillary Clinton and Barack Obama.

Mass immigration and diversity identity politics have been tools of the global elitists, radical Left, and Democratic Party for decades to fragment American society and replace traditional American values and our constitutional republic with a godless socialist kleptocracy. Deception has been the radical Left's most important weapon since the end of the 1960s. Race-baiters and antagonists like Al Sharpton and Jeremiah Wright pose as civil rights activists; anti-American radicals and domestic terrorists like Bill Ayers are portrayed by the left-wing media as patriotic progressives; and Socialists and Communists who have infiltrated every element of our society pose as Liberals and progressive social activists.

Unfortunately, a hallmark of their success is that many Conservatives have bought into their ploy and deception over the years and continue to naively refer to them as Liberals and Progressives when they are in fact corrupt, self-serving radicals and revolutionaries more interested in enriching themselves and serving their special interests than serving the people and common good. Then there are also some republican rhinos inside and outside Congress—career politicians who are apparently more concerned about their own self-interest and lust for power than they are about defending America and their president. They have demonstrated cowardice, indifference, and in some cases even openly support this all-out assault on America.

Actually, the new Democratic Socialist Party appears to be a loose coalition of Communists, anarchists, nihilists, atheists, militant secularists, and social justice advocates that Saul Alinsky himself laid the foundation through his experiences as a community organizer in the 1940s and carried it into the 1950s and 1960s. Alinsky was considered by many a practical theorist for Progressives who had supported the communist cause and had to regroup following the collapse of the Soviet Union; he was a Marxist and considered by some the Lenin of the post-Communist Left. Alinsky also pioneered the alliance of radicals with the Democratic Party ending two decades of confrontation climaxing in the radical Left's riots at the Democratic National Convention in Chicago in 1968.

Violence, defying the rule of law, rioting, killing cops, and bombing military facilities have always been part of the radical Left's legacy and modus operandi. The militant groups of the 1960s and 1970s were led by left-wing ultraliberal domestic terrorists, the likes of Tom Hayden, Abbie Hoffman, Jerry Rubin, Bill Ayers, and Bernardine Dohrn, and the domestic terrorist group the Weather Underground.

Ayers, a friend and confidant of Barack Obama, before and during Obama's years as a community organizer and entry into politics as a state senator in Illinois, was leader and cofounder of the Weather Underground, a self-described communist revolutionary group and self-proclaimed guerrilla organization. It was the radical left-wing militant faction of the countercultural group Students for a Democratic Society (SDS), created in the 1960s to promote social change by any means. The Weather Underground's manifesto, *Prairie Fire*, issued in 1974, was certainly in line with Alinsky's Rules for Revolution, providing some insight into why former president Obama and the radical Left continue their relentless attacks and subversive tactics to undermine President Trump and the institutions and values we hold so dear. The manifesto states, "Our intention is to form an underground, a clandestine political organization engaged in every form of struggle, protected from the eyes and weapons of the state, a base against repression, to accumulate lessons, experience and constant practice, a base from which to attack."

By 1975, the Weather Underground had claimed credit for twenty-five bombings including the US Capitol, the Pentagon, the California Attorney General's Office, the State Department, a New York City police station, and Gulf Oil headquarters in Pittsburgh. By the mid-1980s, the Weather Underground was essentially history. As we all know, history repeats itself. In this case, is it purely a coincidence, or have we been witnessing and are we now confronting

THE POLITICS OF DECEPTION: TARGET AMERICA

a genuine resurgence of the radical Left—a revolution in political affairs, domestically, and internationally?

In the 1960s, 1970s, and 1980s, they were hunted down by the FBI and law enforcement agencies as guerrillas and domestic terrorists. They are now at their apex, operating in plain sight, literally being exposed on a near daily basis in the Halls of Congress, the media, the IC, and government bureaucracy, with a political vanguard of two former presidents Clinton and Obama and an Alinsky disciple, Hillary Clinton, still operating in the darkness of despair and a shadow government along with a desperate group of compliant self-serving bourgeois career politicians in Congress and bureaucrats entrenched in the DOJ, FBI, the IC, and foreign intelligence services along with their globalist allies to make their final all-out assault to destroy the America that they hate and replace it with their democratic socialist utopia.

We have suffered through some very horrific and challenging periods of conflict with our Civil War, world wars (Korea and Vietnam), rampant political corruption, racial tensions, and even domestic and international terrorist attacks on our homeland. However, somehow with the grace of God, we drew heavily on the moral and ethical values that we have held so dear as a people and "one nation under God" and not only survived but also worked together and set aside even some of the most deep-seated political differences, rebuilt, recovered, and bounced back with a great sense of hope and enthusiasm for the future.

"For I am convinced that neither death, nor life, nor angels, nor principalities, nor present things, nor future things nor powers, nor height, nor depth, nor any other creature will be able to separate us from the love of God in Christ Jesus our Lord" (Romans 8:38–39).

The lack of civility and the hateful, vicious daily attacks on our duly elected president and those who support him or dare to hold or express conservative views or oppose or disagree with our more radical liberal brethren suggest that there is something more sinister and demonic about the intensity and purpose of these attacks. I am convinced by the nature and scope of the attacks and their near hysterical attempts to unseat the president that we are witnessing and

15

confronting more than an attempted coup by way of impeachment or by other means. As a true outsider to the cesspool of Washington politics and his populist and determined America and America first agenda, President Trump simply poses the most visible and immediate threat, not only to the radical Left's socialist agenda but also to all those corrupt career politicians and bureaucrats who have always put their own aggrandizement first ahead of the common good.

As such, Donald J. Trump as presidential candidate and president-elect has proved to be their worst nightmare and greatest obstacle to achieving their malevolent goals. While their groundless effort to hijack the presidency has been an all-consuming mind-numbing objective, I believe we are witnessing a well-organized and orchestrated attempt at achieving something much more grandiose. In Barack Obama's own words prior to his election in 2008, "We are five days from fundamentally transforming the United States of America." He and his radical left-wing and so-called progressive supporters in Congress and his administration came within one election cycle of achieving it. The evidence is overwhelming. President Trump is simply in the way and a major obstacle to achieving their real objective to hijack the heart, soul, and wealth of America.

When Barack Obama became president, he appointed Alinsky disciple Van Jones, a self-described Communist, as his green czar to jump-start the militant environmentalist movement. Van Jones had served a prison sentence for his participation in the 1992 race riots in Los Angeles, was an activist in the Maoist organization "Standing Together to Organize a Revolutionary Movement" (STORM), and later joined the Center for American Progress, run by none other than John Podesta, former White House chief of staff in the Clinton administration and cochair of Obama's transition team. It was then and remains an Alinsky-inspired revolution in domestic and international affairs by both radical domestic and international forces who have demonstrated flagrantly more aggressive and at times irrational behavior in efforts to undermine our president, our national sovereignty, our cultural values, and our social norms and institutions to capture the wealth and soul of America for their own benefit under the guise of equality.

As president, Barack Obama and his cronies successfully fulfilled a critical stage of the revolution by following Alinsky's model, cautioning his disciples not to confront their adversaries initially as an opposing army, but to join it and undermine it as a fifth column from within, which is exactly what he did during his eight years in office. Equality is nothing more than a slogan of the radical Left. Make no mistake about it, all the rancor has nothing to do with equality, but everything to do with the minority left-wing political establishment's grandiose plan to secure the power and resources of this great nation for their own selfish interests and those of their international allies and benefactors.

The blueprint of the plan comes right out of Saul Alinsky's Rules for Revolution, later changed to "Rules for Radicals," and follows his strategy of deception that he devised to "promote social change." Obama's cronies and Alinsky-like disciples have now infiltrated and corrupted key government agencies, Congress, our education and religious institutions, and even elements within the DOJ, FBI, and IC. Our individual freedoms and rights are under attack by the demons and demagogues of the new Democratic Socialist Party. While the Democrats and Liberal Left have appeared satisfied for some time with beating everyone over the head with their mantra of political correctness, they are now resorting to intimidation, mob rule, and violence against all who dare to oppose them, much like the Bolsheviks of the Democratic Socialist Party who led the 1917 revolution in Russia. Let's not forget that party became the Communist Party of the Soviet Union.

A critical stepping-stone for the success of this plan was the election of Barack Hussein Obama as president "to fundamentally change America." Eight years in office and he almost succeeded by doubling the national debt with next to zero economic growth, cutting military spending while conducting a purge of all senior military officers who dared to disagree with his policies, promoting the highest unemployment rates since the Great Depression, doubling and tripling the number of Americans on food stamps and welfare, and attempting to nationalize the health-care system. He accomplished all this while traveling the globe and apologizing for

American exceptionalism and past sins, thus weakening America's power and influence on the world stage and did so while cozying up to America's enemies and some of the most notorious third-world dictators. The plan was working exceptionally well, with the mainstream media embellishing and applauding his every action and the Russian intelligence services working behind the scenes to ensure his success. Unfortunately, the plan could only be fully realized with a third term for Obama or yet another presidential victory for the radical left wing of the Democratic Party and the coronation of Alinsky disciple Hillary Rodham Clinton.

Such a grandiose plan obviously requires a good cover story, a key element of a good deception strategy, something that will draw the audience's attention to the bouncing ball while the conjurer performs his magic in plain sight and succeeds in fooling everyone—well, almost everyone. Donald J. Trump, his Swampbusters, and the sixty-three million Americans who voted for him had a grandiose plan of their own, to "Make America Great Again" (MAGA), attempt to reverse the negative impact that President Obama and his radical left-wing agenda had on attempting to "fundamentally transform the United States of America," and give America back to the people. To date, President Trump has been successful beyond all expectations, despite the obstructionist policies of the Democrats, who have accomplished absolutely nothing positive. In fact, President Trump has been so successful that he is literally driving the Democrats and their leaders in Congress—Pelosi, Schumer, Schiff, the rabid media, and their hapless supporters—to a level of distraction unprecedented in modern American politics. Their reaction and behavior are not only irrational but also more recently exhibiting signs of mental instability, and behavior by some congressional Democrats certainly worthy of censure and bordering on maleficence.

There's reason for the insanity. Trump's economy is the best in fifty years—best labor market since 1969, GDP consistently higher than 3 percent, wages and income for all Americans at an all-time high, stock market at all-time highs, employment for all Americans including blacks and Hispanics at an all-time high, unemployment for minorities the lowest in decades, and nearly eight million fewer Americans on food stamps.

Unfortunately, the Chinese-originated coronavirus (COVID-19), manufactured in their biological warfare facility in Wuhan (Biosafety Level 4/BSL-4 laboratory), was likely released while experimenting with this and other dangerous pathogens on animals from local marketplaces where it first manifested itself. Xi and his Chinese Communist Party (CCP) comrades wouldn't hesitate to sacrifice a few thousand Chinese citizens, or care about collateral damage in the rest of the world if able to target the US, trigger panic on Wall Street, undermine our economy, and influence the 2020 presidential elections in support of the left-wing Democrats. I certainly would not rule out the possibility that the complex-DNA coronavirus was also selectively dispersed in places like New York City for maximum impact on our financial markets as part of a well-planned Ministry of State Security (MSS)—Chinese intelligence service—covert influence operation. Not only does it provide President Xi with a face-saving opportunity to retaliate as he publicly threatened to do in response to last year's tariff hikes, but also gives him, the CCP and MSS the ability to maintain plausible deniability.

An ingenious but diabolical way to employ a dangerous pathogen as a bio-warfare agent against the US accompanied by a well-orchestrated deception plan. That plan simply used the highly contagious nature of the complex-DNA coronavirus itself as a cover story for its employment as a biological warfare agent, knowing that the virus would also spread elsewhere, providing cover to further obscure the real target of the virus, the United States. Xi and the CCP withheld and suppressed information for months about the virus, its nature and severity, from local citizenry and the rest of the world. They used a compliant World Health Organization to slow the declaration of a pandemic until March 11 and serve as its own propaganda tool by quickly praising Chinese Maoist-style containment efforts in Wuhan as a model for the world. CCP controlled state-media propagandists, quickly followed with accusations that the virus originated with American athletes at the world military games in Wuhan to further shield Xi and the CCP from any criticism at home. They also used the rabid Trump-hating mainstream media in the US as a receptive host and conduit to propagate the lies and blame America, its military, and the president for the pandemic, which it did without hesitation.

Who, but a conspiracy theorist, could propose such a scenario? Liberals and race baiters might also ask, Who, but a conspiracy theorist or an Islamophobe, would ever propose a preposterous and "racist" scenario, suggesting that nineteen Muslims—Islamic extremists—would hijack four commercial airlines loaded with fuel and innocent civilians to carry out terrorist attacks on the US homeland? The 9/11 commission report stated that "the most important failure [of policy and intelligence] was one of imagination… The policy [and intelligence] challenges at that time were both linked to this failure of imagination." It's easy and more comfortable to accept things at face value and much more difficult "to think out of the box," considering the unconventional and trust-your-gut instincts based on years of intelligence experience and training, while also always being mindful of the potential for deception. Like the Russians, the Chinese are masters of deception, which has always been an integral element of their doctrine and strategy and is practiced in all their military, political, diplomatic, and economic relations.

Remember, the economic boom was built on President Trump's policies on fair trade, renegotiating lopsided trade agreements with China and others, streamlining cumbersome government regulations on small businesses, and lowering corporate and individual taxes on all Americans. The president and Republican-controlled House and Senate, at the time, accomplished much of this by way of hard-fought negotiations and passage of the Tax Cuts and Jobs Act of 2017 against all-out Democrat opposition. Like President Reagan, President Trump's policies reinvigorated American morale, reinvigorated the U.S. economy, reemphasized individual freedom, restored a strong military, and put the needs of Americans and America first reducing reliance on government. President Trump knows and understands that in the words of President Reagan, "Government is not the solution to our problems; it is the problem" (First inaugural address—January 20, 1981). "Government's first duty is to protect the people, not run their lives," speaking at the national conference on building and construction trades (AFL-CIO) on March 30, 1981—the day of the attempted assassination of the president. These policies ran counter to everything Obama and the Democrats were trying to achieve—a permanent welfare class, forever in debt to the Democrats, more intrusive government, and dumbing down America—and apologizing to both our enemies and allies for American exceptionalism. Schumer had been there since 1983 and Pelosi since her coronation in 1987, succeeding Philip and wife Sala Burton who won reelection just before her death and had designated Pelosi as her successor. Schumer and Pelosi were both there during President Reagan's second term, attempting to obstruct and undermine his "America first" policies and reportedly were involved in some effort to impeach in the 100th Congress with the Democrats controlling both House and Senate majorities. As such, they are certainly both candidates as poster "octogenarians" for term limits and censure or expulsion for their purely partisan response to the pandemic.

COVID-19 offered yet another opportunity for the Democrats and Wall Street financiers and media moguls, who have more interests in China than America—like multi-billionaire Bloomberg and globalists like Soros—to manipulate the markets for their own benefit and politicize the pandemic to promote the agenda of the radical left. From Pelosi's, Schumer's, and their Democrat lieutenants' perspective in Congress, it's just another crisis to make the most of politically to press their militant socialist and secularist agenda with zero concern for its victims, following the script from the Obama administration to "let no 'good' crisis go to waste," politically or otherwise.

Pelosi wasted little time attempting to stuff the historic two-trillion-dollar-emergency-stimulus legislation for all Americans with billions for her special interests "holding up" the bill in Congress for several weeks. While she dithered and fiddled with her very sick partisan approach to the crisis, businesses, churches, and schools were closed and tens of thousands of American lives were on the line, with the numbers of deaths and those temporarily forced to leave their jobs, rising exponentially. Something she and her Democrat socialist colleagues could only dream about before COVID-19. Even during the peak of the pandemic, she was stirring her witch's caldron of deceit with her toad, Adam Schiff, to launch another investigation; this time, to attempt to discredit the president and his administration's handling of the COVID-19 crisis, while the president, vice president, and everyone else are still working tirelessly, attempting to mitigate its impact. Such an investigation in the midst of the pandemic is premature and would only be a hindrance and distraction to all concerned. This kind of blatant partisan-political chicanery and behavior is reprehensible. She and Schiff are both worthy of censure for such irresponsible and unscrupulous behavior during a declared national emergency with so many sufferings.

I'm sure she and her puppeteers in Mr. Obama's shadow government are celebrating and urging her on. Just imagine, the militant secularists and socialists have succeeded in taking God out of our schools, out of government institutions, including Congress, and have managed through the courts to subordinate our religious rights and moral values to many of their secularists dictates. Now the "Wuhan BSL-4 laboratory-produced virus" released on the world closed our churches during the most sacred time of the year for all Christians and the militant secularists, Satan and non-believers are no doubt rejoicing. Yet, they are engaged in the most ignorant and profane form of self-deception if they think that this temporary physical barrier will ever separate the good shepherd from His sheep.

> If God is for us, who can stand against us? Since he did not spare even his own Son but gave him up for us all, won't He also give us everything else?... Who then will condemn us? No one—for Christ Jesus died for us and was raised to life for us. (Romans 8: 31–33)

> Can anything ever separate us from Christ's love? Does it mean he no longer loves us if we have trouble or calamity, or are persecuted, or hungry, or destitute or in danger, or threatened with death?... No, despite all these things, overwhelm-

ing victory is ours through Christ, who loves us."
(Romans 8: 35–37)

You can also count on Pelosi and the Democrats to always be out front playing the blame game, while never accepting responsibility for their dithering. They are more culpable and guilty than anyone else for the dramatic impact of the pandemic on Americans and America because of their "do nothing obstructionist" tactics and pure politics response to the pandemic. Their fixation and overindulgence on their phony impeachment hearings are just one case in point. Most of the mainstream media outlets were also beating that drum every day and were the first to eagerly jump on the Chinese Communist propaganda bandwagon that inevitably followed the virus' spread, blaming America for the pandemic. This was the case even when it was clear to everyone, except the fake news media and the congressional Democrat polluters, that Chinese President Xi and the Chinese Communist Party (CCP) were responsible for unleashing this dangerous virus on America and the rest of the world.

Actually, Pelosi, Schumer, Schiff, and the Democrats have conveniently and eagerly exploited the crisis in such a blatant manner that it gives one pause and reason to believe that there must be some degree of collusion between the Democrats, DNC, its billionaire supporters, media moguls, and the Chinese to undermine our economy, our democratic electoral process, and our president—purely for political advantage leading up to the Presidential election.

Chinese President Xi Jinping is publicly on record for threatening retaliation for last year's tariff increases, and his calculated decision to prevent leading US manufacturers from exporting their medical safety and protective gear from China to the US clearly reflected his hostile intentions. There is also some evidence reflected in Chinese scientific studies and papers written about the coronavirus in early 2019 that suggest Xi already had a treatment regimen—other than Maoist-style imposed social isolation—identified for the virus before releasing it on the rest of the world. Early high-dosed intravenous Vitamin C injections, for example, were already being used successfully as a protocol in China for treatment of acute respiratory distress syndrome (ARDS) and prevention of viral replication with its benefits being suppressed by President Xi and the WHO. WHO reportedly went out of its way to convince Google, Facebook, and other media giants to suppress this and the results of some Chinese clinical studies as "wrong information." There were also reports that a National Institutes of Health (NIH) grant of nearly four million dollars to study the coronavirus was initiated by the Obama administration in 2015 with part of it going to China's Wuhan BSL-4 laboratory responsible for the release of the virus. You can be sure that the Vitamin C regimen and others like it that may have been identified during research supported by the US grant were not likely to be acknowledged or shared without significant concessions from President Xi's and the CCP's victims, especially the US. If true, these revelations would only further support my analysis that the release of the virus may have been part of a well-planned and orchestrated deception and covert active measures operation.

In the midst of all the turmoil, the Obama's and Clinton's have been strangely quiet, but have no doubt been fully engaged behind the scenes in orchestrating much of the Democrats' sham impeachment proceedings and disgraceful response to the pandemic, while trying to maintain the appearance of being aloof and disengaged. I'm sure it will not be the case as we draw closer to the Democrat Convention in August, where there are bound to be some real surprises for all concerned. Maybe an open or contested convention contrived by the Obama's, Clinton's, and the DNC. Let's not forget that the Democrat Party also has its superdelegates, who are free to support any candidate for their presidential nomination. Bernie was "burned" in 2016, and despite the lukewarm endorsements from Obama and Clinton Biden may still feel the burn in 2020.

Meanwhile, despite Chinese suppression of information about the virus, the sham impeachment proceedings, which only "ended" on February 6, with a Senate acquittal and all the dithering in Congress by Pelosi and colleagues, President Trump took decisive action and declared a public health emergency over the coronavirus on January 31, closed the borders to travelers from China and put American travelers under quarantine. Only when the president declared a state of national emergency on March 11, and the president's ban was extended to travelers from Europe, did the Secretary General of the World Health Organization finally declare the coronavirus (COVID-19) a pandemic. Not only did they further disgrace themselves, along with the fake news media for criticizing and scorning the president and foreign leaders for the travel bans, accusing them of being xenophobic, but they continued to obstruct and fiddle with the historic two-trillion-dollar-emergency-relief bill, which was finally approved by the Senate on March 26. The audacity of the power-hungry Democrats has been despicable and only underscores that Pelosi and the Democrats in Congress are in this for themselves and their special interests, and to hell with the Constitution and the rest of America or the common good. Nothing would make them happier than to achieve Obama's goal of remaking America into a Third World single-party socialist state, with them and their revolutionary Alinsky disciples and vanguard in charge.

Just prior to the Chinese unleashing the coronavirus on the world, Forbes had stated recently that for the first time in a generation, manufacturing jobs are returning to America, nearly three hundred thousand in 2018; taxes have been lowered for corporations and middle-class Americans; new trade agreements, competitive tariffs, elimination of red tape, and streamlining of regulatory policies have all made America much more competitive in the world marketplace and a recent approval rating for the president of 53 percent! All of these were accomplished in his first three years in office, not only without any democratic support but also in the face of unyielding democratic opposition, left-wing subversion, and negative, rabid anti-Trump media propaganda. The CNN-manufactured poll results in October 2019 stating that the "majority of Americans" wanted the president impeached are not only left-wing propaganda but also blatantly subversive and treasonous. If there was any legal recourse to prosecute the media for treasonous propaganda and propagating lies and fake news, CNN and MSNBC would be at the top of the list of polluters. This has been the case during the pandemic as well. There were political cartoons shortly after President Trump's election victory that pointed out that if Trump cured cancer, the Democrats and media would accuse him of putting all those research scientists, doctors, and health-care providers out of business. I would add that if President Trump walked on water, the Democrats and media would accuse him of not knowing how to swim.

Even now, three years after losing the election in 2016, with their irrationality at a fever pitch, they engaged in yet another desperate attempt at deception and misdirection with the assistance of politically motivated allies in CIA and the left-wing media to unseat the president under the guise of an obviously manufactured whistleblower-inspired impeachment inquiry. I can't imagine why the current leadership in the IC, FBI, and DOJ or republican leadership in Congress don't take these radical Trump haters to task. Nor do I understand how anyone could be so naive or gullible to take any of these purely politically motivated ploys seriously. In this case, even the DOJ evaluated and rejected the legal merits of the complaint, and the IC Inspector General (ICIG) acknowledged that there were indications of an "arguable political bias" on the part of the complainant and followed by evidence of a direct relationship with the former Obama administration.

This whistleblower strategy is so obviously bogus that I'm not sure how anyone could take it seriously, let alone our new DNI Joseph Maguire or our ICIG Atkinson, who had previously judged that it had no merit. Yet the whistleblower's complaint based on erroneous third- and fourth-hand accounts of the president's private telephone conversation with a foreign leader became the basis of the House impeachment inquiry and yet another democratic-sponsored conspiracy. How could anyone other than the Democrats and anti-Trumpers treat this hearsay and politically motivated innuendo as credible? It was even more suspicious that the complaint also directly referred to the DOJ's investigation into the true origins of Russiagate, which was sidelined by the impeachment inquiry that clearly directed attention away from any involvement by the Obama administration or Joe Biden in Russiagate. Let's not forget the involvement of former CIA director Brennan, DNI Clapper, and the FBI and DOJ anti-Trumpers who perjured themselves by lying to the Foreign Intelligence Surveillance (FISA) court to obtain a warrant under false pretenses to spy on a presidential candidate and then falsely accused candidate and president-elect Trump of colluding with the Russians. Remember the quote first attributed to Winston Churchill, "Never let a good crisis go to waste." It was also used by Rahm Emanuel, Mr. Obama's chief of staff (2009–2010), and the Democrats have almost perfected its orchestration as a form of deception. So while they target President Trump and the Republicans for all kinds of manufactured misdeeds, they successfully cover their own real corruption with media support to obscure the truth and show the fake with their propaganda, misdirection, and fake news.

In this case, using the impeachment inquiry agenda and media hype, they managed to keep hidden the true source of Russiagate and buried Joe Biden's quid pro quo in 2016, to have the Ukrainian prosecutor Shokin fired while investigating a case against the Ukrainian energy company Burisma who was paying then vice president Biden's son fifty thousand a month to sit on its board of directors. Mr. Biden was guilty by his own admission by bragging about threatening the Ukrainian president in 2016 to withhold a billion dollars in loan guarantees for Ukraine resulting in Shokin's dismissal. As Obama's Ukraine point man, Joe Biden, would also have been involved in the Obama administration providing $53 million—in taxpayer dollars—to support Ukraine's growing energy industry, as well as $1.28 billion in aid provided to Ukraine between 2014 to 2016, according to the US Agency for International Development. As Obama's administrative interlocutor with Ukraine, Biden should have been and should be held accountable for how the money was used. Peter Schweitzer's book, *Profiles in Corruption*, documents how Biden's family and friends cashed in on his deals with China, Iraq, Kazakhstan, and Latin America. So his questionable dealings with Ukraine and his $1.5 billion deal with Chinese President Xi and the State Bank of China, private equity firm deal, with son, Hunter, while Vice President should come as no surprise. I wonder what Joe and the Obama administration promised Xi for that sweetheart deal. As such, Mr. Biden should have been the subject of an investigation into bribery, extortion, and abuse of the authority of the Office of the Vice President. Once again, like a conjurer, direct the audience's attention away from the real source of corruption on the part of the Biden and Obama administration and project it onto President Trump by manufacturing yet another crisis with some anti-Trump whistleblower alleging President Trump's involvement in the same kind of quid pro quo that Mr. Biden was guilty of himself. As bizarre as it is, even a little unsophisticated, well-placed, and well-orchestrated misdirection and projection can fool "all of the people some of the time, and some of the people all of the time." Most individuals believe what they want to believe and therefore hear and see only what they want to and tune out everything else. Even the most responsible and rational people are sometimes unable to see through the deception and obvious hypocrisy and double standards.

I have a theory of my own, based on my analysis of the facts and some circumstantial evidence. From a strategic perspective, I believe that it's quite possible that the Obama White House and witting support from Trump haters in the DOJ, FBI, and CIA were directly engaged with the Russians and Ukrainians in the Russiagate active measures and deception campaign to undermine both the Trump campaign and rig the 2016 election in favor of Hillary Clinton. VP Joe Biden may well have been used as a point man with the Ukrainians and/or Russians in manufacturing the Steele dossier to support their allegations of Russian interference in the 2016 election and Trump campaign collusion. Vice President Biden's close relationship with the Ukrainians resulting from his role as the Obama White House's policy lead for Ukraine-US policy gave him the access and made him the ideal source and conduit for such a deception campaign. He had legitimate cover as Obama's policy point man, and it gave Mr. Obama and the Clinton the six degrees of separation and plausible deniability they needed. While it all backfired on them, they did succeed in having a media and congressional circus come to town along with the Mueller investigation that dragged on in plain sight while publicly attempting to discredit and undermine the president during the first three years of President Trump's administration. All this ended up with the groundless and totally partisan House impeachment inquiry and hearings and Senate acquittal of the president.

Don't think for one minute that Hillary, Bill, and Obama are satisfied because there are many more battles ahead as the historical record and trail of dead bodies clearly indicate. Remember, impeachment was never the end they are seeking, only a means to that end. Don't be surprised if you see Hillary come out from the dark recesses of the shadow government to run again or join forces with Biden or yet some "mystery" candidate as I believe she might do—whatever it takes to get back in the White House given her uncontrollable and insatiable lust for power.

One commentator recently joked that if Bloomberg and I add Biden or whomever gets the nomination and gets her as his VP candidate, he better have a taste tester. That would not only apply to the trail of dead body thesis but also say as much about his lack of character and intelligence.

In regard to Russiagate, let's not forget that in March 2018, the US House Permanent Select Committee on Intelligence (HPSCI) produced a 150-page report before Mueller presented his independent special counsel report stating, "We have found no evidence of collusion, coordination or conspiracy between the Trump campaign and the Russians." What's more important is that the HPSCI and its ranking member Devin Nunes also announced, "We now know that there was no official intelligence used to start the counterintelligence investigation," of candidate and president-elect Trump. So I believe that the collusion and conspiracy was an Obama- and Clinton-inspired ruse, with the support of John Brennan and the CIA, DNI, Clapper, and the merry gang of Trump haters in the FBI and DOJ with their Russian and Ukrainian intelligence operatives and Bolshevik allies.

As such, when you connect all the dots, this all makes the bogus whistleblower complaint and Pelosi's preemptive impeachment inquiry a classic case of misdirection to draw attention away from Biden's abuse of power and acts of bribery and extortion in dealing with the Ukrainians and lay the groundwork to discredit the findings of the US DOJ investigation into the origins of Russiagate by dramatically fixing all eyes and ears on the bogus impeachment inquiry against the president, based on the fake, manufactured whistleblower accusations by yet another CIA, White House, or DOS leaker and Trump hater.

This nonsense and drama have all the trappings of the bogus Russiagate investigation in the absence of any real official intelligence. It was also based on invented intelligence based on the phony Democratic Party-funded dossier, obtained from "Russian sources" to launch the illegal spying and active measures campaign by CIA and FBI Trump haters against presidential candidate Trump and President Trump with the aid of the Russians and probably the Ukrainian intelligence services.

I'd also argue that the lies and innuendo used by Feinstein and her culture of death comrades during the Senate confirmation hearings to derail the confirmation of justice to the Supreme Court and prolife Catholic Judge Brett Kavanaugh fit the same modus operandi. Neither of these Democratic Party-inspired show trials and hateful displays of political deceit had anything to do with seeking the truth, but everything to do with the subversion of our president and character assassination and demonization of Judge Kavanaugh. Heads should have rolled and indictments for this treachery should have been handed out to every one of those false witnesses.

The Mueller and congressional investigations of Russiagate both involved testimony by the IC, FBI, and DOJ Clinton supporters and in the latter case democratic-funded and coached feminists and prochoice activists, all of whom perjured themselves in testimony before Congress and the American people, the latter at the direction of Feinstein and the Democrats. Perjury is a felony and carries a possible prison sentence of up to five years and fines. So where is the accountability or the justice or equality under the law and the prison sentences? By the way, someone needs to investigate Senator Feinstein and several other establishment-career politicians about their knowledge of the coronavirus and its severity. According to Senate records and financial disclosures, Feinstein, a California Democrat, sold $500,001 to $1 million worth of stock in a company called Allogene Therapeutics on Jan. 31, less than a month before panic about the virus caused markets to plunge, while her husband sold another $1,000,001 to $5 million worth of Allogene shares on Feb. 18. Several other career politicians from both sides of the aisle were also involved in major sell offs of stocks in companies that tanked as a direct result of the market plunge. Seems like some had "insider information," both about the severity of the virus and its likely impact on the market, and didn't want to share it.

Let's see if Pelosi and Schiff bother to address this issue in their partisan investigation about warnings about the coronavirus and America's readiness and ability to address it, and the fact that Pelosi, herself, ignored the president's and HHS's declaration of a public health emergency and sent her own constituents into Chinatown to celebrate Chinese New Year. Fat chance!

"Those who are capable of tyranny are capable of perjury to sustain it" (Lysander Spooner, 1808–1887).

"Lies and secrets, Tessa, they are like a cancer in the Soul. They eat away what is good and leave only Destruction behind" (Cassandra Clare, *Clockwork Prince: The Internal Devices #2*).

Ukrainian President Zelensky has flatly denied that any pressure or quid pro quo was involved in his conversation with President Trump. But that didn't keep the left-wing media or paid for hire whistleblower from erroneously portraying and inventing it as part of the president's conversation with President Zelensky. Nor did it keep the Speaker of the House, Pelosi, who is clearly suffering from "anti-Trump derangement syndrome," from announcing a formal impeachment inquiry even before she read the transcript of the telephone conversation that President Trump released to the public. This is all just another example of how Alinsky disciples Obama and Clinton and their purveyors of subversion and treachery operate with their radical domestic establishment allies and agenda, international globalists and socialist benefactors and supporters, and foreign intelligence services. They all have long preferred a weaker United States of America—economically, militarily, and culturally—and will stop at nothing to subvert the power and authority of our president, our Constitution, and our sovereignty and rule of law. The Democrats have proven that they are masters of demagoguery, deception, and the big lie.

There is also a very demonic and perverse pathology associated with the unbridled hate and deliberate attempts by the Democrats to sew division and discord in all of their vain attempts to subvert a president who has accomplished so much for America and Americans and truly has the people's and nation's best interests at heart. All of their energy, everything they say and do, is negative, destructive, and obstructionist in nature. You don't have to be a psychologist or intelligence analyst to recognize that all the Democrat's manufactured crises are little more than desperate attempts to redirect attention away from their own subversive attempts to tear down and destroy America while covering up the scandals and corruption of sixteen years of Clinton and Obama who used their administrations to enrich themselves, first by selling America to the Chinese under Clinton and then to the Russians, a gang of third-world tinhorn dictators, and globalists like Soros under Obama. They are trying to relive the past by rejecting the realities of the present to include the fact that they lost the 2016 election despite their big fix and are creating their own illusion of a bizarre future world, where they are the political vanguard and bourgeois-entitled minority but everyone else is equally poor and enslaved in the ultimate egalitarian socialist welfare state.

If you've listened at all to the democratic presidential candidate debates, my description is not all that far afield. Democrats and left-wing bleeding-heart Liberals all have one thing in common—they have utter contempt and disdain for the American people and electorate, our Constitution, and electoral process. Behavior by House Speaker Pelosi, who tore up the President's State of the Union Address for all to witness, and statements made by Representative Jerrod Nadler, New York Democrat and House Judiciary Committee Chairman, that "we (the Democrats) cannot rely on an election to solve the 'Trump problem'" are both examples of their arrogance of power and utter contempt for the American electorate. They also reflect their desperate intentions to hijack our presidency, undermine the electoral process, and once again attempt to steal the 2020 elections as they did unsuccessfully in 2016. They actually believe that they know what is best for all of America and that they would prefer a one-party authoritarian Democratic Socialist Party dictatorship to our democratic republic and constitutional democracy.

Mark my words, they are Bolsheviks and elitists who consider the American electorate a bunch of deplorables and only they as the political elite are deserving and capable of leading and deciding what is best for us, our families, and America within their godless society of the future. Obama's agenda epitomized that of a third-world dictator and had his America on the path to third-world status, politically, socially, economically, and militarily.

Democratic presidential candidate Joe Biden will guarantee an arrangement with the Ukrainians and Russians to finish the job by undermining Trump again in 2020 to ensure a democratic victory with him as the nominee and son Hunter as his running mate. Liz Warren will be his Secretary of Commerce to exterminate all monopolists and capitalists like all good Marxists would do. Cory Booker will be his attorney general and confiscate all guns from law-abiding American citizens, take away our right to self-defense, and hand the guns over to criminal and alien drug lords in another fast and furious operation (which by the way, Obama's attorney general Holder was found in contempt of Congress for failing to provide any details of the operation). Bernie Sanders, the self-proclaimed Communist, will be his Secretary of the Treasury and will eliminate all billionaires, triple all Americans' tax burden to pay for free stuff for the millennials, and provide free health care, welfare, education, and recreation for fifteen to twenty million illegal migrants to expand the voting base of the Democratic Socialist Party. Many of them and their loyal comrades will take up positions in the new elitist dictatorship to tear down the border wall, open our borders, abolish ICE, and restrict air travel and red meat consumption by killing off livestock, like cows who give off too much methane gas. These geniuses wonder why their party is over, and all of this is coming back to roost in the laps of the Democratic Party leadership.

The presidential election of 2016 was a gift from God but has only given us a short respite from the wiles of the radical Left—perhaps a bit of divine intervention if you believe in such things as I do. In any case, there is no time to rest, as the presidential election of 2020 may well determine what America will look like for our children, grandchildren, and all future generations. The Democrats are already scheming to steal that election as they recently attempted in 2016 and 2018 and their candidates more radical than ever. The Republicans are holding fast to tradition. Now the gulf between the two and differences in their platforms and agendas are starker than ever. The ideological battle lines between Republican and Democrat have already been drawn. And the choices from my perspective as a Catholic, father, grandfather, and patriot are crystal clear—good versus evil, right versus wrong, light versus darkness, the culture of life versus the culture of death, individualism versus collectivism, jobs versus welfare, God and family first versus godless and me too first, spirit of Christ versus spirit of the antichrist, American exceptionalism versus American mediocrity, rule of law versus lawlessness, less government versus more intrusive government, capitalism versus socialism/communism, and liberty versus tyranny.

Indeed, we are at the moment of critical mass. The radical Left will stop at nothing and will more aggressively pursue its revolution to destroy America and the values and institutions we hold so dear using every means of subversion and deception possible with the aid of the media and Russian intelligence services to achieve its socialist/communist goals. The SVR, formerly the KGB First Chief Directorate, responsible for intelligence and espionage activities outside the Russian Federation, and its military affairs espionage counterpart the GRU are reported to have more agents operating within its primary target, the United States, now than at the height of the Cold War. The very idea that the KGB was disbanded in December 1991 was itself disinformation and fake news. President Yeltsin simply reorganized the KGB and separated the Federal Security Service responsible for internal security and the First Chief Directorate, now the SVR, which is as vigorous in its foreign operations as ever. You can be sure that former KGB foreign intelligence officer Russian president Vladimir Putin and his former KGB/SVR and Communist Party comrades, not to mention his cronies in organized crime, recognized an opportunity of a lifetime to aggressively exploit America's domestic political move to the left under the Obama administration.

As masters of deception, they have employed every tool of deception available in their active measures toolbox—propaganda, information warfare, espionage, and influence peddling operating in the United States during Obama's tenure nearly unopposed and with great success.

While there has been a plethora of arrests made for espionage in the last couple of years, most of them were spying for the Chinese, People's Republic of China (PRC) Ministry of State Security (MSS). The only individual of note to be accused of spying for the Russians during the Obama administration was Edward Snowden, a former CIA employee and contract employee with the National Security Agency (NSA) who provided highly classified information about NSA surveillance to the media. While he wasn't technically working for the Russians or Chinese or any other foreign intelligence service as far as we know, his unauthorized disclosures of highly classified information to the media caused grave damage to national security and directly impacted on our ability to collect intelligence while providing all our potential adversaries and terrorists valuable information to counter our technical collection capabilities and improve their D&D capabilities. He sought and was granted asylum in Russia by President Putin to avoid prosecution. So, you may be asking, where have all the spies gone?

Between the arrest of Katrina Leung and her FBI handler James J. Smith in 2003 and Ed Snowden in 2013, there were no arrests of Americans spying for Russia or China or any other foreign intelligence service of any real consequence. Katrina Leung had a career as a triple agent working for the Chinese MSS, while the FBI believed her to be one of their own assets. When Special Agent James J. Smith reopened an espionage case that the FBI was already pursuing against Leung in 1982, she was believed to be working for the MSS in Los Angeles and Smith supposedly attempted to double her. However, he was more interested in sex than doing his job as a counterintelligence officer who is supposed to be catching spies and not sleeping with them. For two decades (1982–2003) during their affair, he regularly carried highly classified information to their trysts where she promptly copied and provided the information to the MSS, while she provided a stream of directed or contaminated intelligence relating to the PRC to her "FBI handler Smith." Smith in turn convinced his colleagues and superiors the intelligence she was providing was prescient while critically compromising the FBI's Chinese counterintelligence program. When they were both arrested in 2003, Smith was charged with gross negligence in allowing an FBI asset access to classified material, but he and Leung pleaded not guilty. Both entered into plea bargains in 2005 and received slaps on the wrist. Smith got a three-month home confinement and a hundred hours of community service. Leung was sentenced to three years' probation, a hundred hours of community service, and a $10,000 fine. This is what we call "taking care of your own." This was not the first and would not be the last time the FBI mismanaged its counterintelligence assets or misjudged the loyalty of its own officers.

Hillary Clinton was found grossly negligent in using her personal unclassified computer and server to handle highly classified intelligence impacting on national security and was never charged with even violating her secrecy agreement, when every foreign intelligence service on the planet that was interested could have had access to her e-mail account and computer server. Any officer with the CIA, DIA, NSA, or any other IC organization would have been prosecuted to the full extent of the law. That is exactly what happened with the four most recent cases of espionage.

Kevin Mallory, who was convicted of violating his top secret security clearance at least twice, claimed he was acting as a freelance triple agent and sold secrets to the Chinese for $25,000. He was convicted of espionage for the Chinese and sentenced to twenty years in prison. Mallory was a risk-taker according to those who knew him and in deep financial difficulty running a consulting firm that was failing after leaving government service. I don't claim to know much about the Mallory case, but I can't help but wonder how many more moles and malcontents there are in the IC spying who have not been caught, when you consider that espionage is an equal opportunity employer and how disparate the penalties have been for spying and lying. Clearly, the FBI and DOJ have not set the bar very high when it comes to dishing out penalties to high-profile political figures like Hillary Clinton.

Candace Marie Claiborne, a State Department employee with a top secret security clearance, had extensive contacts with Chinese intelligence agents for nearly twenty years and provided them with sensitive national security documents in exchange for $20,000, with lavish gifts and travel. She was arrested in 2017 and sentenced in 2019 to forty months in prison, three months supervised release, and a fine of $40,000.

The most recent and one of the more bizarre cases involved Ron Hansen (no relation to the infamous FBI traitor and spy, Robert Hanssen), a US Army veteran and former DIA officer fluent in Mandarin and Russian, who was recruited by DIA in 2006 to work as a case officer to recruit and manage foreign agents. Working out of a commercial office in Beijing, he ended up contacting and pitching himself to Chinese intelligence and between 2013 and 2016 reportedly received more than $800,000 from the Chinese for services rendered. During this same time, he allegedly also tried to pitch himself to the DIA and FBI on several occasions as a double agent who would ultimately act on behalf of the United States. Hansen is charged with espionage, bulk cash smuggling, and structuring monetary transactions and was sentenced to ten years in Federal prison.

The most serious of these cases was former CIA officer Jerry Chun Shing Lee, who worked as a CIA officer from 1994 to 2007 and went into business on his own in Hong Kong and received payments of hundreds of thousands of dollars during the period 2010–2012. He had access to the names of CIA assets working in China and may have been responsible for the deaths or arrests of a dozen or more Chinese citizens secretly cooperating with the CIA. Lee was arrested in 2018 and sentenced in May 2019 to 27 years in lieu of life for a plea bargain.

Why am I going through this exercise about Americans committing espionage against America with no arrests made during almost an entire decade (2003–2013) overlapping the Obama administration? I'm doing so to suggest that the Obama administration was more interested in having their intelligence resources and FBI spying on their political opponents than doing what they are paid to do, protecting our national security interests by surveilling and catching those spying on America for hostile foreign adversaries. I was teaching and training intelligence officers from throughout the IC during this period. In the post 9/11 period, the CIA and other IC organizations were in a literal hiring frenzy due to the massive retirements of our baby boomer employees, the establishment of the Office of the Director of National Intelligence, significant expansion of our counterterrorist mission, and military and intelligence operations in Iraq and Afghanistan.

At the same time, all of our "horizon" retirement transition classes were full and waitlisted, while many of our intelligence training courses, including my own, were typically full and often waitlisted. The training pipeline and retirement pipeline were in overload. Many of my colleagues and I talked about our agencies and others vetting process and expressed concerns about hiring not hundreds but thousands of new recruits during this period. If our human resources and training programs were in overload, our hiring and vetting processes must have also been stretched thin. CIA was not alone. All the key IC agencies and even some of the military services were engaged in a similar recruiting and hiring frenzy. I can remember the advertisements running on radio and TV about "joining the National Clandestine [Intelligence] Service (NCS)." I can't remember any time before or since that the agency turned to marketing and recruiting on radio and TV, especially for the NCS, our former Directorate of Operations (DO) responsible for CI and our Human Intelligence (HUMINT) collection programs. My colleagues and I were astounded.

As much as we believed in some degree of transparency, you are bound to attract some very bad actors and agents of hostile foreign intelligence services well trained and well versed in how to penetrate the US IC. Unfortunately, President Obama and his Secretary of State Hillary Clinton were less interested or concerned about potential foreign intelligence penetrations or employing the resources of the IC against our potential adversaries than they were in using those resources to spy on political opponents and our allies. They did so while cozying up to our adversaries and apparently used those intelligence resources like their personal propaganda machine to buttress their story lines and narratives about everything from the takedown of Osama bin Laden to Benghazi and the Arab Spring, the Iranian nuclear deal, the Russian invasion of the Ukraine and annexation of Crimea, and the Uranium One scandal.

Not surprisingly, the mainstream media in the United States has been their closest ally and conduit for spreading disinformation and propaganda to promote their own national and international interests at the expense of America's. One of the key objectives has been to support the efforts of the Democratic Socialist Party and radical Left to impeach President Trump since they failed to keep him out of office and usher in another four to eight years of hardcore socialism with close associates Bill and Hillary Clinton. This would have accomplished what every Soviet or Russian leader from Stalin and Khrushchev to Yeltsin and Putin and others had attempted and failed to accomplish. Khrushchev made it clear in a meeting with Western diplomats in 1956, in his comments directed at the United States and others present, "Whether you like it or not, history is on our side. We will 'bury you.'" Like all good Communists, he actually believed that communism would eventually replace capitalism as the preferred economic system in the Western world, but not without active measures to undermine the US economy and military and bring them more in line with its own or worse. Putin, like all good dictators, would be made president for life, and our left-wing mainstream media would plaster his face on the front page of every magazine and newspaper and declare him man of the century. We could in turn kiss our republic and freedoms goodbye.

Let's face it, the truth of the matter is that MAGA is anathema to the kind of weak America that every leader in the Soviet Union and Russia, from Stalin to Putin—not to mention China, yet—would ever want to have to deal with. They have always sought and continue to seek to deal with the United States, economically, militarily, and politically from a position of strength, which they have yet been able to fully achieve. Not only does effective D&D act as an effective 'force multiplier' on the military battlefield, but also it works to the advantage of the deceiver, Putin and Russia in this case, in political and economic affairs.

There was collusion, there is collusion, and there will continue to be collusion, both witting and unwitting, behind the scenes and in plain sight with the political party, which has been a safe haven for Communists, socialists, anarchists, and America haters for decades, the Democratic Party and now my preferred title the Democratic Socialist Party.

When it comes to collusion, Mueller was just looking in all the wrong places. Why wasn't Mueller or the FBI and DOJ investigating Clinton and Obama's involvement in the Uranium One deal or Biden's abuse of his office as vice president to support his son's corrupt dealings with a Ukrainian energy company or his influence peddling and corruption to land his son Hunter a sweet $1.5 billion deal from the state-owned Bank of China for his private equity firm though he knew nothing about China or private equity. Obviously, the hypocrisy, double standards, and as we now know Obama's sycophants in the FBI, CIA, and DOJ were working overtime to hide their real subversion and corruption and keep the public's attention on the fake manufactured Trump collusion conspiracy. Mueller's investigative techniques were also flawed. He was clearly engaged in an effort to get the president and was never really interested in searching for the facts or the truth. This I can and will attest to from personal and professional experience.

Meanwhile, on its way to get back to the White House in 2020, with touchy-feely Joe Biden as its preferred front-running candidate, the Democratic Party has now revealed its true identity as the Socialist and Communist Party of Gus Hall, Bernie Sanders, Kamala Harris, Ocasio-Cortez, and comrades Schumer, Pelosi, and "Wild Bill" de Blasio, not to mention their vanguard, Alinsky disciples Hillary Clinton and Barack Obama. They are all more desperate than ever and as vicious as a bunch of cornered raccoons and as frustrated and nervous as a herd of cats in a room full of rocking chairs. They now present a clear and present danger to our electoral process and national security with their fanatical, desperate, and groundless attempts to unseat our duly elected president, Donald Trump.

Their increasingly vociferous and hateful threats, publicly and on social media, against the president and his family and those who support him are unprecedented in modern American politics. Defeated presidential candidate Hillary Clinton has even given her personal approval and encouraged mob attacks on Republicans, who have been shot, beaten, run out of restaurants, and harassed at their homes and even in the Halls of Congress. In her words, "You cannot be civil with a political party that wants to destroy what you stand for." The irony in her statement is that this is precisely what she and the radical Left stand for and want to do, to destroy America and establish their socialist utopia. These are not the words of a political reformer; these are the words of a Bolshevik and Alinsky revolutionary. This is now the political platform of the new Democratic Socialist Party, which is what she and the Democrats stand for. I suspect that she and Obama have been orchestrating all the subversion and attempts to hijack the presidency and will continue to do so throughout this presidential election cycle. Once again, if you are connecting the dots as I have been, you can't help but come to this conclusion.

By the way, threatening the president of the United States and government officials is a felony, and those responsible should be held accountable and prosecuted to the full extent of the law. They have gone far beyond the limits of their First Amendment rights, and their rants in many cases are clearly seditious in nature. I am genuinely concerned that one of these unhinged fanatics will make an attempt on the president's life even if they succeed in their groundless and ludicrous attempts to impeach in the House. So what are the FBI, DOJ, or Homeland Security that oversees the Secret Service doing about it? As far as I know, not much. At a minimum, his protective detail should be bolstered during this presidential election cycle. More than three years of constant negative media coverage, propaganda, and fake news as well as the many attacks on social media that are now being treated as the new norm are just fanning the flames for violence of one sort or another. We all know that the radical Left is prone to violence and have encouraged antifa and others to violence in the past. "If Fascism ever comes to America, it will come in the form of Liberalism" (*Ronald Reagan, 60 Minutes* interview, December 1975).

It's also another example of how the Democrats and radical Left attempt to turn reality on its head to fit their agenda with the ends always justifying the means. This makes the lawlessness and the kind of double standards that we have seen applied to everything long before and since the 2016 election a new norm for them. Of course, the Democratic Party has always been the party of bigotry, racism, slavery, violence, and double standards. How they have managed to revise history and turn that legacy on its head represents a mastery of the art of lying and one of the grandest deceptions in the history of American politics. The very idea that they claim even today to be the party of President Lincoln is so absurd that it's difficult to believe that anyone, especially our African-American brothers and sisters, would believe or accept it as true. Of course, Joe Biden also repeatedly claimed in his 1988 run for president that he had marched for civil rights, a pants on fire lie. But then as now, lying and cheating in the liberal mind-set to achieve their desired political outcome is acceptable and even admirable. In fact, he did not march, but as any good hypocritical career politician, Biden did actually oppose school busing, which promoted desegregation. He also claimed that segregation was in the best interests of black peoples and that it would "invoke black pride." This guy is just as looney as Ocasio-Cortez, or comrade de Blasio. De Blasio, Democrat Mayor of New York City, the US epicenter of the virus, recently lamented that it was "unfair" and suggested that the Wuhan bio-laboratory produced coronavirus was "racist" because it was attacking blacks and Hispanics in greater numbers, as a percentage of the population in his fair city, than whites!

I wonder what he would say about the Malaysian Tiger, Nadia, at his Bronx Zoo that also tested positive for COVID-19? He obviously doesn't have a clue about the science involved; the fact that the virus is a nonliving entity that must attach itself to a living cell or parasite to replicate, and it absolutely does not discriminate as to race, sex, nationality, or creed. Don't be surprised if this "genius" isn't Biden's running mate in 2020, or maybe one of the Princesses of Darkness Clinton or Pelosi. These are all entrenched Democrat-career politicians who did absolutely nothing to prepare for, or assist, in mitigating the spread of the virus. In fact, in the cases of both comrades, De Blasio

and Pelosi, they actually encouraged everyone in their respective constituencies in New York City and San Francisco to go to Chinatown
to celebrate Chinese New Year (January 25 to February 8, 2020) in
spite of President Trump's and the Department of Health and Human
Services (HHS's) declaration of a public health emergency on January
31. That declaration closed our borders to all travelers coming from
areas of China, Iran, and the Schengen area of Europe to prevent the
spread of the virus. Predictably, Pelosi and the rest of the left-wing
Democrat hypocrites had the audacity to accuse the president of being
xenophobic and played their race-baiter cards, along with the rabid
anti-Trump media and their constituents suffered, as a result of their
own ignorance and failure to heed the warnings.

At this point, a little background on Frederick Douglas, the
African-American social reformer, abolitionist, orator, and statesman
of his time along with a simple quote from Mr. Douglas should suf-
fice to unveil which party is the true party of freedom and progress
and what the Democratic Party really stands for.

After escaping from slavery in Maryland, Frederick Douglas
became a national leader of the abolitionist movement and was a
strong supporter of President Lincoln, the first Republican Party
president, and the Republican Party was united in supporting the
abolition of slavery. It was the Abolitionist Party. On the other hand,
the Democrats staunchly opposed President Lincoln and the abolition of slavery. The Democrats unanimously opposed issuing the
Emancipation Proclamation and overwhelmingly opposed his efforts
to pass the Thirteenth, Fourteenth, and Fifteenth Amendments to our
Constitution and the Civil Rights Act of 1866. Frederick Douglas's
response to the reality of the situation at the time is underscored in
one of his famous quotes, "I am a Republican, a black, dyed-in-the-
wool Republican, and I never intend to belong to any other party
than the party of freedom and progress." This is a simple and endur-
ing fact and truth, and not even 150 years of lies and deception by
the Democrats can change it.

Remember Jesus's words, "Seek the truth and the truth shall
make you free" (John 8:32).

# CHAPTER 2
# Deception 101

*O, what a tangled web we weave, when first we practice to deceive!*
—Sir Walter Scott (Marmion,
1808, canto 6, stanza 17)

*But if we practice for a while, we'll get a wizard's knack for guile.*
—Barton Whaley (January 11, 2010)

Deception is not new. It's been with us since the beginning of time, rearing its ugly head in the garden of Eden where Satan manifested himself as a serpent and convinced the woman (Eve) to eat of the forbidden fruit from the tree of life and she gave it to her husband the man (Adam) who also ate it. The serpent promised her that their "eyes would be opened" and they would be like God who knows "good and evil." We all know the rest of the story—their eyes were opened, they were naked, and they tried to hide themselves from God. But God found them naked, and because of their disobedience, they were banished from the garden wearing only fig leaves. The snake, who previously stood upright and could converse with human beings, also enjoyed the reputation of being shrewder and more cunning than all other creatures. Because of its deception, God condemned the snake to crawl on its belly and eat dust all the days of its life. "I will put enmity between you and the woman, and between your offspring and hers, they will strike at your head, while you strike at their heel" (Genesis 3:1–15).

It's not surprising that Saul Alinsky acknowledges in his Rules for Revolution that Lucifer was the first radical known to man who rebelled against the establishment, God, and as such successfully gained his own kingdom. What he doesn't acknowledge is that kingdom is hell.

Like Adam and Eve, we've all been exposed to or encountered some form of deception and may have even practiced it on occasion, whether wittingly or unwittingly. Deception can be high-tech, low-tech, or no tech at all. The insect and animal world are full of mostly harmless examples of mimicry and camouflage directed at their own predators or prey. The snowy owl's beautiful white feathers and the polar bear's white fur help to hide them in their arctic habitats for hunting. The walking stick looks like a twig and used its disguise to hide from predators, and the katydid looks like the leaves it feeds on. We are constantly bombarded with deceptive practices, some subtle and some very obvious, in marketing, advertising, and sales. Have you ever bought a used car? They don't call them used anymore; they are "certified preowned" and given that alleged "hundred-point bumper-to-bumper inspection." How about negotiating the price for your trade-in on a new vehicle? You know the salesperson is going to have to talk to his manager in the glass cage to get approval and then come back with an apology and a token counteroffer.

The pharmaceutical giants with their nonstop drug commercials have cures for just about every disease and ailment ever documented with acronyms we've never heard of. There are also the many diet look and feel great commercials promising unbelievable results with testimonials from only those who had very positive results. Most of them are required by law to have warnings that the drugs or diets in some cases can do more harm than good, but those warnings are subtle and almost always place responsibility for negative results squarely with you and your doctor. It should come as no surprise that you can sue any of them for failing to live up to your expectations in our litigious society, so we also have all the law firms with their TV, radio, and billboard offers of free consultations and promises that their clients receive more compensation than others.

Whether we are aware or not, we deal with false advertising, marketing gimmicks, misinformation, media disinformation and sensationalism, propaganda, lies, half-truths, and misrepresentation all to get a hook in us to buy into promises for power, prestige, easy money, better health, better sex, and a better, longer life. The truth is that we are not in control—God is. You can place your trust in the doctors, the drugs, and the miracle cures promised by the pharmaceutical companies or the lottery and lawyers or you can embrace that simple act of faith and place your trust in God. Where there is no faith, there is no hope. It's very apparent that many of us have turned away from God and our Judeo-Christian values that our Founding Fathers embraced and extolled in our Constitution that made this country great. This is tearing us apart.

> God who gave us life, gave us liberty. Can the liberties of a nation be secure when we have removed a conviction that these liberties are a gift of God? Indeed, I tremble for my country when I reflect that God is just, that his justice cannot sleep forever. (Thomas Jefferson, author of America's Declaration of Independence and our third president)

The object of deception is to hide the real, the truth, and show the fake or "tell the big lie." Lying is a very basic form of deception. It can also be quite complicated, but once mastered, it can be artfully employed with the guile of a wizard or Satan himself, as the opening poem suggests. There is no shame in lying in politics or so it would seem, not only in the eyes and minds of most career politicians but also in many of their pernicious supporters.

Perhaps one of the more recent and egregious examples is when Harry Reid, former Senate majority leader, lied to the media, the Senate, and national electorate about presidential candidate Mitt Romney's tax history and returns, claiming he paid no taxes for ten years. As absurd an accusation it was, many believed it. It is often said that if you tell the lie often enough and are convincing enough, it can take on a life of its own and is perceived as real or true. Reid later stated that "it was necessary" and he was proud that his lies may have cost Romney the election in 2012.

However, the Judge Kavanaugh hearings over his appointment as the next Justice of the Supreme Court rate as one of the most blatant and despicable displays of deceit and deception to derail such an appointment in recent history, including that of Clarence Thomas. The eleventh-hour allegations and innuendo by Democratic Party activist C. B. Ford and her obvious alliance with Senator Feinstein were nothing less than an attempted character assassination to prevent Judge Kavanaugh's confirmation. It was not only a farce but also a Shakespearean tragedy due to the pain, suffering, and anxiety it caused Judge Kavanaugh and his family, when the *real* motivation for all the lies and obfuscation and obstruction of justice was that he is a prolife Catholic and it was their desperate partisan effort to protect Roe v Wade. Show the fake, tell the big lie, and do everything you can to obscure and hide the real, the truth. The ends always justify the means with the radical Left.

A well-known radio talk show host once commented that Liberals have mastered the art of lying better than Conservatives can tell the truth and that Republicans are losing the war of words. He was actually on to something more significant about the art of lying and how it has made revealing the truth or telling truth from fiction more difficult. There is an online resource, for example, politifact. org, that offers a Truth-o-Meter or analytic technique to fact-check politicians' statements, which it claims can no longer be accurately rated as purely true or false. That's an understatement. The tool still must rely on the subjective analysis of those applying it. Whether you subscribe to it or not, the fact is that the tool itself is a representation of the degree to which secular relativism has impacted our basic value system and has skewed our perception of what is true and what is false, what is right and what is wrong, what is good and what is evil.

According to the online tool, the art of lying has become so complex in mixing truth and lies that the scale PolitiFact uses has six categories of political rhetoric—true, mostly true, half true, mostly false, false, and "pants on fire." I'd say Harry Reid's bold-faced lies about Romney would qualify as pants on fire by his own admission, as would Feinstein's deceitful efforts to derail Judge Kavanaugh's confirmation. So while there is still only one way to find the truth and speak the truth, there are now at least five times as many ways to lie and obscure the truth. The progressive liberal mind-set takes this to the extreme and will even argue that there is no truth and everything is relative and based on perception and opinion.

> So, Pilate said to Him, "Then you are a king?" Jesus answered, "You say I am a king. For this I was born and for this I came into this world, to testify to the Truth. Everyone who belongs to the Truth listens to my voice."
> Pilot said to Him, "What is Truth?" (John 18:37–38)

During the Last Supper Discourses with his disciples, Jesus answered this question,

> Thomas said to Him, "Master, we do not know where you are going, so how can we know the way?" Jesus said to him, "I am the Way and the Truth and the Life. No one comes to the Father except through me. If you know me, then you will also know my Father." (John 14:5–8)

Jesus also warned his disciples,

> If the world hates you, realize that it hated me first. If you belonged to the world, the world would love its own; but because you do not belong to the world, and I have chosen you out of the world, the world hates you. (John 16:18–20)

For those nonbelievers and those career politicians and their supporters who will always deny Christ, lying, committing perjury, and giving false testimony and cheating and stealing are acceptable, especially when it serves to promote your own self-interests, whether they be political, economic, or social. They have and are attempting to apply this mind-set to alter and change every facet of our culture and society and even rewrite our history. The liberal media's penchant for rushing to judgment before making any effort to validate or corroborate what they report and then politicize it applying their bias and mind-set to everything they report is an excellent example of how this works. In doing so, they set themselves up as the perfect practitioners and ideal hosts and conduits for demagoguery and deception.

As such, most of what they produce is now treated as fake news, disinformation, and propaganda and rightly so. An even more disturbing and sinister product of the more radical liberal bias literally attempts to alter reality, make what is fake real, what is evil good. And lying, cheating, stealing, and killing are all acceptable under certain conditions, conditions that they dictate. Opposing women's rights to have late-term abortions is wrong or mean-spirited, but aborting and killing fifty to sixty million human beings, an entire generation of American citizens, is right and good. This now includes murdering babies at birth and selling their body parts. The point, and the real danger, is that once we lose our ability to differentiate between truth and fiction, the real and the fake, good and evil, or are indifferent to pursuing the truth, we become more vulnerable to demagogues, dictators, and the demons of deception.

> Beloved, do not trust every spirit but test the spirits to see whether they belong to God, because many false prophets have gone out into the world. This is how you know the spirit of God: every spirit that acknowledges Jesus Christ come in the flesh, belong to God, and every spirit that does not acknowledge Jesus, does not belong to God. This is the spirit of the antichrist, who, as you heard is to come, but in fact is already in the world... They belong to the world; accordingly,

their teaching belongs to the world and the world listens to them. We belong to God, and anyone who knows God listens to us, while anyone who does not belong to God refuses to hear us. This is how we know the spirit of Truth and the spirit of Deceit. (1 John 4:1–6)

Good intelligence analysis and good journalism should seek ground truth, and the importance of seeking the truth can't be overstated. One of CIA's very own slogans that you can find on one of its challenge coins reads, "And ye shall know the truth and the truth shall make you free." Of course, most Christians and believers know that this statement originated with Jesus and can be found in John 8:32. The truth that Jesus speaks about is meant to represent God and Christianity, and the freedom refers to freedom from all worldly impediments such as sin, ignorance, and misery. There is no doubt that our mainstream media would be well served to follow this advice, but it would have to abandon its blatant partisan political agenda and engage in some serious research and analysis to seek the facts and the truth in what they report.

Unfortunately, real journalism is dead and has been for many years. We are now confronted with and exposed to politically motivated and opinionated talking heads who do no research or analysis and are trained and paid only to read what their producers have scripted for them on their teleprompters. However, they are not alone in their lack of professionalism and discipline.

Our very own (former) director of the CIA, who should be a standard-bearer for good intelligence analysis, obviously also failed to grasp its importance or meaning. President Trump legally relieved him of his position as director and later his security clearances, but the president could hardly free or relieve him of anything more, least of all his love affair with socialism or Alinsky disciples Hillary Clinton and Barack Obama. We know how and why Mr. Brennan became the director of the CIA. He was former president Obama's intelligence advisor during his 2008 presidential campaign, a favorite of Bill and Hillary Clinton, and a dyed-in-the-wool Liberal who voted for Gus

Hall, the US Communist Party (CPUSA) candidate for president in 1976. By his own admission, this occurred about four years prior to Mr. Brennan joining the agency in 1980 as a career trainee.

I'm still unsure how Mr. Brennan managed to get through what at that time was a very rigorous CIA interview and polygraph process. I experienced it myself in 1978 while I was being recruited by CIA. If memory serves me, Gus Hall was indicted and imprisoned for "conspiracy to teach and advocate the overthrow of the US government by force and violence" and was a recipient of the Order of Lenin from the Soviet Union. One of the many intrusive but necessary questions anyone would be asked in an interview and lifestyle polygraph back then was whether you were a member of or ever *supported any* organizations or individuals that advocated the overthrow of the US government. If you voted for Gus Hall in 1976, the answer to that question would have to be a resounding yes, that is, unless you lied or were given a pass by the polygrapher. Brennan claims he was forthcoming and still got the "pass."

Polygraphs are not admissible in a court of law, because they are not foolproof. If you give a polygraph to someone in a psychiatric hospital with a serious case of psychosis, who really believes they are Napoleon Bonaparte, it is unlikely that there would be any indication of deception on their part on a polygraph. As a cradle Catholic and one educated in a Catholic elementary school, my Catholic guilt always showed through on a polygraph. If I ever had even the slightest doubt about my answer to a question, it would show up. During that 1978 polygraph, in answer to a question as to whether I had ever violated anyone's trust in me, I thought of my dear mom and the times I hid something I had done wrong from her. After a pause and examination of conscience, I actually remembered and confessed to taking a dollar from my parent's bedroom dresser when I was five years old to buy all the kids in the neighborhood (the projects) candy at the local convenience store. I explained that I was disciplined and punished. Nevertheless, I was promptly accused by the polygrapher of being untrustworthy and asked if I violated the trust of all I came into contact with. My response was a firm no. It was one of the most intrusive polygraphs I would ever take in my career.

My point is that if they had known that Mr. Brennan voted for Gus Hall, I believe that should have been a red flag to security and all but disqualified him from being granted a top secret clearance and employment with the CIA or any agency within the IC. Yet what could possibly possess an educated twenty-one-year-old apparently interested in a career with CIA to vote for the Communist Party candidate for president when the Democrats had Liberals Jimmy Carter and Walter Mondale as that party's candidates? Apparently, they weren't Liberal enough.

I was assigned to DIA as a young navy lieutenant, after returning from a year in Vietnam as an intelligence liaison officer and advisor (February 1972 to February 1973) and had a bachelor's of arts degree in political science and a master's of arts degree in international relations, and yet in 1976, I knew next to nothing about Gus Hall, except that he was a Communist. What more did anyone need to know about Gus in 1976 that would get you to vote for him or support him, unless you shared his ideology and politics? I don't believe that this is something that can be dismissed as youthful naïveté. While I am saying that John Brennan is probably the most unabashedly left-wing partisan director of the CIA in the agency's history, I'm not suggesting that he is a Socialist or Communist or is necessarily an agent or operative of the Russian government or intelligence services. Then again, he wouldn't be the first high-ranking CIA officer to betray his country and the president he is supposed to serve, regardless of party affiliation.

The case of senior CIA officer Harold Nicholson, who also came to work for CIA in 1980 (same year as John Brennan) after a short stint in the army (Brennan never served in the military), raised serious questions about the deficiencies in the hiring and vetting practices of the agency that would allow for such a highly placed mole. He served overseas in various posts as a counterintelligence officer, deputy chief of station, and chief of station in Romania before serving as a branch chief in the Counterterrorism Center in Washington DC. He was recruited by the Russian intelligence service apparently during one of his overseas assignments and compromised national defense information and sensitive imagery intelligence and computer data to the Russians until his arrest in 1996. To date, Nicholson is the highest-ranking CIA official to be convicted of espionage.

Some of our most unlikely candidates for spying have also been coached to beat the poly, as one Ana Belén Montes had been by the Cuban intelligence service. When she came to work for the DIA in 1985, she had already been recruited and trained by the Cubans while holding a clerical job in the DOJ. There are ways to beat the polygraph, but you have to be schooled. Anna Montes, who was a highly decorated and respected senior analyst at DIA (1984–2001), spent all her spare time spying for the Cuban intelligence service and received such schooling to beat the poly on several occasions, including one she had to take to receive access to a very sensitive special access program (SAP). Unlike Ames and Hanssen who began spying in 1985 for the KGB for big bucks, she was motivated by ego and US policy toward Cuba, which she opposed.

Another obvious problem is that individuals in high places even in the IC like the director of the CIA and the director of National Intelligence, in this case, lost sight of their responsibility and accountability to the president and the American people who elected him and got caught up in their own partisan political ambitions for more power and prestige at the expense of anyone who got in their way. John Brennan's adolescent temper tantrums and scandalous seditious public comments about the president, while still director of the CIA, were proof enough of his disloyalty and fact that he was not working for this president or the American people. I'd have to argue that he "blew his cover," as we would say in intelligence parlance. If he was not working for this president and the American people, who was he and who is he working for? The Russians? Obama's shadow government? We do know now he's another left-wing talking head for all the left-wing media outlets.

If you start connecting the dots and the players, you can't help but identify a very conspicuous thread, yet one still hiding in plain sight, not only Mr. Brennan and his support for a communist candidate as influential as Gus Hall (who ran for president in 1972, 1976, 1980, and 1984) and his efforts to subvert the president but also Barack Hussein Obama and Hillary Rodham Clinton, both Saul

Alinsky disciples. All are apparently engaged in the activities of a post-Obama administration shadow government about which books have been written. An article circulating on the Internet erroneously attributed to the late conservative columnist Charles Krauthammer described the community organizing project Organizing for Action (OFA). Regardless of who wrote the article, much of what is reported about OFA is true, and it fits nicely with the hundreds of Alinsky-inspired community organizations in urban areas throughout the United States.

The OFA claims tax-exempt 501(c)(4) status but is the successor to Obama's 2012 reelection campaign, and its policies and agenda are those of the former president and are strongly allied with the Democratic Party, despite its claim of being nonpartisan. It also continues to maintain Obama's website and Twitter account. They trained over ten thousand organizers during its first two years, and some estimates put their number as high as thirty thousand.

Unlike political parties that are limited in the amounts of individual contributions they can obtain, OFA can accept unlimited contributions, and they can advocate for policies unregulated by campaign finance laws. While groups like OFA must spend at least half of their funds on social welfare programs (kind of like the Clinton Foundation's false claims) to be eligible for tax-exempt status, enforcing this requirement is nearly impossible. Just as political parties could once exploit the soft-money loophole, OFA can now take advantage of ambiguity and deception in hiding campaign-related expenditures.

On February 3, 2020, the Government Accountability Office (GAO) issued a report addressing the issue of campaign finance enforcement largely ignored by the mainstream media, which was more interested in wallowing in Pelosi's and the Democrats' House presidential impeachment show trial and trying to cover up the true source of the Iowa caucuses debacle. I believe the caucuses were rigged by the Democratic National Committee (DNC) months in advance and software sabotaged to once again undermine presidential candidate Bernie Sanders's campaign as it did in 2016. It turns out that the CEO and COO of the software company responsible for the caucus' application glitch, Shadow Inc., both worked on Hillary Clinton's 2016 presidential campaign, and we all know how much Hillary and Bernie adore each other. We can only hope that Bernie who led the field of democratic socialist candidates and has since endorsed Biden will finally see the light and run as an independent.

As for the GAO report, $8.6 billion was raised during the two-year period, January 2017 through December 2018, to influence federal elections. GAO reports that the system for oversight is convoluted and enforcement weak with multiple steps dependent on party loyalties and an unwillingness to hold anyone accountable. This opens the way for fraud and abuse in exceeding contribution limits and makes it easier to funnel foreign contributions into campaigns.

Like the Clinton Foundation, OFA will likely be the recipient of contributions by global benefactors like Soros and possibly foreign intelligence services, like the Russians who contributed to Clinton's campaign in 2016 and Chinese, who would both stand to benefit immensely as stakeholders in the democrats' efforts to undermine President Trump, our Constitution, and our political system. Both the Russian and Chinese intelligence services must consider Donald Trump and everything his MAGA and America first policies stand for anathema to achieving their own political, military, and economic goals. On the other hand, they must also view the agenda and policies of the radical Socialist Democrats as being much more compatible with their own. OFA will probably be at the forefront of proselytizing and marshaling the party's grassroots and expanding its base while selling their vision of a socialist utopia with empty promises of a *mega* welfare state, along the lines of Saul Alinsky or Vladimir Putin or "Nicky" Maduro or Hugo Chávez or Fidel and Raul Castro, all good buds of former president Obama. They are or were, in the cases of Fidel and Hugo, all authoritarian dictators who used all the same promises of a socialist utopia to enrich themselves while burying their citizenry in abject poverty.

This is an undeniable fact and truth about the product of socialism and tyranny that accompanies it. According to Marx, as he explains in *the Communist Manifesto*, socialism is only a stage in the transition to communism; it's not an end in itself. Marx refers to this transition state as the dictatorship of the proletariat. This stage was not intended to be a dictatorship by one or a few men, as it has always turned out to be, but a democracy where the majority exercised dictatorship over the minority or remnants of the middle class and bourgeoisie. Once his vision of a stateless communist society is achieved, the mode of distribution changes from each receiving in accord to what he produces to "from each according to his ability [to produce], to each according to his needs," the productive and the haves providing for the nonproductive have-nots.

His vision of his communist society is one where force and selfishness disappear and man would live by the "grace of the iron laws of history" rather than with the grace of God in perfect freedom and harmony. We know this is impossible without the grace of God, for while all things are possible with God, nothing is possible without God. This vision of freedom and harmony of Marx's is ancient and not entirely ignoble. Nevertheless, it is only a vision and one proven historically to be dangerous and unachievable. It is based on the *fallacy* that evil arises only from economic institutions when in fact and truth, men are motivated and corrupted as often by the lust for power, jealousy, and hate as they are by property or wealth. Since this society is also a godless society, history is replete with examples of how tyranny and corruption accompany socialism and communism, and anyone who would promote an economy or society built on either is ignoring history and God.

Edmund Burke warned, "The only thing necessary for the triumph of evil is that good men do nothing."

## The Benghazi Debacle

Former director of National Intelligence Jim Clapper's testimony at the Benghazi hearings, which took place two years after the tragic event, was to say the least a jewel of equivocation. I've known the former DNI since he was the director for Intelligence (J2), US Forces Korea (USFK), and have worked for him at various times in my career and held him in high esteem. When I saw his performance at the Benghazi hearings, he convinced me either that he had a serious memory lapse or that he had been totally coopted by the Obama administration. He was clearly attempting to avoid saying anything that would contradict the Clinton-Obama narrative concerning the YouTube video that was claimed to be responsible for prompting "those 'spontaneous' protests."

Those so-called protests ended with an all-out coordinated assault by the militant group Ansar al-Sharia on our diplomatic post and annex in Benghazi with heavy weapons rockets, mortars, rocket-propelled grenades, antiaircraft machine guns, truck-mounted artillery, and automatic weapons. These are not the kinds of weapons that a handful of misfits who are out looking to kill a few Americans on a Tuesday night stroll would have at their disposal.

It seems incomprehensible to me, a forty-six-year career intelligence professional, that the DNI, given his distinguished military career and professional intelligence background and all the resources at his disposal, couldn't figure that out. I still don't understand how he could possibly continue to support the phony YouTube narrative, even if it may have cost him his job. It is almost always more difficult to be truthful than to just go with the flow. He and the director of the CIA, Secretary Clinton, Obama, and his National Security Advisor Susan Rice had two years to prepare for those hearings; and it should have been obvious then and certainly is now that they were not interested in seeking the truth or sharing it, but rather stuck to their phony narrative for purely partisan political reasons.

As then secretary of state Hillary Clinton suggested in her infamous rant during the Benghazi hearings, "The fact is we had four dead Americans [Ambassador Stevens, a Foreign Service officer, and two American CIA contractors]. Was it because of a protest or was it because of guys out for a walk one night who decided that they'd go kill some Americans? What difference at this point does it make?"

The fact that the DNI and later the director of the CIA, John Brennan, bolstered the big lie and cover story was to say the least disappointing and could more accurately be characterized as pejorative. It represented the politicization of intelligence at its worst—something that all good intelligence analysts are trained and cautioned to avoid at all times and the likes of which I had never witnessed or experienced in my career. It turns out that John Brennan probably did more to institutionalize his own partisan and liberal political viewpoints on CIA's workforce and products than any previous director of the CIA. Even more disturbing were the publicly aired personal attacks by Mr. Brennan, Mr. Clapper, and other senior FBI and DOJ officials against the president. In particular, John Brennan's rants and outlandish attacks and totally bogus accusations that the president was an agent of the Russian government and was guilty of treason were way out of line. Given Brennan's early history as an apparent pro-Communist Gus Hall groupie and the fact that he was Obama's intelligence advisor and remains a Trump-bashing pro-Obama and pro-Clinton devotee, I would contend that Mr. Brennan is a much more likely candidate as a Russian agent of influence. Like Nicholson, he may well have been working for the Russian intelligence services long before he became director of the CIA. It is now pretty obvious that his attacks on President Trump were an attempt at misdirection to deflect and project onto the president what he and his coconspirators were guilty of themselves, not only colluding with Putin and the Russians but also hiding behind a vail of secrecy to spy on and subvert opposition political candidate Trump and overthrow a democratically elected President Trump. That is treasonous and takes me back to my question about how he managed to get through his interview and polygraph in 1980.

Even if you choose to discount my conjecture, as senior leaders in the IC, they are supposed to perform their duties and responsibilities independent of any political or partisan views or ideology. Never in my career was I ever confronted with such disloyalty, blatantly public and in your face disloyalty and disrespect for the president of these United States and the American people who elected him. My conservative colleagues and I in the IC never voted for Jimmy Carter and never liked DCI Admiral Stansfield Turner who decimated our human intelligence capability during his tenure. I didn't vote for the Clintons or former president Barack Hussein Obama, but I never ever engaged in negative private commentary about them, let alone criticize them in public, which I'm certain would have prompted an official reprimand or our dismissal.

The idea of actively subverting and undermining the president of the United States because you didn't vote for him and didn't like him would never have crossed our minds. We considered such action that Gus Hall advocated then as we do now treasonous. So why aren't the Democrats and a former president and the leaders of the IC, the FBI, and DOJ and Congress, all who have engaged in such conduct for the past three years and are continuing today, held accountable? It is the ultimate in hypocrisy and double standards, and the mainstream media has been their greatest ally in promoting the fake—the lies and innuendo—and ignoring the real and their responsibility to report the facts and seek the truth.

Their other allies include the Russian and Chinese intelligence services and globalists like Soros who also stand to benefit from their subversive activities to destroy our way of governing and undermine our Constitution and our rule of law. If these liberal misfits are allowed to continue unimpeded, we will be living in a totalitarian state, a dictatorship and tyranny of the minority. They are the Bolsheviks of the twenty-first century, whether as witting or unwitting participants in this revolution. This is precisely where the left-wing Democratic Socialist Party is hell-bent on taking us, and they and their Russian and Chinese foreign intelligence service allies are only one or two election cycles away from achieving their collective goal.

> Freedom is never more than one generation away from extinction. We didn't pass it on to our children in the bloodstream. The only way they can inherit the freedom that we have known, is if we fight for it, protect it, defend it, then hand it to them with the well 'taught' lessons of how they in their lifetime must do the same. And if you and I don't do this, then you and I may well spend our sunset years telling our children and our children's children what it once was like in America when men were free. (Pres. Ronald Reagan)

We are an open society, so it's relatively easy for our potential adversaries to acquire the knowledge they need about our strengths and weaknesses, capabilities and vulnerabilities. We're pretty much an open book. I used to joke with my students that our adversaries are like Bill Belichick, coach of the New England Patriots, who was accused of covertly spying on his opponents in 2007 by the NFL in what was called Spygate. I'd tell them that our adversaries like Belichick have our playbook. Not only do they have knowledge of our intelligence collection capabilities and vulnerabilities, but also they have a very good appreciation for how we think and how we do business. Therefore, it's also important that we have some appreciation for how our potential adversaries gain that knowledge. It is much more difficult for us even when using the most sophisticated collection and analytic techniques to assess an adversary's capabilities and intentions, especially if they are employing D&D against us and are closed societies or hard targets like Russia, China, Iran, and North Korea, as we in the IC refer to them. Increased knowledge leads to improved D&D. Improved D&D and knowledge of how we do business reduces our intelligence advantage and makes us more vulnerable to surprise. It's a little like the opponent changing their plays at the line of scrimmage when they have seen your defensive alignment and they call an audible. If you know the audible, you can react in time to beat it, but if you don't, your defense is more vulnerable.

Another undisputed fact is that the deceiver always has the advantage over the target of the deception, unless the deception is terribly flawed or it is compromised. D&D go hand in hand. Denial is simply the act of hiding the object or preventing observation or access to what it is that is being hidden and is largely passive in nature. Deception requires the active manipulation of data, information, and stimuli to alter the perception of the target audience in a manner that supports the objective(s) of the deception and thereby benefits the deceiver.

Deception is a mind game. Richards Heuer points out in his groundbreaking book, *the Psychology of Intelligence Analysis*, that Deception is 90 percent applied psychology. If you know who your target audience is and how they think and have even the slightest appreciation for their cognitive biases and how they react to certain stimuli, then you are in a better position to manipulate their perceptions and their actions and reactions.

We used a simple paradigm in my classes, both the D&D fundamentals and advanced deception planning and analysis course—first, to better understand the anatomy of a good deception plan and, second, to better equip my students to recognize, analyze, and dissect a deception.

- See-Think-Do (S-T-D): Plan a deception
- Do-Think-See (D-T-S): Analyze a deception

The deceiver identifies the goal or purpose of the deception, the target of the deception, and establishes the objectives they want to achieve, that is, what the target of the deception must do or not do that will allow the deceiver to achieve his goal. Considering the current mind-set of the target, the deceiver then is going to determine what the target must think in order to act as desired and what the target must see and hear to think and act or react in the desired manner. In implementing the deception, the deceiver must decide which facts or objects are to be hidden and which shown. He then creates the observables he wants the target to see to support the story or narrative and the picture he wants the target to construct (perception) from the deception activities while deleting, hiding, or sufficiently obscuring the signatures of the real object or thing to be hidden. At this point, he identifies the conduits and means available to get the deception activities and stimuli to the target, systems, organizations, media, and people.

We only show the target what we want them to *see* or observe (the fake) so they will *think* that what they perceive is real and therefore act or react in a manner to support the deceiver's goal and objectives and do or not do what is desired. To paraphrase, we show them what we want them to see/hear/observe to get them to think in a way that will get them to do/act/react in a manner that supports the deception. We monitor their reactions and actions and other feedback, media and public and official statements, to adjust and fine-tune our deception or terminate it and go to plan B or C if it appears to be foundering.

It also stands to reason that we need to have some understanding of those cognitive biases that impact on our own perception of reality and our intelligence analysis. In order to raise my students' awareness of those cognitive biases, I invited one of the agency's clinical psychologists to test them and give a presentation on those biases most common and bothersome in our profession and what we could do to mitigate their impact on our perception and analysis. Many of these are addressed and explained in Heuer's book. We did this early on the morning of the first day of class. Several of these perceptual distortions are worth mentioning and are relevant to our discussion about our vulnerability to deception and impact on our analysis. These are as follows:

- Thoughts largely based on assumptions and past experiences powerfully influence how a situation is perceived and our consequent feelings and actions.
- People do not respond to objective reality, but rather to their perception of reality.
- Perceptions, even when grossly distorted, are the person's real world and the starting point from which they evaluate a situation, explore options, and make decisions.
- We tend to perceive what we expect to find, and our perceptions are powerfully dependent on our assumptions and preconceptions.
- It takes more information and more unambiguous information to recognize an unexpected phenomenon than an expected one.
- The tendency to perceive the expected is stronger than the tendency to perceive the desired.
- Mind-sets are quick to form but are resistant to change.
- Once a conclusion is drawn, it is difficult to view new or contradictory data with an open mind.

- It takes far more compelling evidence to change an existing view than to initially form one.
- New information is assimilated to existing images; gradual, evolutionary change often goes unnoticed.
- A new analyst or independent observer may generate more accurate insights than more experienced colleagues.
- Failure to generate multiple possible explanations increases gullibility.
- Get information of various types and from multiple sources.
- Seek multiple, varied, independent channels of information to corroborate incoming data before passing it along.
- Avoid mirror imaging, our tendency to assume that the person, group, or potential adversary being analyzed thinks and acts like we would under similar conditions.
- Projecting onto others your own rationale and explanation for their behavior or expected actions or reactions.

I'm sure you'll agree that many of these perceptual distortions and cognitive challenges were present in the actions and behavior described in chapter 1 and with the Mueller investigation.

While some students may have considered this nothing more than psychobabble, they all realized by the end of the course how important it was to have a better appreciation for the psychological factors impacting on their susceptibility to D&D and their ability to mitigate its impact on their analysis.

This was followed by a day and a half of intense training in adversarial D&D capabilities including state and nonstate actors, their strategies, doctrines, and techniques. Some are very sophisticated and some not so much. We reviewed lessons learned in cases where their knowledge of our capabilities and vulnerabilities enabled them to significantly improve their D&D employment strategies over the years and their sources of information and knowledge about us. Some of those sources of knowledge include espionage by enemies and traitors within and foreign intelligence service operatives, unauthorized and authorized disclosures from sources within the IC and congressional staffs, and intelligence exchanges with foreign intelligence services and sources and activities outside the IC, Congress, and the media and scientific and academic exchanges and even diplomatic démarches.

The bottom line is that increased foreign knowledge equals improved D&D for potential adversaries. What separates us in the IC and the information that we provide the president and senior policymakers from those media outlets like CNN or Fox is that we collect secrets by secret means. Therefore, if we can't protect our sources and methods and they are compromised, our ability to provide reliable and verifiable intelligence to our president and his senior advisors is compromised, and our intelligence advantage over our adversaries is reduced or lost.

By the end of the second day of our three-day course, the majority of students are feeling pretty confident that they know just about everything they need to know about deception, especially adversarial D&D. To remind them that they and their cognitive biases are part of the problem and to reinforce the fact that the basic elements of a good deception are psychological and that the deceiver always has the advantage, we brought in an illusionist or professional magician at the end of day 2. While some thought this was quite amusing, I explained up front that he was not with us to entertain, but to demonstrate that he would successfully manipulate our perceptions and fool us or deceive us, despite the fact that they knew that was his goal.

This wasn't the first time CIA had hired a magician to support its mission. John Mulholland, a famous American magician, was hired in the early 1950s to write a manual to support CIA officers' field operations against a Soviet adversary who was adept at espionage and D&D. Mulholland's transcripts were discovered in the CIA archives, declassified, and published as *the Official CIA Manual of Trickery and Deception* in 2009.

My good friend and colleague, retired navy commander, Dick Christian had been practicing magic since he was seven years old and accepted his first dollar as an illusionist at age eleven. He performed his entire life, except for a twenty-year hiatus during his navy career, but even then he had occasion to use his skills.

Dick would begin his presentation with a short lecture about illusionists and conjurers and told the story of the war magician Jasper Maskelyne, a British stage magician in the 1930s and 1940s who was credited by some, including himself, with extravagant claims of cities disappearing, armies relocating, and dummies proliferating (tanks, aircraft, and ships) and the use of dazzling lights to conceal the Suez Canal from German bombing attacks. Some historians support Maskelyne's claims, while others don't. My students found them fascinating nonetheless.

Of course, the Allies did develop a sophisticated deception plan to support our D-Day operations nearly seventy-six years ago, June 6, 1944. He described how we deceived the Nazis into thinking that the Allies were invading at Pas-de-Calais, keeping General Rommel and his German heavy-armored divisions in check in the area of Calais, while our invasion on D-Day proceeded farther south at Normandy. He shared the story of how General Patton's Ghost Army with all its dummy armor and artillery as part of Operation Fortitude and Bodyguard successfully misled the German High Command as to the location and timing of the invasion and General Patton's role in the invasion. The operation was successful for several reasons, as follows:

- British intelligence cultivated double agents as channels for disinformation to the enemy.
- All German agents in England were doubled as conduits of disinformation to the German High Command.
- The use of Ultra to decrypt messages between the German intelligence service and the German High Command.
- General Patton as the general the Nazis feared the most and believed would lead the invasion remained in place in England in plain sight of German reconnaissance with his Ghost Army.

All this created enough uncertainty to delay Nazi decisions and delay German reinforcements and the movement of reserves to the area of the Normandy invasion for some time. It was just enough time, despite very heavy Allied casualties, for the Allies to establish their beachheads at Normandy and move inland and later liberate Europe from Adolf Hitler and his Nazi war machine.

Dick also shared his personal experiences as a navy commander and commanding officer of a destroyer escort (DE) in the Mediterranean. To demonstrate how low-tech can be just as effective as the very sophisticated D&D campaign used by the London Controlling Section (LCS) to support the Normandy invasion, he explained how he and his sailors succeeded in penetrating a carrier battle groups' outer defenses during a major exercise in the Mediterranean. He had his crew altered the running lights on the destroyer to match those of a merchant ship, operated only under cover of darkness, maintained radio silence, and when underway were powered by a single engine and a single screw/propeller and, when challenged, simply responded, "No English." As far as the commander of the CBG was concerned, he was dealing with a harmless merchant ship. At first light with the DE, now well within the CBG defenses, the signalmen on the DE signaled, "Bang, bang, bang, gotcha." And that's how a little old DE with an imaginative commanding officer and crew defeated a carrier battle groups' defenses, using a little bit of D&D to hide the real and show the fake.

By the time Dick got through his full complement of illusions, both physical and mental, my students knew they were in the presence of a master of illusions and deception. They would always give him a standing ovation. It also brought them back to reality and the fact that deception was 90 percent applied psychology and that they and their cognitive biases were part of the problem, which made them all more susceptible to adversarial D&D and self-deception. It also made them more receptive to adopting some of the structured analytic techniques available, like the analysis of competing hypotheses, to assist in mitigating the impact of those biases on their analysis.

On the final day, we considered case studies that proved to be some of the more significant and difficult D&D problems that the

IC had encountered and dealt with—some successfully and some not so successfully.

I'm going to begin with the Indian nuclear tests in May 1998, because much has been written about it and the fact that I was directly involved as the Deputy National Intelligence officer for Warning assigned to the National Intelligence Council at CIA headquarters in monitoring and analyzing preparations for those tests. We knew the Indians had tested their first nuclear device underground in the Thar Desert (Pokhran Test Range), code name Smiling Buddha, in May 1974, so we knew they had the capability to test again. But in this case, we were more concerned about their intentions and the likelihood of them doing so again. For their part, policymakers want to know both—will they test and if so, when will the tests occur (preferably date and time)? Capabilities are much easier to monitor with our high-tech collection systems than intentions, and we may never have enough detailed information to predict the timing of such an event with any degree of confidence. Ascertaining Indian intentions would have required some very good human intelligence, but that was not in the cards.

Our primary goal on the Warning staff was to provide enough strategic warning of the event to allow some action by the policymakers to influence the outcome, prevent the test, or failing that prevent surprise to the president, other senior decision-makers, and the policy community to allow them to mitigate the impact of the event. We did have one significant political indicator that a test was more likely to occur as a result of general elections held in March 1998, when the nationalists right-wing Indian People's Party, the Bharatiya Janata Party (BJP), took control of the coalition government and Atal Bihari Vajpayee regained his position as prime minister. They were known to be strong supporters of India's nuclear weapons program and desire to declare India a full-fledged nuclear state. We provided such an assessment a week or so prior to the tests with little effect.

India conducted five nuclear tests between May 11 and May 13, 1998, and Prime Minister Vajpayee declared India a full-fledged nuclear state in a press conference immediately following the tests. While there was increased activity associated with preparations for testing, there was much more that we would have expected to see but weren't observing. We also knew that there were occasional bursts of activity at the test sites in 1982, 1995, and 1997. Despite the absence of some key pieces of evidence or indicators, we did advise senior decision-makers and policymakers of the potential for an impending test and our assessment that it was more likely given the strong nationalist stance of the BJP. However, without more detailed evidence, we would not be able to meet the expectations of those senior officials. While there was a whirlwind of diplomatic activity to dissuade the Indian government from testing and attempts to keep Pakistan from following suit, both conducted tests that month, with Pakistan testing five weapons on May 28 in response to India's tests and one for good measure two days later. It turned out to be both an intelligence and warning failure and a policy failure. This is all revealed and detailed in the book *Weapons of Peace: The Secret Story of India's Quest to be a Nuclear Power*, written by *India Today* deputy editor at that time Raj Chengappa. You can find it in your local library.

There is an important distinction that I want to make here between our analysis and our assessment that also needs to be explained. Our analysis is based on facts and available evidence and is evidence based. Our assessments are an extension of our analysis to include what we believe. While assigned in the Pentagon years earlier as a senior Warning analyst, I had the opportunity to brief Gen. Colin Powell, when he was chairman, Joint Chiefs of Staff. He used to ask his intelligence briefers, "Tell me what you know, what you don't know, and what you think." That is the essence of the difference between analysis, what we know based on the evidence, and our assessment, what we think. He was also interested in what additional collection initiatives we were taking to bridge or narrow the gap between the two, what we don't know.

What we didn't know in the case of the Indian nuclear tests was that in some of those previous years where there was activity associated with preparations to test, they were accompanied by US démarches to convince the Indians not to test, and some of the signatures we relied on to analyze and assess those preparations were shared with Indian officials. As you may know, a typical diplomatic démarche would require sufficient evidence to convince the Indian officials that we gotcha or caught them in the act. We'd call this an authorized disclosure to support a major policy objective. Regardless, those démarches compromised some of our key signatures and intelligence sources and methods.

Each episode taught the Indians what to do and what not to do to deny and deceive us. They simply hid or disguised with good cover and camouflage what they didn't want us to see (the real) and showed us only what they wanted us to see, just enough of the real to keep us guessing along with the fake. A key takeaway from this experience was that in conducting our analysis, when there are major gaps in our information, we always need to consider the possibility that D&D is being employed against us. Admiral Jeremiah, who was commissioned by DCI George Tenet to examine the reasons for the intelligence and warning failure, concluded in his report that "the absence of evidence does not equate to the evidence of absence." His point would initially elude those who were unfamiliar with the potential impact of D&D on our collection and analysis but proved to be right on the mark and good advice. Put another way, gaps in our intelligence are not always the result of limitations in our technical and human intelligence collection capabilities, but rather created or manufactured for the successful employment of D&D against us.

However, as stated earlier in this chapter, even the most well-educated and well-informed Americans tend to be ahistorical and most often fail to recognize and build upon the lessons of history. This has been the case in two more current examples of adversarial D&D, which came to us from North Korea and Iran, both official members of the axis of evil, even before Pres. George Bush coined the phrase, and both skilled practitioners of D&D.

I like to think of them as the rogues who roar or the neighborhood bullies who are just as desperate for attention on the world stage as the desperate Democrats in Congress who openly support them and applaud their causes and their brutal murderous regimes over our president's attempts to confront them and promote America's national security and that of our allies in the regions.

Iran has already initiated nearly a dozen attacks on US and allied installations in Iraq and the region including the December 3, 2019, rocket attack on al Asad airbase; attacks on Israel; attacks on civilian shipping in the Strait of Hormuz; shoot down of our unmanned drones; and attacks on Saudi oilfields. These attacks and those on US military facilities in Iraq in early January 2020 following our surgical missile strike that killed Iranian general and "butcher" Soleimani underscore their lawless behavior and demonstrate how desperate the maligned Khamenei regime is to rally the Islamic Revolutionary Guard Corps (IRGC), its security forces, and attempt to focus its domestic populace's and world attention on its confrontation with the United States, which is considered by all radical Muslims to be the Great Satan. Of course, the United States doesn't pose any real threat to Iran and the Iranian people. In fact, the president and his senior advisors' handling of the rogue Iranian regime has reflected tremendous restraint and discrimination and proportionality in the application of military force.

The president clearly demonstrated this restraint and his decision made public not to attack military targets in Iran when he realized that just over a hundred innocent civilians would also be killed due to IRGC D&D tactics of collocating military and civilian facilities to guarantee some level of civilian collateral damage for good press and propaganda. This tactic was practiced by the Nazis, by North Vietnam, by Saddam Hussein during both gulf wars, and by Assad in Syria and the Stalinist-like North Korean regime and is practiced by all dictatorial regimes who value their military forces and power over the lives of their civilian population. They employed these measures to complicate our targeting, intimidate neighbors, enslave their populace, and ensure regime survival with the ends always justifying the means.

These D&D tactics and practices like them are in clear violation of jus in bello principles of warfare and are morally reprehensible, but we always have to remember we are not playing by the same set of rules and we are dealing with tyrants and terrorists. That is a fact of life, whether we are negotiating with them or in crisis or conflict with them. In addition, in any dealings with the Iranian regime, if you don't understand their concept of taqiyya/kitman (concealment/disguise), you are at a disadvantage from the outset. D&D are cultural and religious imperatives with the Iranians and Shiites.

"Islamic law [sharia] exists to serve the interests of the Muslim community and of Islam. To save Muslim lives and for the sake of Islam's survival it is obligatory to lie, it is obligatory to drink wine" (Ayatollah Ruhollah Khomeini, speech [July 31, 1981]).

A former Islamic studies professor at the American university in Beirut highlighted the ongoing mainstream nature and pervasiveness of taqiyya as an Islamic political tool in a contemporary treatise stating that:

"Taqiyya is fundamentally important to Islam and practically every Muslim sect agrees to it and practices it... Taqiyya is mainstream...and very prevalent in Islamic politics, especially in the modern era" (Sami Mukaram, *At-Taqiyya fi 'I-Islam* [Dissimulation in Islam] [2004]).

Iran's threat to continue its full-scale nuclear weapons development program without a deal on their terms, nuclear blackmail, drove the dynamics of the negotiations from start to finish, and Foreign Minister Zarif proved himself a master of taqiyya and deception in pressing his threats. At the beginning, he warned that "the only way to ensure that the Iranian nuclear program 'remains' peaceful is to allow the program to develop in a peaceful international context." Given the nature of the deal, or Joint Comprehensive Plan of Action (JCPOA), July 14, 2015, I'm convinced that former president Obama and Secretary of State Kerry and the other US negotiators either didn't have a clue about taqiyya or were so eager to strike a deal at any cost and declare victory that it became a political imperative with Obama whose presidency was coming to an end.

Let's not forget who the players were in these negotiations, the P5 + 1, the United States, China, Russia, Britain, France, and Germany. Keep in mind that the Russians have been major benefactors in supporting Iran's nuclear and other strategic weapons programs over the years and have been close economic and trading partners. Russia has also sold Iran advanced military hardware, while Iran has shared its drone and other military technology with the Russians.

China and Iran have improved military relations and cooperation in recent years as well. Both China and Russia have blamed the United States for increased tensions in the region and began conducting combined naval operations in the Indian Ocean and Gulf of Oman in late December 2019.

Just a few months before the historic arrangement was reached, a report by the International Atomic Energy Agency (IAEA) was leaked to *the New York Times* (February 20, 2015) and indicated that the agency "remained concerned about the possible existence in Iran of undisclosed nuclear related activities involving military-related organizations, including activities related to the development of a nuclear payload for a missile." Earlier, in November 2014, IAEA issued an independent report concluding that despite their disingenuous protests to the contrary, the Iranian regime continued to engage in "systematic," "vigorous" combined military and dual military-civilian efforts "such as enrichment, warhead weaponization, and delivery systems at some stage, whose ultimate goal was procuring a nuclear weapons capability."

Both the Obama Plan of Action arranged with Iran and the Clinton-Holbrooke 1994 Framework Agreement with North Korea to freeze its nuclear weapons program were little more than political expedients to mollify the regional bullies through pandering, declare a partisan political victory, and kick those hot button issues down the road. You don't have to be an intelligence officer or diplomat to recognize that we're now confronted with two renegades with nuclear weapons and long-range intercontinental ballistic missiles that are now or soon will be capable of carrying a nuclear payload to targets in the United States, Europe, and Asia.

The deals themselves lacked any real guarantees of unencumbered access to all nuclear-related facilities by the IAEA and UN-sponsored inspection teams and amounted to little more than extortion on the part of the rogues who got everything they demanded in terms of sanctions relief and billions in frozen assets and aid, much of which undoubtedly was reinvested in their nuclear and strategic weapons development programs and military modernization and, in the case of Iran, also more funds to support terrorism in the Middle East and the rest of the world.

Unfortunately, German chancellor Merkel quickly announced her opposition to President Trump's decision to withdraw from the JCPOA and announced that German and EU sanctions relief would remain in force. Of course, Germany's relations with Iran goes back to the early nineteenth century, and it was Germany that countermanded US efforts during the Clinton administration to impose international sanctions on Iran for its nuclear ambitions back in the mid-1990s. It has been an uphill struggle to convince Germany, Britain, and France, with the latter expressing serious concerns about the deal during negotiations, to follow the US lead. Instead, all have sought innovative deceptive ways to undermine US sanctions and continue vigorous trade relations with Iran.

I predict that these very shortsighted and economically driven decisions rather than security-driven policy decisions will eventually come back to haunt them. The truth of the matter is the 2015 deal only emboldened and encouraged increased Iranian meddling in the region while still allowing Iran to pursue its uranium enrichment and strategic missile programs, which as noted above will eventually give Iran the capability to strike targets in Germany and throughout Europe, a fact that the leadership in Germany, France, and Britain will have to face and accept responsibility for some time in their lifetimes.

President Trump was right to withdraw from the JCPOA, which was a sham, and his decision to confront Iran head-on is precisely the most appropriate foreign policy approach to deal with a renegade and bully who violates all the basic rules of international conduct. You don't deal with a bully by appeasing or pacifying them as did Clinton with North Korea and Obama with Iran. You need to stand up to them and bloody their nose if necessary. This is especially true when they pick on their weaker neighbors or worse yet kill innocent civilians and attack Americans and US facilities, which they have been flagrantly guilty of since the Iranian Revolution in 1979.

Let's not forget the siege and takeover of the American embassy in Tehran in November 1979 and the Iranian hostage crisis that

occurred during President Carter's tenure. Fifty-two American diplomats and staff were held hostage for 444 days while negotiations
dragged on, and a single rescue attempt in April 1980 failed with
the loss of eight American servicemen in a helicopter-air transport
collision. Five aircraft were also abandoned when the mission was
aborted. It was no surprise given the state of the economy that Jimmy
Carter lost the 1980 presidential election in a landslide to Ronald
Reagan in November, and it was no coincidence that the hostages
were released on January 20, 1981, then president Reagan's inaugu-
ration day.

I'm tempted to give President Reagan full credit because of his
hardline stance against negotiating with the Iranians. I believe his
tough talk probably convinced Iran that they needed to strike a deal
with the Carter administration before President Reagan took office
and so they did. Therefore, the real credit must go to President Carter
and his advisors who submitted to blackmail and extortion, giving
the Iranians everything they demanded, sanctions relief, release of
all frozen Iranian assets, and millions of dollars in aid and repara-
tions. The same pattern of negotiations and results were brought to
us by President Bill Clinton with the Clinton-Holbrooke Framework
Agreement with North Korea in 1994 and then again by President
Obama with the Obama-Kerry Iranian nuclear arrangement or
JCPOA in 2015.

As commander in chief, President Trump's decision and autho-
rization for the military operation on January 3, 2020, to take out
Iranian general Soleimani, who was responsible for directing much of
the murder and mayhem in the region, while in a military motorcade
in Baghdad, absolutely met the basic requirements of jus in bello
principles of proportionality and discrimination. It put the regional
bully Iran on notice. The proportion of means to a just end must be
conscientiously calculated as part of a realistic assessment of proba-
bility of success, and the principle of discrimination that prohibits
direct intentional attacks on noncombatants and nonmilitary targets must be met. It was clearly met in this case. Soleimani and his
Republican Guard Forces Command (RFGC) thugs were responsible for thousands of American deaths and those of innocent civilians

and were in Baghdad to orchestrate the New Year's Eve attacks on the American embassy. And they were responsible for planning and organizing additional attacks on other diplomatic posts and US military facilities and personnel in Iraq and the region. He and his thugs posed a clear and imminent threat to those facilities and personnel. The Trump administration's strategy has wisely employed a combination of diplomatic, economic, and military action to send a very clear message to the lawless rogue and regional bully that it, Iran, will have to deal with and confront the United States directly if it continues its aggressive hostile and destabilizing activities.

Military force has been employed as a last resort and has strictly avoided targets that would cause collateral damage or kill innocent civilians. Even the economic sanctions that have been ratcheted up are largely targeted against the Iranian regime, senior leadership, and those individuals and entities associated with the regime, while diplomatic initiatives are ongoing to garner greater support from our European and regional allies to support the US strategy.

"Let every nation know, whether it wishes us well or ill, that we shall pay any price, bear any burden, meet any hardship, support any friend, oppose any foe in order to insure the survival and the success of liberty" (Pres. John F. Kennedy).

The greatest threat to Iran and the Iranian people comes from within Iran, the Khamenei regime and IRGC, whose support for terrorism and relentless pursuit of its strategic nuclear weapons and missile development programs at all cost already pose a grave threat to Iran's regional neighbors, while the brutality of the regime in denying its citizens the freedoms and liberties they are demanding cannot be ignored. Keep in mind that Iran is ruled by tyrants, corrupt kleptocrats, and an unyielding oppressive authoritarian theocracy. According to the New-York-based Center for Human Rights in Iran, the regime has killed and imprisoned thousands. In recent demonstrations expressing outrage over the shoot down of a civilian Ukrainian airline and deaths of Iranian students and other Iranian passengers onboard in December 2019, Iranian authorities killed and wounded an unknown number of protestors. Last November 2019, Amnesty International reported that over three hundred protestors were killed as a result of demonstrations opposing a shutdown of the Internet by the regime to attempt to hide their brutality from the outside world. The facts and the truth, more Iranians have been killed, imprisoned, and executed by their tyrannical corrupt government than any outside force or enemy.

Yet it's not much unlike what is ongoing in America today with the Democrats in the House of Representatives, the greatest obstructionists of freedom, justice, and the rule of law since the Civil War. They are the Jane Fonda's of the twenty-first century, colluding and offering aid and comfort to our enemies while manufacturing crisis after crisis, to focus the publics' attention on sham partisan show trials, first on Russian collusion, then Justice Kavanaugh, and finally on the impeachment of the president in their vain attempts to draw attention away from their own failings and corruption. All this while President Trump continues to successfully address the most important domestic and international issues confronting America and Americans but only with the grace of God and the support of enough brave republican senators and congressmen who also care more about America than their own personal agendas.

All the Democrats' lies and deception have been channeled into an embarrassing and farcical obstructionist and divisive agenda, which demonstrates nothing but disdain and contempt for the American people, our electoral process, and our democratic republic, all because they lost in 2016 and know they can't win in 2020. Bloomberg, Biden, and all the democratic candidates have one thing in common—they are all career politicians, liars, and demagogues and demons of deception. They have demonstrated their hate and lack of civility with their opponents and with one another in a dramatic fashion during the democratic candidate debates. They have made a mockery of our national character, our electoral process, and our nation. Every corrupt obstructionist Democrat up for reelection in 2020 needs to be soundly defeated and their corrupt political careers ended.

Exactly what populist Pres. Donald Trump, never a politician or bureaucrat, set out to accomplish in clearing the swamp. It has proven to be much more difficult due to the entrenched nature of those career politicians on both sides of the aisle in Congress, but most notably the Democrats. Candidates like Bloomberg buying his way into the primaries with his billions, and TV ads full of misrepresentations. Berating the intelligence of America's farmers, treating women in his employment as second-class citizens, and his "stop and frisk" program while mayor of New York City clearly aimed at Blacks and minorities must all be made known to reveal his true character. The democratic candidates are certainly doing their part in their debates to show their true character, pillorying one another like a bunch of undisciplined teenagers. We need to do our part at the polls in November and help make clearing the swamp more than a slogan and make it a reality. We need to take back the House of Representatives and clean house by removing the most obnoxious and radical career politicians up for reelection this year like Pelosi, Schumer, Schiff, and Nadler along with the squad. They all need to be soundly defeated by wholesome God-fearing untainted conservative candidates entering politics for the first time. Thankfully, there are many of them entering races across the country.

> Who among you is wise and understanding? Let him show his works by a good life in the humility that comes with wisdom. But if you have bitter jealousy and ambitions in your hearts, do not boast and be false to the Truth. Wisdom of this kind does not come down from above, but is earthly, unspiritual and demonic. For where jealousy and selfish ambition exist, there is disorder and every foul practice. But the wisdom from above is first of all pure, then peaceable, gentle, compliant, full of mercy and good fruits, without inconstancy or insincerity. And the fruit of righteousness is sown in peace for those who cultivate peace. (James 3:13–18)

# CHAPTER 3
# Foreign Knowledge, Espionage, and Spy-Catching

*The life of spies is to know, not to be known.*
—George Herbert (Anglican priest
and poet, 1593–1633)

Espionage, while not the only source of foreign knowledge, has been the most damaging. And 1985 has often been referred to as the Year of the Spy largely because of the arrest of four individuals and their accomplices—one each from the navy, FBI, CIA, and the NSA, demonstrating in a very big way that espionage and the Russian intelligence services are an equal opportunity employer. From my perspective with forty-six years as an intelligence officer, 1985 should have been labeled the Year of the Wake-Up Call for all four organizations, who up until then refused to seriously consider the possibility that one of their own would ever turn against them. As it was then, it is now. We never learned the lessons of the Year of the Wake-Up Call. Putin and the Russians are probably more engaged now in espionage and active measures than they were during the Cold War, and we have more agents of the Russian intelligence services operating within our government and bureaucracy than anyone could possibly imagine.

Some of the earlier espionage cases that you don't hear much about—Walker, Miller, Howard, and Pelton—all had personal and significant financial problems that should have been red flags to their employers and that each were potentially serious security risks.

*John Walker* was a US Navy chief warrant officer and communications specialist who spied for the Soviets for eighteen years (1968–1985). Walker had access to cryptologic key lists needed to decipher top secret naval communications and provided these key lists to the Soviets, allowing them to decipher more than one million encrypted naval messages. These provided the Soviets with highly sensitive information related to weapons and sensor data, naval tactics, and the locations of naval surface, submarine, and airborne operations and training.

The totality of what was compromised was described as providing the Soviets "war-winning information." Walker also successfully recruited one of his students, Senior Chief Petty Officer Jerry Whitworth, a senior chief radioman, his older brother Arthur, a retired navy lieutenant commander and military contractor, and son Michael, an active-duty seaman, all with access to highly classified naval communications and intelligence. Walker may have received compensation of over $2 million. Walker was arrested in May 1985, only after his daughter and ex-wife made several attempts to convince the FBI of his spying.

*Richard Miller*, a twenty-year veteran, the first FBI agent in its history to be caught spying, was viewed as a loser by his colleagues and was officially reprimanded for being overweight and selling Amway products out of the trunk of his car. He was excommunicated from the Mormon Church for having an extramarital affair, was separated from his wife and eight children, and was in heavy debt. Instead of dismissing him, his FBI bosses assigned him to a position in the Los Angeles field office in Counterintelligence in 1984, where he retained access to highly classified information. He was supposed to be monitoring and catching spies, but instead was compromised by one—an attractive modern-day Soviet mate hare, Svetlana Ogorodnikov, who had immigrated to the United States with her "husband" Nikolai and settled in Los Angeles in 1973. Both were actually access agents of the Soviet KGB. She was your classic honey trap who convinced him through their sexual encounters to sell secrets to the Soviet Union. His spying career was short-lived, but he allegedly collected $50,000 in gold and $15,000 in cash before he and his honeypot were both arrested in May 1985, just before a second meeting with the KGB was to take place in Vienna, Austria.

*Edward Lee Howard* was hired by the CIA at the age of thirty in 1981 and was later joined by his wife Mary. Both were trained by the agency as case officers in the counterintelligence tradecraft. Howard had admitted during the hiring process to using drugs, including cocaine. How he ever got through the rigorous interview and polygraph process and why he was ever hired is a mystery to me. Maybe he had the same polygrapher that passed on John Brennan. His career was shorter-lived than any I'm aware of. He was dismissed when he failed a routine polygraph in 1983, before being posted to the American embassy in Moscow. What makes Howard's case interesting is that he was motivated by vengeance and disgruntlement over his dismissal, and his spying career was shorter-lived than his more than two-year career with the CIA. However, prior to the failed poly and in preparation for his posting in Moscow, he was given access to extremely sensitive and detailed files with the names of Soviet agents working for the CIA. Following his dismissal, he simply passed them on to the KGB resident in Washington DC.

That resident was Vitaly Yurchenko, who allegedly defected to the United States in 1985. The most noteworthy of those agents compromised by Howard was Soviet scientist Adolf Tolkachev, who was doing sensitive Soviet research and testing of stealth technology. Tolkachev and many of the others compromised by Howard were promptly arrested and executed. Howard later eluded CIA and FBI surveillance and escaped to Helsinki and then on to Moscow, where he received a hero's welcome and remained until his "untimely" death in 2002.

*Ronald Pelton* served in the US Air Force as a Russian language voice intercept processing specialist and was assigned to the NSA, before being hired as a civilian. He was employed for fourteen years before filing for bankruptcy and resigning in 1979. Pelton faced mounting financial problems and in January 1980 contacted the Soviet embassy in Washington DC. Although the FBI had the Soviet embassy under surveillance, they were unable to observe or identify him. Pelton, like Howard, was debriefed by KGB resident Vitaly

Yurchenko, where he disclosed the details of an extremely sensitive NSA and US Navy operation, Ivy Bells, a program to wiretap undersea cables to monitor Soviet military communications and track Soviet submarines. Additional debriefings were conducted with the KGB in Vienna, Austria.

During his very short defection, Vitaly Yurchenko also provided information to the FBI about Pelton recalling meeting and debriefing Pelton in 1980. After several months of surveillance, bugging his car and house, and unable to collect any incriminating evidence, a sting operation was conducted that resulted in his arrest. As for Yurchenko, it is still believed that he was a redoubled agent, who defected in order to give up Howard and Pelton to protect a much more valuable KGB asset, Aldrich Ames.

The most notable cases during my career were CIA Senior Counterintelligence Officer Aldrich Ames working within CIA's Soviet Division and FBI Special Agent Robert Hanssen also working in Counterintelligence at FBI headquarters.

Actually, not only did Ames's and Hanssen's spying careers overlap, but also they both began in 1985, Ames in April and Hanssen in October, and were both handled by the same Soviet KGB resident agent in Washington DC. Incredibly, Senior KGB colonel Victor Cherkashin, who was chief of counterintelligence at the KGB residency in Washington DC in 1985, had the good fortune as a KGB officer to be their spy handler. In his book *Spy Handler*, Cherkashin is described as the man who recruited both Ames and Hanssen, but the fact is both were walk-ins or volunteers, and there was little recruiting involved or necessary.

Cherkashin described one brief meeting with Ames in Chadwick's restaurant in Georgetown, Washington DC, as having dramatically altered the landscape of US-Soviet espionage. It was at that meeting in June 1985 that Ames wrote down a list of names of virtually every CIA asset working within the Soviet Union, to include a number of KGB and GRU officers who Cherkashin personally knew and had worked with. Among those was a former colonel of the KGB (Committee for State Security) and resident-designate (station chief in US CIA terms) assigned to the Soviet embassy in London in 1982,

Oleg Gordievsky. Gordievsky was suddenly recalled to Moscow in 1985 under suspicion of being doubled by the British intelligence service MI6. Aldrich Ames had given him up as one of a dozen or more US/British assets being run against the Soviets. Ames also provided a plastic bag full of sensitive intelligence reports disclosing even more details about CIA operations. Most of those CIA assets named by Ames were later arrested and executed. This was only the very beginning of the most damaging nine-year espionage case ever discovered in the history of the CIA.

A number of these cases were initially believed to have been exposed by Edward Lee Howard, when he fled to Moscow to avoid prosecution. However, there was convincing evidence that one of the objectives of Vitaly Yurchenko's arranged defection to the United States from August to September 1985 was contrived by the KGB to protect Ames by giving up Howard and Pelton. Ironically, it was Ames who initially met Yurchenko and debriefed him upon his arrival in the United States at Andrews Air Force Base, very drunk and very concerned that Yurchenko might reveal his identity, but never did so.

According to the CIA Office of Inspector General (OIG) report, senior agency management should have been held accountable for permitting an officer with obvious problems such as Ames to continue to perform such sensitive duties with nearly unrestricted access to a wide range of highly sensitive intelligence. Among those issues identified in the OIG report, which his managers were aware of, included sleeping on the job, alcohol abuse, security problems, financial problems with heavy debt in the early 1980s followed by unexplained bank account deposits, a cash purchase of a $540,000 house, and failure to file required contact reports with foreign nationals or foreign travel reports. A psychological profile of Ames that was prepared as part of the investigation indicates a troubled employee with a significant potential to engage in "harmful activities"—of course, none more harmful than espionage. The report goes on to state that it was difficult to understand the repeated failure to focus more attention on Ames earlier when his name continued to come up throughout the investigation. He had access to all the compromised cases, his financial resources improved substantially for unestablished reasons, and his laziness and poor performance were rather widely known. All these are critical CI indicators any one of which should have drawn attention to Ames. Combined, they should have made him stand out.

Another more recent case of espionage deserves mention here, former Air Force enlisted counterintelligence specialist Monica Witt, who worked in the Air Force Office of Special Investigations (OSI) from 1997 to 2008. She was trained as a Farsi language specialist and spent time in the Middle East engaged in both Signals intelligence collection and human intelligence operations. According to the indictment, while assigned to OSI between 2003 and 2008, she had access to extremely sensitive intelligence associated with a Special Access Program (SAP) involving US counterintelligence operations in Iran and true names of recruited agents and their US handlers. The indictment states that the SAP involved a sophisticated agent communications program that if compromised would allow the Iranians to identify and locate the recruited agents. When she left OSI in 2008, she continued to work in that program with a civilian intelligence contractor until 2010. Not only did she compromise the special communications program, but also she traveled to Iran on several occasions and produced anti-American propaganda videos and films in 2012 and 2013 prior to her apparent defection to Iran in August 2013. The FBI had her under investigation and surveillance for several years prior and had questioned her and even tipped her off in 2012 that she was targeted for recruitment by Iranian intelligence, when in fact she was already an Iranian asset. Yet no arrests or charges were filed until after her defection.

The compromise of the communications program may have also been responsible for the arrest of more than a dozen CIA assets in China. However, the arrest and conviction in May of 2019 of former CIA Case Officer Jerry Chun Shing Lee, who worked for the agency in China and elsewhere from 1994 to 2007, was also indicted on similar charges. Following his resignation, he lived in Hong Kong as a private businessman and met frequently with Chinese intelligence in 2010 and made cash deposits in his Hong Kong bank accounts of hundreds of thousands of dollars over the next three years.

*The New York Times* reported on May 20, 2017, that the Chinese government began systematically dismantling CIA intelligence operations in China in 2010, killing or imprisoning more than a dozen CIA assets and crippling intelligence gathering there for years afterward. Lee and an unnamed accomplice were implicated, but some also believed the Chinese had gained knowledge of the special communications program compromised by Witt from Iran and hacked the communications the CIA used to communicate with its assets in China. I'd also add that it's a common practice for the Iranians, Chinese, and Russians to share such sensitive intelligence if it helps their mutual counterintelligence operations against their common enemy, the United States.

As pointed out earlier, espionage is an equal opportunity employer but isn't the only source of foreign knowledge and potentially valuable intelligence available to our adversaries, both state and nonstate actors. Former DCI George Tenet had reportedly stated on more than one occasion that unauthorized disclosures and leaks provide a veritable treasure trove of intelligence for our adversaries just as damaging as espionage. In an interview with *USA Today* in 2002, he stated that unauthorized disclosures "have become one of the biggest threats to the survival of US Intelligence."

In the intelligence discipline, when we are discussing leaks and unauthorized disclosures, we often refer to the Lunev Axiom. When classified intelligence is exposed in the press or media, it's basically the equivalent of intelligence gathered through foreign espionage. The axiom reflects statements by former Soviet military intelligence officer Col. Stanislav Lunev, who in 1992 became the highest-ranking GRU officer to defect to the United States. He had stated that while assigned to the residency in Washington DC, he "was amazed—and Moscow was very appreciative—at how many times [he] found very sensitive information in American newspapers." Lunev later offered, "In [his] view, Americans tend to care more about scooping their competition than about national security, which made [his] job easier." While bits and pieces of such information may not in themselves be harmful, it is the cumulative impact of these and other compromised sources of information that our adversaries and terrorist groups are able to pull together that pose a serious threat to our national security. Press leaks that reveal intelligence techniques, sources, and methods give adversaries the opportunity to develop D&D countermeasures, resulting in a decline in the effectiveness of intelligence collection efforts and raising the potential that intelligence collection can be subjected to manipulation and rendered ineffective. The problem is more acute today, because leaked materials are now easily disseminated and researched electronically, allowing rapid compilation and comprehensive review. Remember, improved foreign knowledge of sources and methods lead to improved D&D and countermeasures reducing the effectiveness of both our intelligence collection and analysis and the credibility and veracity of that intelligence.

We also refer to what is commonly called the Gertz effect. Bill Gertz is an American editor, columnist, and author of several books addressing national security issues that are generally very insightful and, in some cases, also very revealing, in a not so helpful manner, on matters dealing specifically with US intelligence and counterintelligence capabilities and vulnerabilities. The problem is that Gertz always seems to be looking to generate an eye-popping type of reaction to his revelations about our national technical and human intelligence collection systems and programs, our most sensitive covert intelligence operations, our collection and analytic vulnerabilities, and our defensive and offensive counterintelligence capabilities. With him, it always seems to be a no-holds-barred approach to his investigative journalism. He and journalists like him can hide behind their First Amendment rights and argue that such transparency, even when it involves exposing highly sensitive intelligence sources and methods, is necessary and in the public interest. The fact is that intelligence sources and methods compromised only improve our *Enemies* knowledge. Ironically, *Enemies* is the title of one of his many books about how America's enemies steal our vital secrets and get away with it. He typically blames it on negligence and incompetence while saying nothing about his own unauthorized disclosures and damaging revelations.

I have only purchased and read two of Gertz's books, *The China Threat* and *Enemies*, and used them in the two courses that I taught on D&D, as worst-case examples of unauthorized disclosures in the public domain. Both books begin with and contain references throughout to top secret intelligence reports, communications, studies, and programs that neither he nor the general public have a need to know. The real irony is that in *Enemies*, he criticizes the IC for allowing itself to be victimized by Chinese, Russian, and other foreign intelligence services and berates our track record for catching the many spies within our midst, when he and other investigative journalists who claim to be crusaders for reform are themselves guilty of acting as the equivalent of highly trained foreign intelligence operatives.

Gertz is given credit by fans and critics alike for having great insider insights into the dark world of spying and spy-catching when in fact he has obtained his highly classified intelligence from his own moles and mules inside the IC, congressional staffs, and other unnamed government entities. In one of his more infamous and controversial compromises, he somehow obtained and included at the back of his book, *The China Threat*, a highly classified section of a National Intelligence Estimate (NIE) on China, before the NIE was even published. Gertz has been subpoenaed to appear in court in the past to reveal his sources without much success. In 2006, Gertz wrote a story about the prosecution of a Chinese spy ring in California, Chi Mak, his wife, brother, and two other relatives who were convicted by a grand jury for conspiring to export US defense technology to China, including data on an electronic propulsion system that could make submarines virtually undetectable. Gertz simply attributed the information to "senior Justice Department officials," but even such a vague attribution suggests that he must have a large pool of moles and leakers embedded throughout our government bureaucracy, who if ever identified should and I would hope would be prosecuted to the full extent of the law. While courts have held that the Espionage Act and other relevant statutes allow for convictions for leaks to the press, the government has never prosecuted a traditional news organization for its receipt of classified or other protected information.

While Gertz and journalists like him are more a part of the problem than the solution, they and the spies in our midst are not alone in compromising sensitive US intelligence. There are also those who leak and direct highly classified intelligence to the media for partisan political and ideological reasons. Some may actually be agents of the Russian, Chinese, or Iranian or other foreign intelligence services who have penetrated our intelligence agencies, the Congress, the DOJ, military services, and even the White House staff as was the case during the Obama administration.

This was made very apparent to me immediately following the covert operation to take down Osama bin Laden on May 2, 2011, shortly after 1:00 a.m. Pakistan time (2000 UTC) and just after 3:00 p.m., Sunday, May 1 (Washington DC time). President Obama formally approved the plan, which had been in the making for months, just after 1:00 p.m. Eastern Daylight Time (EDT). Once on the ground, the raid on bin Laden's compound in Abbottabad, Pakistan, took only forty minutes, from about 3:30 p.m. to 4:10 p.m. EDT. Bin Laden's body was positively identified, and President Obama addressed the nation about the successful raid around 11:30 p.m., Sunday night, while bin Laden's body was buried at sea within twenty-four hours to comply with Islamic law.

This was a unilateral US covert operation, which excluded any notification of the Pakistani government or intelligence services due to real concerns about compromising the mission. Since it was a covert operation, it also required presidential approval, or a presidential finding, which specifies in writing why the action is necessary and how it directly supports identifiable foreign policy and national security objectives of the United States. The operation was directed by then director of the CIA Leon Panetta from the CIA Operations Center and supported by Admiral McRaven, USN commander of the Joint Special Operations Command, and carried out by Navy SEAL team 6. The raid culminated a ten-year manhunt for bin Laden, who was credited for being one of the masterminds of the al-Qaeda 9/11 attacks on America that killed and injured thousands. What was not transparent to the American public was the significant investment of intelligence resources to support years of intensive intelligence collection and analysis to find bin Laden and his top lieutenants.

My targeting students and I got a firsthand look at how intense this collection and analytic effort was as we were fortunate enough to have key members of the "hunt for bin Laden" targeting team brief us in class on a regular basis. These analysts were instrumental in laying the groundwork and identifying the bin Laden courier that led the IC to the Abbottabad compound and resulted in the successful operation.

The following day, Director Panetta, Admiral McRaven, and members of their staffs presented a highly classified briefing in the Bubble (CIA's auditorium), which was also broadcast on CIA's classified internal closed-circuit TV network for a few senior administration officials and CIA personnel, detailing the intelligence, operational planning, and decision-making process leading up to the successful execution of the operation.

I had just started preparing for one of my classes that day teaching and facilitating a course in the fundamentals of D&D and was able to watch the entire briefing on the classified closed-circuit TV network with my colleagues in CIAU. When I returned to my apartment after work that day, I was shocked to see a big chunk of that highly classified presentation on the evening news, in some instances repeating some of its most sensitive points almost verbatim. It was then, and remains, one of the most egregious examples of a leak or disclosure I had ever experienced firsthand. Unfortunately, I wasn't alone in my assessment.

On day 2 of our class, one of the key issues we addressed was terrorists' use of D&D, and our speaker on that subject had already completed her own initial analysis indicating that about 80 percent of the top secret presentation was compromised on the evening news. Of course, it would be very useful to other terrorist organizations and improve all potential adversaries' knowledge of our operational, collection, and surveillance capabilities and improve their D&D techniques to counter them. The nagging question on the minds of my students, my colleagues, and myself was, whether this disclosure could possibly have been authorized or accomplished for purely partisan political reasons? We could not understand how something so sensitive with so much invested over so many years could be compromised in such great detail with the media gaining access and sharing it with the world in less than twenty-four hours.

We all realize the push for transparency, but the president's address should have been enough information for the general public and media, that the mission was a success and Bin Laden was killed by Special Operations forces in a nighttime operation with no American casualties other than a damaged helicopter. That should have ended the public exposure with no further need to know, authorized or required. On the one hand, there were those who accused President Obama of taking more credit for the take down than was due and milked it for all he could for his 2012 reelection campaign, with the November elections just a few months away. The highly publicized photo of the president with Hillary Clinton and his national security team in the White House situation room at least made it appear to the uninformed that they were controlling the operation, while they were really only getting live near-real-time updates from Operation Neptune Spear. On the other hand, there were those like Admiral McRaven who heaped lavish praise on the president for his decision-making and determination to get bin Laden despite the risks.

The fact and the truth are that Obama was not the first president to go after bin Laden who continued to be the face of the worldwide terrorist threat and number one on the FBI's Most Wanted List. A 1986 Presidential Finding signed by Pres. Ronald Reagan authorized worldwide covert action against terrorism. Unfortunately, during the Clinton administration, according to the 9/11 Commission Report, President Clinton failed to follow up on at least four excellent opportunities to kill or capture bin Laden. It was also on Clinton's watch that terrorists launched a series of attacks on US interests at home and abroad—the World Trade Center attack in 1993; the attack on Khobar Towers, US Air Force barracks, in Saudi Arabia three years later; 1998 bombings of US embassies in Kenya and Tanzania; and the attack on the USS Cole in Aden, Yemen. Each of these were carried out with no effective response and turned out to be precursors of the 9/11 attacks.

It was actually George Bush, following the 9/11 terrorist attacks on the World Trade Center and Pentagon where I was assigned as the Deputy Defense Intelligence officer for Global Trends and Projections and lost seven of my colleagues in DIA, who issued a Memorandum of Notification calling for bin Laden to be either captured or killed. He also authorized billions in additional funding for the CIA and other IC agencies along with the military services to prosecute the Global War on Terrorism.

Khalid Sheikh Mohammed, number three in the al-Qaeda leadership, and several other top lieutenants were killed or captured during the Bush administration. In contrast, when President Obama entered office in 2008, one of his first official acts as president was to direct that there no longer be a Global War on Terrorism, but directed that we refer to it as Overseas Contingency Operations. One of his apparent rationales was to avoid offending Muslims world-wide, since Muslims were only responsible for 90 percent of terrorist attacks especially against America and American interests worldwide (sarcasm intended). The Bipartisan 9/11 Commission had even crit-icized President Bush for using the term Global War on Terrorism, arguing that it was too vague and that the enemy is not just some generic evil. They stated that the catastrophic threat is much more specific; it is the threat of Islamist terrorism. Once again, the real experts were arguing for clarity, while President Obama and com-pany preferred obfuscation to hide and deny the real threat.

In facilitating and teaching courses in D&D and deception planning and analysis at the CIA University, we focused largely on our adversaries and their employment of D&D against us in all spheres of our strategic relations, political, diplomatic, military, and economic. My students were career civilian and military intel-ligence officers from throughout the IC who needed to understand the D&D doctrines, strategies, and capabilities of our adversaries to advance their own strategic political, military, and economic objec-tives and counter our own. It became even more important following the terrorist attacks on our homeland on September 11, 2001, that alerted us to the fact that we could no longer just concern ourselves with state actors' use of D&D, but needed to address terrorists and other nonstate actors' use of D&D.

I also became painfully aware and concerned as an informed observer during President Obama's tenure and more so during the 2016 presidential campaign and election of President Trump that nowhere has deception been more prevalent than in our very own domestic political environment. It had never been a major concern of mine or my students, because CIA's charter and our concerns were to collect and analyze foreign intelligence. In fact, the agency is proscribed along with other US intelligence agencies by Executive Order 12333 from collecting and retaining information on US persons or companies operating in the United States. This includes anyone with a valid US visa or green card holders, which was the case with the 9/11 attackers.

The only exception that I'm aware of is when terrorist activity is suspected. In order to pursue the collection of such information, which would be readily shared with the FBI and DOJ, approval would have to be obtained from the special FISA court established by the passage of the Foreign Intelligence Surveillance Act of 1978 that we have heard so much about concerning domestic spying by the FBI on President Trump and his campaign.

I believe it's very important in our analysis to consider some key events in history that may help us separate the truth from fiction and connect the dots to better understand how we have arrived at where we are today, a very dangerous and volatile domestic political environment. It's an environment teeming with hate, demagoguery, and deception, which can only lead to more violence. I say this because one of our vulnerabilities is that Americans tend to be shortsighted. We ignore the lessons of the past at our own peril and focus on the here and now. We also tend to be very nearsighted focusing on the next election cycle and not much beyond that. Patience is also a virtue that seems to be in short supply with the demand for instant gratification and quick fixes being the order of the day in our problem-solving and decision-making. Then there are the millennials who seem to be very technologically savvy but are in many cases lacking interpersonal and communications skills and have very short attention spans. I can attest to this after spending thirteen years in the classroom with young adults.

Our potential adversaries are well aware of these qualities and have and will take advantage of them in their normal course of doing business with us and in their strategies employing D&D against us. While not the only source as discussed, their success is in large part based on intelligence obtained over the years through espionage, which provided them detailed knowledge not just of our collection capabilities and limitations, but of how we do business. Remember, increased knowledge leads to improved D&D and active measures, propaganda, and covert influence operations are all tools of deception.

As previously noted, three of the most damaging spies and traitors during my career—Walker (navy), Ames (CIA), and Hanssen (FBI)—spied for the Soviet Union and gave up information individually and collectively that proved to cause grave damage to US national security. All were what we refer to as walk-ins or volunteers due to the fact that the Soviets never really had to do much in terms of recruiting any of them and each had their own motivation for spying, money, revenge, sex, or some combination thereof.

Neither Aldrich Ames or Robert Hanssen, the most damaging of all spies during my career, were motivated ideologically with an affinity for socialism or communism. We all thought we left that behind in the late 1940s and early 1950s with Sen. Joseph McCarthy, who rooted out the Rosenbergs and other dyed-in-the-wool Communists in Congress and Hollywood. Not so, as it now appears that they are back in greater numbers than ever in Congress, federal, state, and local governments as well as our social, religious, and educational institutions.

I'm sure many of us would like to deal with these radical left-wing alien misfits like hero Russell Casse did in the movie *Independence Day*. "Hello, boys. I'm back." Right after, he would proclaim, "All right you alien a——, in the words of my generation, up yours!" After all, it is very clear, they have turned to violence and intimidation to serve their own political agenda of deceit, intolerance, and hypocrisy and are propagating a culture of death and the spirit of the antichrist. One might argue that we have to fight fire with fire or follow the Old Testament Mosaic Law of an eye for an eye, which simply meant that when dealing out justice to wrongdoers, the punishment should fit the crime. The eye for an eye rule did not authorize or sanction vigilante justice. Neither is the rule binding, nor should it be practiced by Christians, which Jesus's sacrificial death abolished (Romans 10:4). We cannot allow ourselves to be dragged down into the abyss with the Democrats and radical Left and lower ourselves to their immoral, unethical, and uncivil standards of behavior.

In Martin Luther King, Jr.'s words, "Darkness cannot drive out darkness, only light can do that. Hate cannot drive out hate, only love can do that."

And in those prophetic words of the great apostle of Christ, Saint Paul, in his second letter to Timothy (2 Timothy 4:1–6),

> Beloved, I charge you in the presence of God and of Jesus Christ, who will judge the living and the dead, and by his appearing and his kingly power: proclaim the word; be persistent whether it is convenient or inconvenient; convince, reprimand, encourage through all patience and teaching. For the time will come when people will not tolerate sound doctrine but, following their own desires and insatiable curiosity, will accumulate teachers and will stop listening to the Truth, and will be diverted to Myths. But you be self-possessed in all circumstances; put up with hardship; perform the work of an evangelist; fulfill your ministry.

Where there is no love, and hate and evil are suffocating, and reason and compromise simply don't work, you have to take a stand and fight for what is right and just, as the Apostle Paul counseled Timothy. I believe we're at that tipping point right now and need to stand up, speak out, and be counted, not as vigilantes like our opponents and protagonists, but as disciples of Christ and Evangelists and teachers, and confront them through prayer and action and overwhelm them at the ballot box. They call for the "extermination of the monopolists" (Elizabeth Warren's and Karl Marx's words) and are doubling down to take away our freedoms of speech, religion, and right to bear arms and subject us all to the tyranny of their political correctness and militant secularism of the radical left-wing minorities.

"Our lives begin to end the day we become silent about the things that matter" (Martin Luther King, Jr.).

"The only thing necessary for the triumph of evil is for good men to do nothing" (Edmund Burke).

Now, we can add a motivation for espionage, treason, and sedition that most have never considered in our lifetimes, political deception and subversion to undermine our Constitution, to overthrow a duly elected president of the United States, and to transform America into the socialist utopia and dictatorship of the radical Left. There is no tyranny of the majority in America; the tyranny is and will continue to come from the radical left-wing minorities and political correctness police that the Obama administration worked so hard to reestablish and energize during his eight-year tenure in office and continues to do so from his shadow government.

Republican president William McKinley, twenty-fifth president of the United States, who was assassinated six months into his second term in office in September 1901 by an anarchist, once warned, "The tyranny of the minority is infinitely more odious and intolerable and more to be feared than that of the majority."

Nothing could be more appropriate to characterize the political discourse today in America. It is the overbearing minority that dominates this discourse by misleading, intimidating, and tyrannizing the silent majority with lies, deception, and humiliating name-calling. As such, the Democrats are conducting their own form of active measures against the American electorate, manufacturing one phony crisis after another to distract us all from their own flagrant corruption and deceit. Only with the divine intervention of a just, loving, and merciful God did the grandest deception of all fall short of its goal. However, as we all now know, Obama's bureaucratic sycophants like McCabe and the other FBI, DOJ, and CIA coconspirators along with their congressional and media allies have continued their vane attempts to deceive the American people and subvert our president and our national sovereignty. Most of them are acting as agents of the Russian and Chinese intelligence services and corrupt Ukrainian organized crime syndicates.

The SVR, the foreign intelligence service and successor of the former First Chief Directorate of the KGB, responsible for foreign intelligence activities, has been greatly expanded since a reorganization of the Russian intelligence services in 1991 by Pres. Boris Yeltsin. The reorganization itself was an attempt to deceive the United States and our Western allies into thinking that the KGB was being eliminated or dismantled as a relic of the Cold War, but just the opposite was the case. Its resources and capabilities and foreign intelligence activities were assumed by its successor, the SVR. The SVR, like the KGB, is responsible for espionage and active measures (cyberattacks, propaganda, information and covert influence operations, and espionage) in the United States and the West, which have actually been as robust in the post-Cold War era as they were during the height of the Cold War.

In fact, some would argue that the new SVR and FSB are exactly like their predecessors, except now on steroids. Those operations have been complemented and bolstered by the GU (or GRU), the Main Intelligence Directorate of the Minister of Defense and Chief of the General Staff, or military intelligence organization, which is reportedly Russia's largest foreign intelligence agency with several times the numbers of agents deployed in foreign countries as the SVR. Let's not forget that Pres. Vladimir Putin spent most of his early career (1975–1991) as an intelligence officer in the former KGB before entering politics and served for a short time as the director of the Federal Security Service of the Russian Federation (FSB), also a successor of the KGB, responsible for internal state security.

These agents of influence and subversives—like McCabe, Comey, Strzok, Page, and Ohr—have been crawling out of their spider holes and have been exposed and discredited and should be prosecuted. Yet that hasn't deterred the Clinton-Obama mafia that is doubling down to finish the job. McCabe's accusations that President Trump is a Russian provocateur, for example, are a classic attempt at misdirection and dissimulation to hide the real and promote the fake. McCabe and his Trump-hating masters and associates are guilty of exactly what he and others have attempted to project onto our president and members of his administration.

In attempting to do so, even in testimony before Congress, many of these individuals have perjured themselves and should be held accountable. What President Nixon and his Watergate plumbers were guilty of in the 1971 break-in of Democratic Party offices in Watergate pales in comparison to what these Bolsheviks have and are continuing to attempt to openly and blatantly accomplish with their subversion and sedition. They encourage and exhort violence and hate speech with their militant left-wing militias, the antifa, now operating as a domestic terrorist organization on behalf of the Democratic Party apparatus and the radical Left.

Over two years of the Mueller investigation as well as those conducted by Congress and millions of taxpayer dollars later, and not a shred of hard evidence of collusion with the Russians on the part of candidate Trump, President Trump, or his administration. That's because Mueller and his kangaroo court were looking in all the wrong places. I'm even willing to give Mr. Mueller and his largely democratic investigative team members and Clinton campaign donors the benefit of the doubt and not characterize the investigation as a witch hunt, which for all intent and purposes it was.

Setting that aside, it was a seriously flawed investigation. I know from experience that the FBI is incapable of policing their own or are unwilling to police their own and has a poor track record of catching spies, including those within their midst. The investigative techniques applied by Mr. Mueller and his team were much like those applied in the terribly botched mole hunt that ended in the arrest of their very own Robert Hanssen. The lead investigator for that mole hunt was FBI Special Agent and top spy catcher David Szady, who had his team of twenty-five investigators focus single-mindedly on the wrong man for more than two years despite the fact that eight of the twenty-five investigators did not believe the wrongly accused CIA officer was the mole. Szady never apologized and argued that the investigation was a success, because they eventually found the real mole, Robert Hanssen. The DOJ Office of the Inspector General (OIG) did not agree.

As such, the Hanssen case, like Russiagate, is a great example of how not to catch a spy and how not to conduct an investigation. According to the DOJ OIG report of August 2003, the Hanssen case highlighted significant, long-standing deficiencies in the FBI's internal security program, many of which were brought to the attention of FBI management over the years but were not corrected. Before Hanssen's arrest, the FBI's security program was based on trust. Rather than taking the kind of proactive steps adopted by other IC components, such as regular counterintelligence polygraph examinations, financial disclosures, meaningful background reinvestigations, and utilizing audit functions regarding computer usage, the FBI trusted that its employees would remain loyal throughout their careers. According to the OIG report, Hanssen was never required to submit to a polygraph examination or complete a detailed financial disclosure statement during his twenty-five-year FBI career, despite his extraordinary broad access to extremely sensitive human and technical intelligence from across the IC.

In contrast, during my career as an intelligence analyst and operations specialist, I was subjected to a lifestyle polygraph when being recruited by CIA in 1978 and at least six regular CI polygraphs and additional ad hoc polygraphs for access to special programs. These procedures were followed for my colleagues in the CIA and DIA. While the OIG report indicated that the FBI had taken steps to improve its internal security program following Hanssen's arrest, by adopting a regular CI-focused polygraph program, a financial disclosure program, and the creation of a Security Division, some of the most serious weaknesses still had not been fully remedied at the time of the report. Hanssen had also exploited many of the weaknesses in document and computer security to pass sensitive information to the KGB and its successor, the SVR. According to the OIG, those weaknesses continued to expose the FBI to the risk of future serious compromises by another mole.

I'll also give them a break by acknowledging that they are first and foremost a law enforcement agency with its intelligence squads only formally established under Mueller's directorship post 9/11. During my last thirteen-year second career as an intelligence educator with CIA (March 2003 to April 2016), I was asked to put together a team to go out and train Director Mueller's newly formed intelligence squads and special agents at their field offices throughout the United States in the areas of D&D, targeting, and asset validation. I had a team of subject matter experts in D&D from the IC Foreign Denial and Deception Committee (FDDC) that had representatives from throughout the IC. Among the team members was the deputy chairman of the FDDC, an FBI special agent, who knew and had worked with the notorious FBI spy Robert Hanssen and presented a detailed briefing on Hanssen and the volumes of highly classified and sensitive intelligence he compromised and provided to the Russians; my good friend and professional magician, Dick Christian; and a career CIA counterintelligence officer and good friend and colleague of mine, Brian Kelley, who was the CIA officer falsely accused of being the mole that turned out to be Hanssen, the spy in their midst.

Brian had an opportunity to tell his story in a CBS *60 Minutes* interview, and it demands some special attention here as well. Despite the fact that Brian and family members were hounded, harassed, and interrogated on numerous occasions for more than two years, Brian harbored no bitterness toward his FBI protagonist Szady or the team of mole hunters. The ordeal only ended when the FBI reportedly paid $7 million to a Russian intelligence officer for a file that contained an audio tape with the voice of the real mole along with some partial fingerprints. The voice on the tape, which Szady expected to be that of Brian Kelley so he could finally nail him to the cross, turned out to be that of their very own Robert Hanssen.

The incredible rest of the story was that after being completely exonerated by the DCI and failing to get so much as an apology from the agent in charge of the FBI investigation, Szady, Brian agreed to participate in the FBI field office training in hopes that it might prevent another individual from being unjustly accused and harassed by the FBI. Brian joined the team to try to teach and train those FBI officers how to validate assets by employing a systematic process to vet potential assets for reliability and avoid being duped by double agents. We trained over a thousand FBI agents at twelve of the FBI's field offices and Washington HQs, between August 2003 and September 2004.

The importance of this training would become much more apparent after the December 30, 2009, Camp Chapman attack in Khost, Afghanistan, killing seven CIA officers and contractors and wounding six in the most lethal attack against CIA in over twenty-five years. The suicide bomber was a known al-Quaida operative and propagandist, Humam Khalil Abu-Malal al Balawi, who the Jordanian intelligence service were convinced they had "doubled" to penetrate al-Quaida's inner circle in Pakistani tribal areas. It turned out that Balawi was not properly vetted, used the opportunity to gain access to Camp Chapman, and continued to be run as a "triple" by al-Quaida's second in command, Ayman al Zawahiri, himself. The attack may have been in retaliation for an earlier drone strike that killed senior al-Quaida operative, Abdullah Sa'id al-Libi.

The majority of the younger officers were very receptive to the training and amazed and impressed that Brian was willing to devote himself to such training once they became aware that he was the CIA victim of the infamous mole hunt and some very poor investigative work by the bureau. However, there were also plenty of the old school knuckle-draggers who just couldn't let go of their approach of using threats and intimidation to vet and keep their assets or perps in line. Our team received the DCI Meritorious Unit Citation for our work and some extremely positive feedback and evaluations for the training from the field offices, but we received no recognition or even a formal thank you from Director Mueller or FBI HQs that I'm aware of.

Brian was awarded one of the highest CIA civilian career awards at his retirement ceremony in 2007, the Distinguished Career Intelligence Medal. During his final years of active service with CIA and following his retirement until his untimely death on September 19, 2011, Brian was an active participant and stalwart supporter of multiple education and training programs throughout the IC and with the Institute of World Politics. He was a regular guest speaker in my D&D and targeting courses at CIA University. Brian was always one of our most interesting, animated, and popular guest speakers, whose presentations were full of wit, wisdom, and anecdotal stories that would keep our students on the edge of their seats. Brian was an expert in counterintelligence and a master at spy catching, and those who wrongly pursued him were not.

The fact is that there was a great deal more evidence to contradict Szady and the FBI's assumption that it was Brian, than support it. Brian was subjected to numerous interrogations and polygraphs including an FBI-directed polygraph that showed no indication of deception. They even ran a false flag operation, a stinglike op, against him at his home to trap him into agreeing to meet "Russian friends" that would help get him out of the country. He closed the door on the visitor and reported the incident to a senior FBI official the next morning not realizing that it was an FBI operation and that senior official was Szady himself heading up the team of mole hunters. There were also unexplained gaps in times that while Brian was out of town or out of the country, drops were still being made to Hanssen's KGB/SVR handlers, most of them under a wooden bridge in Nottoway Park, Vienna, Virginia, about a hundred yards from Hanssen's home.

While there were several involved in the investigation who had serious doubts that Brian was the mole, the lead agent in charge remained persistent. Rather than treating any of this contradictory evidence as exculpatory, that he was innocent and could not be the mole, they spun it and convinced themselves that he was the perfect spy.

Ironically, years earlier, Earl Pitts had warned the FBI about Hanssen during one of his FBI debriefings. Pitts was a former FBI counterintelligence and case officer, arrested in 1997 for spying for the Russians, who had indicated in one of his debriefings that while he wasn't aware of any other spies in the FBI, he was suspicious of Robert Hanssen. Had the FBI followed up on Pitts's tip, Hanssen most likely would have been caught much sooner. The senior FBI officer who had interviewed Pitts brought it to the attention of Szady and the team in 1999 and suggested they look within the FBI. The FBI disregarded the suggestion, and Pitts's warning was ignored and Hanssen's espionage was allowed to continue for two more years.

Mueller and his FBI agents' investigative pursuits and analysis regarding Russiagate were also skewed from the outset, just as they were in Brian's case. Mr. Mueller and his partisan team were working to prove a single hypothesis, that there was collusion between Donald Trump, his campaign, and the Russians. It was all déjà vu for me, and my thoughts went immediately to my departed brother and colleague Brian. Just as it was then, when they presumed that the mole was in the CIA, and once they erroneously zeroed in on Brian, he was presumed guilty; and all evidence that was collected was focused on proving that assumption, just as it was with President Trump.

Likewise, Mr. Mueller's Russian collusion investigation, his hypothesis wasn't a hypothesis at all. It was just another assumption, and a tainted one at that, reflecting a very serious cognitive bias, which basically results in only considering evidence that supports the hypothesis while discounting or disregarding evidence that might contradict it, very much like the FBI mole hunting investigation. It's one of the most common analytic traps we encounter that make us more vulnerable to intelligence failures, surprise, and deception. If multiple hypotheses are established and considered, we can avoid this pitfall. One of the analytic techniques we used successfully in our D&D and warning analysis that helps to mitigate the impact of our cognitive biases is the analysis of competing hypotheses, which Richards Heuer describes in chapter 8 of his book, the *Psychology of Intelligence Analysis*.

Of course, collusion between the Clintons, Obama, and the DNC was not and never would be considered by such a partisan team of investigators. Nor would they ever consider the possibility that Russian efforts through active measures and covert influence operations would more likely be directed at supporting the candidate or candidates that are most ideologically in line with their own, which were clearly Clinton and Obama. They had to ignore and discount all the scandals during Obama's presidency and Clinton's tenure as secretary of state involving the Russians and Ukrainians and even the Chinese. Alinsky disciple Hillary Clinton was already figuratively in bed with Putin and the Russians. It's also unlikely that there was any consideration given to a null hypothesis, that there was no real collusion, but rather only a Russian active measures campaign to make it appear so, to spurn further divisions in our domestic political environment and discredit our national electoral process. Given the partisan nature of the investigation and mandate to get Trump at all cost, it certainly doesn't appear that there was one.

Given the fact that after more than two years of investigation, there was no hard evidence of any collusion with the Trump campaign or the president, I would expect the Mueller report to address the absence of evidence as well as contradictory evidence of collusion to support that conclusion. I haven't seen or heard anything that would indicate that a null, no collusion, hypothesis was ever considered.

There was also an even more fundamental problem with the concept of an independent special counsel investigation. I claim no expertise in constitutional law. However, in a recent Hillsdale College publication, *Imprimis*, Prof. John Marini, in his article "Politics by Other Means, the Use and Abuse of Scandals," discusses how the Ethics in Government Act passed by Congress in 1978 established the independent counsel statute that was justified on the grounds that "executive discretion must be subordinate to the law." But that masked its true political purpose, which was to insulate the permanent, unelected government bureaucracy (read shadow government, deep state) from political control. The independent counsel statute was devised to "stand as a bulwark against any president or senior executive branch official who dared threaten the centralized executive bureaucracy put in place by the Democratic Party majorities of the 1960s and 1970s." Thus, it weakened the president's political control of that sprawling bureaucracy and strengthened Congress' hand in managing it. In effect, it also took political and policy disputes out of the hands of elected officials and the people and put them into a category of legal disputes.

We are now hearing career politicians like Pelosi and Nadler arguing that "we cannot rely on an election" to decide who will be president in 2020. These kinds of statements should send chills up the spine of any freedom-loving American. The fact that they are coming from left-wing career politicians is proof positive that they are Bolsheviks and not only intend to discredit President Trump and hijack the presidency but also would probably prefer to discard our democratic electoral process and replace it with their own single-party authoritarian dictatorship. It reflects their absolute contempt for the Constitution and the American electorate who don't and won't support their personal partisan militant secularist and godless agenda.

This may not seem like such a big deal unless you consider as Professor Marini points out that the DOJ has authority over the FBI and federal courts in which its attorneys operate. As such, the DOJ is empowered to access, manipulate, and maneuver federal laws, rules, regulations, and procedures and witness testimony as it may deem desirable to bring most of those it targets to their heels, including a duly elected president of these United States. When you really think of it, Donald Trump came into office as the people's president to drain the swamp, threatening the very deep state establishment that controls the government. There are parallels here, if you try to connect the dots, with the buzz saw that President Nixon ran into following his landslide victory in 1972 promising to use his executive authority to bring the executive bureaucracy under his control and the entrenched deep state struck back. Nixon posed a threat to the political establishment just as candidate and President Trump does today.

Many years after Nixon's resignation, we identified the source who took him down, a high-level FBI official Mark Felt, who was later identified as Deep Throat, who leaked all the classified intelligence to which he had access to Woodward and Bernstein. Why wasn't Felt prosecuted for leaking classified intelligence to the press while so many others have been prosecuted for the same crime? Meanwhile Stephen Kim and Thomas Drake were relentlessly pursued and threatened by the Obama administration and were eventually prosecuted and jailed for sharing classified intelligence with the media. Isn't it interesting that the DOJ and FBI were also at the forefront of the Russiagate investigation with a former director of the FBI, Mueller, and the number one Trump hater, Strzok, as his lead investigator along with a bunch of entrenched DOJ, FBI, and CIA partisan bureaucrats? What will it take to convince the voters of this country that the Democrats are all about double standards, deceit, and hypocrisy and are hell-bent on hijacking the heart and soul and wealth of America for their own demonic and self-serving interests? That is their legacy and that is their game plan.

Therefore, while it certainly appears that there was some level of collusion, it was all taking place in plain sight with the Clintons and the Obamas and all those rats who were scurrying out of their spider holes still trying to save the sinking ship, the Democratic Party, which has sold its soul to the demagogues and demons of the radical Left. I'm amazed that this was not obvious to anyone who is rational and seeking the truth. But then none of them are rational or seeking the truth. Yet, as ludicrous and ridiculous as it all appeared, given enough airtime and fake media coverage, there is an uninformed public and irrational minority of Trump haters, who will take McCabe's, Pelosi's, Schiff's, and others' preposterous allegations to the bank.

These Russian agents of influence in Congress, the FBI, and DOJ, to say nothing of those in the IC, aren't smart enough or shrewd enough to come up with the kinds of active measures and deception campaign that we have witnessed on their own. The Russians are masters of deception and have been successful beyond our imagination in their operations against the United States and others historically and currently. They are clearly at work and operating through those Trump haters and America haters using them as their conduits and dupes and stooges along with their manufactured anonymous sources and whistleblowers for their deception and influence operations, and I predict that they will continue to do so throughout the upcoming election cycle. Perhaps this is the buzzsaw of Obama deceit and deception that former DIA Director and short-lived National Security Advisor, General Michael Flynn, USA and former Trump confidant Roger Stone encountered and were victimized by similar bogus charges by the FBI and DOJ early on in the Trump Administration?

To avoid left-wing accusations that I am Russia-phobic, I'm sure the Chinese, whose spying already rivals the Russians, can also be expected to get into the game big time during the upcoming presidential election cycle. There has been a flurry of American intelligence officers recently arrested and convicted of spying for the Chinese as described elsewhere in this book. One of them even claimed he spied for the Chinese because he hated Donald Trump, but accepted compensation for his spying in any case. What a sorry pathetic coward and liar.

We now also have reports and accusations by Guo Wengui, an exiled Chinese dissident and billionaire real estate tycoon, who is warning that the Chinese Communist Party (CCP) is conducting its own aggressive active measures campaign designed to undermine the reelection of President Trump in 2020. According to Guo, the campaign is being directed by Pres. Xi Jinping and VP Wang Qishan through the CCP and National Security Committee. This is a credible accusation due to the fact that the D&D programs along with the military and intelligence services in Russia, China, Iran, and North Korea are all centrally directed from the highest level of government and the Communist Party. Those of you who think that China and Russia are more democratic and more open as societies are sorely mistaken. The Communist Party still rules with an iron fist in both China and Russia, and their internal security and intelligence services are pervasive and controlling.

Chinese interference in American politics was first disclosed by President Trump in September 2018 (just prior to the midterm elections) and a month later in a speech by Vice President Pence. As would be expected of the Chinese, Pence described China's interference as employing a whole-of-government approach involving political, economic, military, and propaganda to interfere and influence both policy and politics. In a speech the vice president gave on October 4, 2018, Pence stated, "President Trump's leadership is working; and China wants a different American President." Obviously, a Socialist, Communist, or even an Alinsky disciple whose ideological leanings are more in line with theirs and one who could be easily manipulated would be much preferred to a seasoned negotiator like Trump intent on putting America first and keeping America first. He just doesn't fit their mold and can't be bought like the Clintons, Obamas, or Bidens. And thank God for that blessing.

According to Guo, President Trump has already caused a lot of damage to the CCP. In apparent retaliation for his tough trade policies and firm support for our allies in the region, including arms sales to the Republic of China (Taiwan), it plans to use four weapons to attempt to derail his reelection. These include Wall Street financial leaders who have a vested interest in doing business with the Chinese like Mike Bloomberg, politicians and lobbyists in Washington who have been corrupted by agents of the CCP like the former Clinton administration that allowed unfettered access and influence by the Chinese into Washington politics throughout the 1990s in exchange for millions in campaign contributions or the Obama administration with creepy Joe Biden and son Hunter's shady dealings with China and the Ukraine, and the mainstream leftist media with many of its owners having special interests in China and finally by marshaling Chinese and Asian Americans who have increased wealth and political clout. You can be sure that it will also involve Chinese intelligence operatives to conduct influence operations and activate pro-Chinese agents already embedded throughout the government bureaucracy including the IC.

If we consider the circumstances surrounding the coronavirus in light of President Xi's threats and Guo Wengui's "warning," there is very good reason to suspect that the release of the virus was part of a planned Chinese active-measures campaign to undermine our thriving economy and influence our presidential election as I have already proposed.

# Chapter 4
## Spies, Lies, and Russian Active Measures

*There are few subjects about which, so little is known or understood by the general public as the skillful practice of the intelligence tradecraft and art of deception.*
— The Official CIA Manual of Trickery and Deception

All the discord and finger-pointing about Russian collusion, Russiagate, and the millions of taxpayer dollars spent on a frivolous attempt by congressional Democrats and their Mueller investigation to prove the Trump campaign and president guilty of collusion with the Russians, discredit his election, and undermine his presidency are a direct result of Russian active measures, which have been conducted in the United States by the KGB, GRU, and SVR for decades. Christopher Andrew and Vasili Mitrokhin describe and detail these operations in their book *the Sword and The Shield* based on the Mitrokhin Archive described by the FBI as "the most complete and extensive intelligence ever achieved from any source" on the KGB and their worldwide operations. If you want an authoritative source on Russian intelligence services' active measures and influence operations, the Mitrokhin Archive is where you'll find a treasure trove of some of the most closely held secrets of the KGB and GRU.

While Russian active measures here in the United States should come as no surprise to any well-trained intelligence officer, it is one of those weapons in their arsenal of D&D operations—initially refined as a key element of their military doctrine in the early twentieth century *maskirovka*, largely applied to a complexity of measures, cover, concealment, and camouflage intended to mislead the enemy regarding the presence, capability, and disposition of forces. The Soviets and Russian leadership and intelligence services later expanded and incorporated the doctrine to include strategic, political, and diplomatic means applying sophisticated deception campaigns involving active measures, to include media manipulation, disinformation, covert influence operations, propaganda, cyber and information warfare, and assassination to achieve their strategic political, economic, diplomatic, and military goals.

We must also keep in mind that this has also historically included support for foreign communist, socialist, and opposition parties and underground, revolutionary, criminal, and terrorist groups. Many of our shortsighted career politicians and senior government officials and our younger history-deprived generation of millennials are largely unaware of these facts or choose to ignore them and therefore are more vulnerable to being victimized. This is not to excuse them for their behavior or ignorance. And if the FBI and DOJ were so impressed with the Mitrokhin Archives fifteen to twenty years ago, why are they acting like a bunch of schoolgirls going out on their first date with the KGB, FSB, and SVR? As I've pointed out early on in my discourse on the politics of deception, the increasingly hostile political environment and radical left-wing attempts to undermine the president have made them ideal targets and conduits for deception, in this case Russian active measures. Some, but not all, may be described as unwitting dupes. But many like Brennan, Obama, Hillary Clinton, Mueller, Comey, and McCabe are doubtless witting conspirators and agents of influence.

Remember, see-think-do. In fact, Putin played them all like a fiddle, but could not have been so successful if Brennan, Clapper, Mueller, and the FBI anti-Trumpers weren't so intent and focused on using Russian influence operations to promote their own partisan political agendas. They were all blinded by their own self-interest in seeing Hillary Clinton elected. This was also the goal of the Russian deception operations.

Any good deception plan always has a reasonable cover story, like any good illusionist always has something in his act to misdirect the attention of his audience from the real by showing the fake. Remember, Putin and his intelligence services simply hid the real and showed the fake to cover the real goal of their deception plan—and it proved extremely effective—making it appear that there was collusion with the Trump Campaign when just the opposite was the case. But it could only have been so with the knowledge and complicity of some very senior insiders. In order to understand how and why Putin would also employ active measures and influence operations to make it look like the Russians were supporting candidate Trump, you need to consider his actions through the strategic lens of a KGB foreign intelligence officer, which Putin was and remains (once a KGB officer, always a KGB officer) as well as considering some historical precedence.

We used a couple more acronyms in our classes that were very helpful in assessing an adversary's capability and inclination to employ D&D in particular situations. It's another simple analytic technique, like see-think-do and the analysis of competing hypotheses, that we call MOM and POP. Does the adversary have the *motive*, the *opportunity*, and the *means* to conduct a successful deception operation, in this case, in the United States during a presidential election cycle to influence the outcome of that election to support its own strategic political, military, and economic policies and objectives? In this case, the answer is a resounding yes, and anyone who doesn't have blinders on or their head buried in the sand would connect the dots and come to the conclusion that Putin and his foreign intelligence services would be working overtime to get Clinton elected. POP simply refers to *past, operational, practices*, which we know with a high degree of certainty and experience that the Russians are masters at D&D and espionage with their closest competitor, the Chinese.

So just for fun, let's consider a couple of historical examples of Soviet KGB and Russian active measures and influence operations against the United States.

Shortly after the attack on Pearl Harbor and Hitler's declaration of war against the United States, Vassili Zarubin was appointed

KGB legal resident in New York, where he was also responsible for the subresidency in Washington DC. Stalin, having serious doubts about Roosevelt's resolve, summoned him before his departure and told him that his main assignment in the United States was to watch out for attempts by Roosevelt and "US ruling circles" to negotiate with Hitler and sign a separate peace. Zarubin's recruitment strategy was straightforward—he simply demanded that the leaders of the Communist Party of the USA (CPUSA) identify supporters and sympathizers in government establishments suitable for work as agents. Eugene Dennis, a Moscow-trained Comintern agent who became CPUSA general secretary, reported that a number of secret party members were joining the first professional American intelligence agency, the Office of the Coordinator of Information, reorganized in June 1942 as the Office of Strategic Services (OSS), which became the CIA with the passing of the National Security Act of 1947. Among the first Soviet agents to penetrate the OSS was Duncan Chaplin Lee, who became personal assistant to its head, Gen. William Joseph "Wild Bill" Donovan. Donovan and others in the Roosevelt administration apparently had a rather relaxed attitude about Communists. Donovan reportedly once said that he'd "put Stalin on the OSS payroll if I [he] thought it would help [us] defeat Hitler." Donovan wasn't alone in his lax attitude toward Communists. There was a major gulf between the intelligence supplied to Stalin on the United States and that provided to Roosevelt on the Soviet Union. Virtually, every branch of Roosevelt's administration had been penetrated, while the OSS didn't have a single agent in Moscow. After Roosevelt's death three months into his fourth term, his third-term vice president Henry Wallace indicated that had Roosevelt died earlier (during his third term in office), Wallace's intention was to make Laurence Duggan and Harry Dexter White, both reactivated prewar Soviet agents, his secretary of state and secretary of the treasury, respectively.

Another example more analogous to Russiagate, according to the Mitrokhin Archives and other sources, is about Moscow following the presidential election of 1960 with great interest. Soviet Premier Nikita Khrushchev regarded the republican candidate Richard Nixon a McCarthyite friend of the Pentagon "hawks" and was anxious that Kennedy win. The Washington KGB resident Aleksandr Feklisov was ordered to propose diplomatic or propaganda initiatives, or any other measures, to facilitate Kennedy's victory. The residency tried to make contact with Robert Kennedy but was politely rebuffed. Khrushchev's view of Kennedy changed after CIA's abortive and inept attempt with the Cuban Brigade at the Bay of Pigs in April 1961 to topple Fidel Castro. Kennedy himself, following a summit with Khrushchev in Vienna to discuss the three-power status of Berlin, believed that Khrushchev thought that anyone as young and inexperienced as Kennedy, who could get into a mess like the Bay of Pigs, could "be had." In May 1961, GRU Colonel Georgi Bolshakov, operating under cover as head of the Washington bureau of the TASS news agency, began regular meetings with Atty. Gen. Robert Kennedy. Bolshakov convinced Kennedy that they could set up a direct channel of communication between President Kennedy and First Secretary Khrushchev, short-circuiting the ponderous protocol of official diplomacy. While Robert Kennedy was convinced that an authentic friendship existed, he forgot (or didn't realize) that he was dealing with an experienced intelligence professional who had been instructed to cultivate him.

In March 1962, Castro urged the KGB to set up an operation base in Havana to export revolution across Latin America, and in May, Khrushchev decided to construct nuclear missile bases in Cuba, the most dangerous gamble of the Cold War. As the construction of the missile bases in Cuba began, Bolshakov continued to provide reassurance, probably as part of a deliberate deception plan, that Khrushchev would never countenance such an aggressive policy. Interestingly, CIA's Board of National Estimates had produced a Special National Intelligence Estimate (SNIE) published in September that came to a similar conclusion, though DCI Doug McCone disagreed with that judgment. When U-2 reconnaissance revealed the existence of the bases in mid-October, thus beginning the Cuban missile crisis, both Robert and President Kennedy knew they had been played, and President Kennedy felt personally deceived. He was personally deceived.

As for the Kennedy assassination, I have my own theory and analysis. The Soviets claimed they were not involved, but the KGB secretly funded Oswald and went to great lengths to conduct active measures and influence operations to blame the assassination on a right-wing conspiracy involving the CIA using E. Howard Hunt of Watergate fame as a coconspirator with Lee Harvey Oswald the shooter. The KGB even forged a letter from Oswald to Hunt, a former CIA intelligence officer, to establish a connection between CIA and President Kennedy's assassin. This is classic deception 101 and makes for great press and takes the heat off the Soviets and KGB, but it's largely fake. The truth lies somewhere between the Bay of Pigs and Cuban missile crisis, where paranoia by Castro about another US attempt to invade Cuba or eliminate him and his regime, and vengeance and lost face by Khrushchev who had to back down to a young inexperienced US president during the Cuban missile crisis converged to add up to assassination.

We have to be careful not to mirror image, and remember, the Soviets/Russians and their intelligence services don't play by the same rules. Assassinations are perfectly acceptable, and plausible deniability can be achieved through well-planned and well-orchestrated deception operations and active measures. In this case, according to the Mitrokhin Archives, it turns out that CIA was already implementing a plan to take out Castro, and the KGB was probably aware of it. Allen Dulles, the then recently retired director of Central Intelligence on the Warren Commission, withheld this information from the commission. FBI Director J. Edgar Hoover also held back information and was surprised to learn that Oswald had written a threatening letter to the FBI upon his return from Russia and had met with KGB and Cuban intelligence operatives in Mexico City just prior to the assassination, yet Oswald did not appear on the FBI's security index of potentially disloyal citizens. Hoover was afraid that if that became public, it would destroy the FBI's reputation. While the information withheld may not have changed the Warren Commission's conclusion, when it became public in the 1970s, it encouraged the belief that there had been other cover-ups, which pointed to the involvement of the IC.

The Watergate scandal and reports of intelligence abuses spawned a whole new series of conspiracy theories. Although most of the abuses had been ordered or authorized by successive presidents, the belief grew that in the words of Sen. Frank Church, chairman of the Senate Select Committee on Intelligence, the CIA had been "behaving like a rogue elephant on the rampage."

Oswald, a former marine and sharpshooter, though a witting participant, was a dupe. He spent time in Moscow with his handlers and Russian wife and in Mexico City with his Cuban and KGB interlocutors just days before the assassination. A few months before, he was reported to be in New Orleans, where he set up a one-man branch of the Fair Play for Cuba Committee and was distributing pro-Castro leaflets. Oswald had a love affair with communism, was a Marxist, and preferred the lifestyle in the Soviet Union to that in the United States and prided himself as being an agent of the KGB. He was psychotic, as even the KGB realized, but as such a perfect stooge and fall guy. The very idea that he acted alone, as the Warren Commission report concluded, is absurd. While there have been numerous conspiracy theories surrounding the president's assassination, none that I have researched seriously considered the KGB's role or the strategic interests and motivations of the Soviets and Cubans at that time. Castro and Khrushchev both had good reason in their own minds and longer-term strategic and policy interests to have President Kennedy assassinated.

As such, the Soviets had strong reasons of their own to deflect responsibility for the assassination from Oswald who had defected to Russia in 1959. They were quick to try to distance themselves from the assassination by employing a series of active measures by planting conspiracy theories of their own to pin the blame on the CIA and right-wing conspirators. The right-wing conspirators were supposedly three leading southern oil magnates and financier associates of Jack Ruby's, who Ruby reportedly met with shortly before the assassination. Ruby was also the shooter who fatally wounded Oswald shortly after Oswald was taken into custody. To cement the CIA connection, the KGB forged a letter from Oswald to E. Howard Hunt, making it appear that Oswald was seeking Hunt's permission to move ahead with the assassination plot. The forgery was so good that the FBI and Oswald's wife (widow) were convinced it was his handwriting.

I would even go so far to say that President Kennedy's own vice president and successor Lyndon Baines Johnson was also culpable in President Kennedy's death that day in Dallas. Both he and Texas governor Connelly knew as did President Kennedy himself that he was "heading into nut country." In Vince Palamara's book *Survivor's Guilt*, he points out with detailed accuracy that the last-minute change in the motorcade route that took it directly under the Book Depository was unnecessary from a security standpoint, lacked supporting personnel, and violated protocol. The leaking of alternative routes to the press and incredible lack of protection at its most exposed point cried out for a much more thorough investigation than the Warren Commission ever provided.

One group had purchased a full-page ad in the *Dallas Morning News* on the day of President Kennedy's visit accusing him of being a communist stooge. How could any sane person or persons accuse the president who had ordered the failed Bay of Pigs operation to take down Castro and his regime and forced Khrushchev and the Soviets to back down during the Cuban missile crisis of being a communist stooge? It was indeed nut country. LBJ and Kennedy were also constantly at odds over civil rights and other issues. LBJ had the ego and temperament of a man who probably thought he should have been president and may have been concerned that he might not even be on the Kennedy ticket in 1964. After all, the reason the president was in Dallas that day was to kick off his reelection campaign and raise money in Johnson's home state of Texas, which Kennedy and Johnson barely carried in their razor-thin victory over Nixon in 1960, and things weren't looking any more promising. The presidential election in 1960 wasn't the only one the Soviets interfered with, and it wouldn't be the last. KGB active measures surrounding President Kennedy's assassination were and remain a key element of their many decades' long operations in the United States.

Moscow's assessment of anti-Sovietism in the United States changed radically in the early 1970s. In 1968, the Kremlin had been so anxious once again to prevent the election of the veteran anticommunist, Richard Nixon (as they were in 1960), that it had secretly offered to subsidize the campaign of his democratic opponent, Hubert Humphrey. Once in office, however, Nixon and his brilliant National Security Advisor and later Secretary of State Henry Kissinger rapidly emerged as the architects of détente, and more Soviet-American agreements were signed in 1972–1973 than in the entire forty years of diplomatic relations reestablished between Moscow and Washington by Roosevelt in 1933. According to the Mitrokhin files, Moscow was dismayed when Nixon was forced to resign and suspected that his resignation was forced not so much by public indignation, but by a conspiracy by the enemies of détente, in particular the Jewish lobby.

Service A—the active measures branch—of the First Chief Directorate of the Ministry for State Security, or KGB, was also heavily engaged in active measures in the 1960s and 1970s to foment and exploit racial tensions in the United States. Civil rights leader Martin Luther King, Jr. was a target of those operations, in attempting to link the aims of the civil rights movement to a worldwide struggle against American imperialism by spreading propaganda using the CPUSA that secret party members within King's entourage would guide his policies. It seems that these active measures achieved some success. It turns out that the FBI was also conducting surveillance and active measures against the civil rights leader for years, attempting to discredit him with Hoover accusing King and his entourage of being secret members of the CPUSA. Hoover even obtained approval for wiretaps from Attorney General Robert Kennedy in 1962. Sounds eerily familiar, like Russiagate, doesn't it? This made Dr. King the only prominent American to be the target of active measures by both the FBI and the KGB, which we knew of, that is, until presidential candidate and our current president Donald Trump also became such a target and victim.

Could the FBI then have had their very own King-haters, bigots, and hypocrites like J. Edgar Hoover himself, or have been duped by very effective KGB active measures working with the CPUSA to discredit and take down Dr. King? Or did the FBI simply benefit from those KGB active measures that helped to justify their own operations using wiretaps to spy on the very popular civil rights leader? Maybe a combination of both.

Ironically, in the case of Russiagate, we experienced a similar but more blatant pattern of behavior and active measures by the Russian SVR, Ukrainian intelligence service, and Trump haters in the FBI and DOJ, with the active participation of the CIA to discredit President Trump's campaign and his election as president. They obtained a FISA warrant under false pretenses and perjured themselves in the process to spy on a US presidential candidate and duly elected president. The truth about the phony Steele dossier based on some anonymous Russian or Ukrainian source and the entire Russian collusion ploy that originated with and was financed by the Clinton campaign and Obama shadow government is now a matter of record. Nevertheless, the damage has been done and millions of taxpayer dollars spent and the big lie lingers on with the left-wing media and hypocrites in Congress. Yet none of the conspirators who were all part of manufacturing the deception and perjured themselves have been punished.

In the case of Dr. King, failing in their first attempt to influence him, the KGB aimed instead at replacing him with more radical leaders through a disinformation campaign to discredit him and his lieutenants in the African and US media by accusing him of being an Uncle Tom. A disinformation campaign was conducted to accuse him, among other betrayals of his race, of receiving subsidies from the government to tame the civil rights movement and prevent it from threatening the Johnson administration.

Similarly, failing in their collusion ploy and groundless multi-million-dollar Mueller investigation, the Democrats in the House hatched yet another deception by manufacturing the whistleblower ploy regarding the president's telephone conversation with the Ukrainian president regarding rampant corruption and Biden's admitted involvement in a quid pro quo while vice president, which he bragged about, to withhold billions in aid to have an investigation of corruption implicating his son and possibly other Obama administration officials terminated. It demonstrated just how insanely desperate and unimaginative the Democrats really are using Biden's quid pro quo and son's corrupt dealings with the Ukrainians, projecting it on to President Trump, and using it as the basis for their groundless impeachment ploy. You can't make this sort of pathetic partisan politics of deception up. It was all built upon more lies, innuendo, and hearsay without any substance. The vote cast was totally partisan with 229 Democrats voting yes, three voting no, and all 195 Republicans voting no. It should be noted here as it has been elsewhere in this book that if a party has enough votes, it can impeach a president for jaywalking, and the Democrats have threatened or attempted to do so with every republican president since Eisenhower. The only exception was Gerald Ford. The desperation and vindictiveness, bigotry, and hypocrisy of the Democratic Party is all part of its legacy but has never been more blatant and anti-American and antidemocratic than it is today.

The KGB, like the Democratic Party, also sought to exploit the violent images of the long, hot summer in August 1965 in Watts hoping that as violence intensified, Dr. King would be swept aside by black radicals like Stokely Carmichael, who they attempted to cultivate and with some success. Carmichael attended a meeting of third-world revolutionaries in Cuba in the summer of 1967, telling them, "We have a common enemy. Our struggle is to overthrow this system… We are moving into open guerrilla warfare in the United States." Traveling on to North Vietnam, Carmichael declared in Hanoi, "We are not reformists… We are revolutionaries. We want to change the American system." As a result of Dr. King's assassination on April 4, 1968, violence and rioting quickly followed, which the KGB had earlier blamed King for trying to prevent. From this point on, the KGB portrayed him as a martyr of the Black Liberation Movement and spread conspiracy theories that his murder had been planned by white racists and the authorities. Remember there was a similar story line that they used following the assassination of JFK five years earlier about a right-wing and CIA conspiracy. Whatever their involvement, you can be sure that the KGB always has a cover story and plan to ensure their plausible deniability.

According to the Mitrokhin files, on at least one occasion, the first north American department of the KGB ordered its New York residency to use explosives to exacerbate racial tensions in New York (Operation Pandora) by planting a delayed-action explosive package at one of the black city colleges and then making anonymous calls to three black organizations claiming that the Jewish Defense League was responsible. The attempt to stir up racial tensions in the United States remained part of Service A's stock-in-trade for the remainder of the Cold War.

The American politician and policymaker most feared by Moscow during the Cold War era was Ronald Reagan during his first term as president. According to the Mitrokhin Archives, active measures against Reagan had begun during his unsuccessful bid for the republican nomination in 1976. The center, the Kremlin, had no doubt that Reagan was far more anti-Soviet than either the incumbent president Gerald Ford or democratic contender Jimmy Carter. Service A was ordered to embark on a wide-ranging quest for compromising material, but apart from confirming and hyping up Reagan's reputation as a Cold War warrior, they were unable to come up with anything more damaging. The Kremlin actually came to believe paranoid interpretations of Reagan's policy and was convinced, particularly during 1983, that President Reagan was planning a nuclear first strike on Moscow. Yuri Andropov, in April 1982, as one of his last acts of his fifteen-year term as chairman of the KGB, directed all foreign intelligence officers to participate in active measures to ensure Reagan's defeat in the presidential election of 1984. Residencies in the US and around the world were ordered to popularize the slogan "Reagan Means War."

While convincing their fair share of students on college campuses, Reagan's landslide victory in 1984 demonstrated that Soviet active measures also have their limitations.

Finally, one of the most ludicrous and devious of Soviet active measures was hatched and planted in 1985 by the KGB and their East German counterparts, the Stasi, claiming that the AIDS virus was an American biological weapon being produced at Fort Detrick in Maryland. Operation INFEKTION was a disinformation campaign run by the KGB to undermine US credibility abroad and create tensions between host countries and the United States over the presence of US military bases, which were often portrayed as the source of the virus in local communities. As crazy and unbelievable as this disinformation campaign was, by 1987, it received coverage in over eighty countries in thirty languages, primarily in leftist and communist media publications, but very damaging to US interests in any case.

What is surprising is that our senior intelligence officials in the IC and the FBI, with all the intelligence analytic and investigative resources available to them, were unaware that this is standard operating procedures for Putin and his Russian intelligence services and were unable or unwilling to expose it for what it really was/is—active measures and covert influence operations. Feeding propaganda, misinformation, and even forging documents and using directed information in the case of the Steele Dossier to generate more discord and division and to subvert our political system and weaken America at home and abroad—this is what the Alinsky disciples Obama and Clinton have in common and why the Democrats have embraced the radical left-wing socialist agenda. They are now and always have been the enemies of America in our midst disguised only as democratic career politicians and bureaucrats whose agenda is to hijack and capture the heart, soul, and wealth of America to advance their own wealth and lust for power.

All you have to do is open your eyes and ears to the facts and the truth. Both the Clintons and Obamas enriched themselves during and following their presidencies and made the best of currying favor not only with their special interests but also with the Chinese and Russians. While I don't put much stock in net worth estimates, every one of the sources I have consulted including federal election disclosures, Snopes fact-checks, Business Insider, Forbes, and others indicate the Clintons' net worth jumped from about $700,000 reported in 1992 to $240 million in 2017, while the Obamas' reported net worth jumped from about $1.3 million in 2007 to at least $40 million according to a GOBankingRates estimate in 2018. According to businessinsider.com, *the New York Post* reported a much higher net worth of $135 million. Each of them collected their $400,000 per year presidential salary and $200,000 per year presidential pension. In contrast, Donald Trump's net worth before running for president according to Forbes was reported at $4.5 billion and has since dropped to about $3 billion. President Trump has also kept his campaign promise "not to accept a salary" according to PolitiFact's Truth-O-Meter. He has donated his $400,000 salary to a variety of government agencies since taking office like the Veteran's Administration, Surgeon General's Office, Homeland Security, and National Park Service.

Clinton and Obama's Alinsky-inspired socialist utopia with them as the vanguards and privileged bourgeoisie would doubtless prefer to establish their own personal authoritarian kleptocracy, much like the corrupt murderous leaders of Iran, Venezuela, or Cuba, who they regularly support and applaud while tearing down America. President Trump has not been deterred by their subversion or waivered from pursuing his MAGA agenda and campaign promises. Rather he has confronted them and their special interests and has opposed and continues to expose their godless anti-America socialist agenda.

Putin recognized the stark and growing ideological differences and sharp divide in our domestic political environment and has and will continue to exploit the situation by directly or indirectly supporting Obama's shadow government and the Democratic Party and its new love affair with socialism and communism. In retrospect, it certainly appears that John Brennan as director of the CIA and DNI Jim Clapper, among other senior officials in the IC, the FBI, and DOJ, used those active measures as a pretext and opportunity to spy on candidate Trump, opposing their favored candidate (Clinton), probably at former president Obama's urging or direction. Former FBI director Comey and Deputy Director McCabe along with former DOJ US Associate Attorney General Bruce Ohr, who was directly linked to British spy Christopher Steele's anti-Trump dossier (originating from Russian or possibly Ukrainian sources with Joe Biden's encouragement as Obama's point man) all should have been fully aware of Russian covert influence operations in the United States, especially during a presidential election cycle.

As such, the idea that they would knowingly use this information to spy on a presidential candidate, deceive the American people, and undermine Donald Trump's presidency is treasonous. Actually, the precedent had been set by their boss, former president and Alinsky disciple Obama and fellow Alinsky disciple former secretary of state Hillary Clinton. Those of you who might argue otherwise need to be reminded about President Obama's and Clinton's State Department effort to covertly unseat Israeli Prime Minister Benjamin Netanyahu during the 2015 Israeli Parliamentary elections. Obama and Clinton, no doubt with some assistance from the director of the CIA, funneled over $350,000 in taxpayer grants to build a campaign to oust Netanyahu. The group, OneVoice, used the money to build a voter database, train activists, and hire a political consulting firm tied to President Obama's campaign. All of it was used to wage the anti-Netanyahu campaign, according to a bipartisan staff report from the Senate Permanent Subcommittee on Investigations. This also took place during President Obama's last two years in office and during the onset of our own 2016 presidential campaign. If Obama was willing to engage in covert influence operations to unseat our closest ally and strategic partner in the Middle East largely because Obama had made private overtures to the Palestinians and saw Mr. Netanyahu as an obstacle to negotiations, there is good reason to believe that Obama wouldn't hesitate to use his minions in the IC, FBI, and DOJ to deceive the American people in an attempt to undermine Donald Trump's campaign and his presidency. Looking at it in hindsight, I'd almost have to draw the conclusion that Obama's effort to oust Netanyahu, though it failed, was a strong indication and precursor to his attempt to engage in a similar effort to ensure Clinton's election, which also failed, thanks be to God.

Remember the acronym MOM (motive, opportunity, and means) and POP (past operational practices). After all, there was a great deal more at stake, from Obama's, Clinton's, and the Democrats' perspective in getting Hillary Clinton elected than there was in achieving an Israeli-Palestinian accord. While this may have been a somewhat cynical assessment then, it certainly has proven itself to be the case, and it fits in perfectly with Obama's foreign policy of cozying up to our enemies and many of the world's dictators and tyrants while apologizing for American exceptionalism and "all our past transgressions" while rebuking our allies.

Let's not forget lovebirds FBI agents Strzok and Page who had an extramarital affair and shared damning e-mails and text messages about efforts to subvert Donald Trump during his campaign and after his election as president. Strzok ran both the FBI Clinton e-mail investigation and the Russian meddling investigation and was a lead agent in Mueller's Special Council Russian investigative team, until he was removed in August 2017, when the text messages and e-mails exchanged with his lover Page raised serious concerns about his anti-Trump and pro-Clinton bias. It's very likely that with Strzok as the lead agent, with his openly expressed biases, not only were decisions tainted by those biases, but also the collection and consideration of evidence. Fact is the investigation was corrupted by a clear anti-Trump bias and flawed from its inception to its conclusion, attempting to prove something that did not exist, with no effort or interest to consider alternative explanations for the Russian interference.

So while all those officials were well aware of Russian intelligence operations in the United States, especially during a presidential election cycle, they chose a campaign of lies and deception while the real collusion was within the Obama administration and with his minions in the IC, FBI, and DOJ, with a hostile anti-Trump media and hostile foreign intelligence service eager to jump on the bandwagon. Even Obama's and Hillary Clinton's criticism of Putin and his reelection as president was a farce and a well-orchestrated act to cover Russian support.

I believe that would have been plan A, to use Russia's interference to buttress Clinton's election prospects, though in their minds and hers, the coronation was a slam dunk. When that blew up in their faces, the ugly, underhanded, dangerous, and probably hastily contrived plan B, pinning the tail on the elephant in the White House began—like a bunch of wild-eyed undisciplined adolescents, who didn't get their way and the win, spun themselves into a fevered frenzy and blindly sought to prove the fake and hide the real by obscuring the truth and proliferated the big lie. This is not conspiracy theory. I'm just performing analysis as I did for more than forty years, considering available evidence, past precedence, and alternative explanations in an attempt to connect the dots and get to the truth. Their plan A and contingency plan B almost worked.

While a critical battle was won by the American people in 2016 with the election of Donald Trump, the war is not over. The radical left-wing Alinsky revolutionaries are on the march and will be doubling down to steal the 2020 election and promote violence to do so as they have historically. The forces of hate and darkness will have to be defeated at the polls in November and continue to be exposed for who they really are and for what they really stand for, an America recast in their image as a socialist/communist mega welfare state or kleptocracy for their benefit and enrichment. Saint Augustine would call this the lust to dominate. But God's will be done, and I believe our kind and merciful God has a different plan.

Putin and his Russian intelligence services will continue their attempts to influence and steal the upcoming presidential election in every possible way while maintaining plausible deniability to support their own strategic political, military, and economic goals. It's also pretty apparent that the Democrats as the party that has sold out to the radical Left and has embraced the wiles of socialism and communism, and their candidates, whoever they may be, will likely be the benefactors of that support as they were in 2016. They will also benefit from Chinese interference who the Clintons sold out to during the Clinton administration in the 1990s. So much has been written about the influence peddling and corruption during Clinton's administration that I won't attempt to address it here. I will recommend a couple of books that really nail it, *the Year of the Rat, How Bill Clinton and Al Gore Compromised US Security for Chinese Cash*, and a book by a fellow patriot and former Secret Service officer Gary Byrne *Crisis of Character*, where he describes his firsthand experience with Hillary, Bill, and how they operated during his eight years in the White House.

Since the Democrats are more desperate than ever to get back in the White House, they no doubt will also be engaged in orchestrating all types of voter fraud as they have in the past. This should make it easy for Putin and the Russian intelligence services and the Chinese or whomever to operate with a safe degree of cover and separation. I fully expect the Democrats and community organizers in the Obama shadow government to marshal all those being cultivated as their new political base—illegals, disenfranchised felons, the unregistered, the dead, and let's not forget the well-trained ballot box stuffers.

As part of his shadow government, Obama has organized his own army called Organizing for Action (OFA) [mentioned earlier in the book] of some thirty thousand strong, dedicated to organize communities for progressive change but, more importantly, to organize and implement the resistance to disrupt and undermine everything that our current duly elected president is trying to accomplish. The organization goes against our democracy and our Constitution and laws and if allowed to proceed will destroy our way of governing and the constitutional republic we know as America. The organization reportedly is funded by a network of nonprofits, which is growing its war chest of over $40 million with some 250 offices nationwide. It all represents a direct assault on our governing and electoral process and is more akin to a deposed third-world dictator's effort to retake the reign of power from the people and their duly elected governing authority.

Millennials usually identified as eighteen- to thirty-four-years-olds, who reportedly will make up 50 percent of the world's workforce in 2020 and be a major force in all future elections may very well determine the outcome of the 2020 presidential election, and for this reason, I am hopeful that this book will reach them and open their minds to the facts and the truth. Many millennials are flirting with the idea that socialism may be both a viable and desirable alternative to capitalism. The fact is it isn't, never has been, and never will be. If they'd only take the time to study history and consider the real fruits of socialism, poverty, misery, and tyranny, in all those places it's been adopted—Venezuela, Bolivia, Ecuador, Russia, China, Cuba, and the list goes on. The term democratic socialism is a form of self-deception, because there is nothing democratic about the slavery and tyranny that accompanies it, with all its hollow promises of a free and carefree life under their socialist/communist banners of equality for all with free health care, free education, free housing, free food, paid vacations from imaginary jobs, and free transportation and all it costs them is their votes and total subjugation and loyalty to the nomenklatura or new radical Left democratic establishment and ruling class and a tyrannical central government for life. What's not to like about all these false promises and lies? Study history. The first Democratic Socialist Party of the twentieth century became the Communist Party of the Soviet Union following the Bolshevik Revolution of 1917. This should be a wake-up call for all.

> Jesus began to speak, first to His disciples, at a time when so many people were crowding together that they were trampling each other underfoot, "beware of the leaven—that is the hypocrisy—of the Pharisees. There is nothing concealed that will not be revealed, nor secret that will not be known. Therefore, whatever you have said in the darkness, will be revealed in the light, and what you have whispered behind closed doors, will be proclaimed on the housetops." (Luke 12:1–3)

Khrushchev and his KGB, like the Pharisees, "whispered behind closed doors" and then proclaimed on the housetops that they would bury us, not with "nucs," but through subversion by infiltrating the Catholic Church, the US Congress, our judicial system, and our educational institutions and by undermining our economy. And they have now succeeded in accomplishing the first four of these with surprising ease! For eight years, they succeeded in having one of their own Alinsky-trained disciples, Barack Hussein Obama, get elected from obscurity as a community organizer through fraud and deception and active measures to the highest office in the land. During his eight years in office, he nearly succeeded in achieving one of his and his Russian and globalist allies' objectives to level the playing field or, in my words, dumb down the United States in every respect, not only domestically by establishing his version of a classless society by eliminating the middle class but also internationally by literally and figuratively bringing America's economic system and Americans to their knees with anti-American billionaires and globalists like George Soros, acting at times as a puppeteer. He did succeed in burying this country in ten plus trillion in additional debt and practically bankrupted our economy while also seizing control of our healthcare system with possibly the worst piece of legislation ever passed by Congress, the Affordable Care Act (ACA), which to no one's surprise proved to be another deception. There was nothing affordable about it, and it has all but died under the weight of its own cumbersome inception. According to the Congressional Budget Office (CBO), enrollment never approached the thirty some million uninsured persons it was supposed to aid with current coverage just over eight million costing the American taxpayers an estimated one point eight trillion for the period 2012–2022.

Let's not forget that former president Obama accomplished this in the middle of the night with total support from the democratic-controlled Congress and Senate, with no republican input or support. But while it ultimately has failed, it proved to be a tremendous distraction for years after its passage in Congress and the mainstream media, obscuring and deflecting attention away from democratic scandals and corruption and equally important progressive objectives, as well as many other facets of the progressive agenda of the Left and their ideological socialist globalists and Russian allies.

A key contingency of this well-planned, if not so well-orchestrated, deception, which the DNC, Clintons, and Putin and the Russian intelligence services never expected to have to implement, was implemented out of necessity when Hillary Clinton, yet another Alinsky-trained disciple, lost the 2016 election despite all the media hype about a landslide victory and efforts by her allies, foreign and domestic, to guarantee her coronation. Putin and the Russian intelligence service colluded with pro-Obama and Clinton agents who were well placed in the White House, DOJ, FBI, and IC. Let's not forget the e-mail leak that helped to expose the DNC and Chairwoman

Debbie Wasserman Schultz for colluding to rig the US Presidential Democratic Primaries in Clinton's favor. Now they would all have to double their efforts to undermine and discredit the duly elected president of the United States, Donald J. Trump.

While they will continue to attempt to manipulate and influence the electoral process, they are now and will continue to be engaged in acts that in any other time in our nation's history would have been considered treasonous and seditious—first, spying on a legitimate presidential candidate and now attempting to undermine and overthrow the duly elected president of the United and even going so far as to provoke and promote violence using their left-wing antifa supporters, not only against those who would dare to support the president but also against law enforcement personnel charged with maintaining law and order. These aren't peaceful protests by reformers, but they are paid Marxists, thugs, and anarchists who are an integral element of the radical Left's program of violence and intimidation against Trump supporters, in particular, and Conservatives in general. It's important to understand that this is all part of the radical left-wing socialist agenda to tear down America, piece by piece, all those institutions and values that make up the very fabric of our constitutional democracy and republic.

Of course, we know now that neither candidate Trump nor President Trump was ever engaged with Putin or the Russians prior to, during, or after the election. While this may all seem a bit redundant, it is sometimes necessary, and I believe this is one of those times when we need to look at the accusations of collusion from as many angles as needed to debunk this left-wing partisan political influence operation for good. Critical thinking and Socratic questioning, which I often used with my students in our classroom deception planning and analysis exercises, both seek meaning and truth. Critical thinking provides the rational tools to monitor, assess, and reconstitute or redirect our thinking and action. This is what educational reformer John Dewey described as reflective inquiry, "in which the thinker turns the subject over in the mind, giving it serious and consecutive consideration." Socratic questioning is an explicit focus on framing self-directed, disciplined questions to achieve that goal. Much like the analysis of competing hypotheses is a method of hypotheses elimination, in that better hypotheses are found by identifying and eliminating those that lead to contradictions. It's pretty obvious that none of the analytic tools I've discussed so far to deal with cognitive biases and analytic pathologies were ever used by Mueller and his knuckle-dragging anti-Trumpers in his investigation. If any of them had been applied, he and his largely democratic associates would have saved the American taxpayers millions of dollars.

If you're really interested in seeking the truth, you need to ask yourself some serious questions. First, were the Russians actively engaged in conducting influence operations during the 2016 presidential campaign? Is there any precedent for such operations during a presidential election cycle? What did or does Donald J. Trump have to offer Putin and the Russians as a candidate or as president? What did or does Hillary Rodham Clinton have to offer Putin and the Russians as a candidate or as president? How might Putin and his Russian intelligence services calculate the risks and benefits of such active measures? The answer to the first question, according to all the anti-Trumpers in Congress, the IC, the FBI, DOJ, and the Mueller investigation, is that the Russians did engage in active measures to influence the election. I agree that this was the case. I have already provided the answer to question two about KGB and Soviet efforts to influence the outcome of the 1960 presidential election in favor of JFK and the 1968 election in favor of Hubert Humphrey and both Ronald Reagan's 1976 failed efforts to gain the republican presidential nomination and his 1984 reelection campaign.

An honest and rational answer to question three is that neither candidate Trump nor President Trump would have anything to offer Putin and the Russians, and although they knew his chances of winning were slim to none, they had to cover their influence operations supporting Hillary Clinton with enough directed information, the Steele dossier, and misinformation to make it look like Donald Trump was their favored candidate. In my words, these die-hard, lifelong Communists would never want, let alone support, the election of a true God-fearing MAGA, motherhood, and apple pie successful billionaire businessman, who they could never influence through bribes or extortion and, if elected, have to deal with his America first policies for the next four to eight years.

An honest and rational and informed answer to question four is the subject of an entire chapter in this book, but just let me say the following with regard to what she had or has to offer Putin and the Russians: Hillary's Russian reset, Uranium One deal, $500,000 donation to the Clinton Foundation for a an hour speech by Bill Clinton in Moscow, and red lines crossed by Russians in the Ukraine, Syria, and Iran while Hillary was secretary of state. These were all great successes for Putin, the Russian intelligence services, and Russian strategic interests and policies. Maybe that explains why the Russians contributed nearly one hundred fifty million dollars to the Clinton Foundation and zero to Donald Trump. This is to say nothing about her character as a self-serving wannabe Alinsky-trained Bolshevik. In counterintelligence terms, Hillary Clinton was and remains a perfect target for extortion and manipulation. Donald Trump was and is a hard target. The Trump collusion story line fits the narrative that the Democrats, DNC, Clintons, and Obama and all their treacherous conniving allies and the mainstream leftist media wanted to hear and promote.

Mueller and his band of merry anti-Trumpers on his special council are just another example of the double standards and hypocrisy surrounding the investigation from its beginning. Thirteen of the seventeen members were Democrats and nine of them contributed more than $57,000 to the Clinton campaign. Not only should it go down as one of the most unnecessary and unscrupulous special council investigations ever, but also it was the most expensive and unproductive at a cost estimated between $25 and $40 million in taxpayer dollars. It's also just another pitiful example of how vindictive the Democrats and radical Left can be when they lose or don't get their way. Deception, lies, spies in our midst, and collusion are all at the hands of the Democrats. Once again, this was all a red herring and elaborate attempt at misdirection and dissimulation to manufacture a reality and illusion that was a farce. There was never any interest in seeking the facts or the truth, but rather to distract and direct attention from their own scandals and the real source of collusion.

The real collusion was always a key element of Obama's and the Clinton's deal with Putin, Medvedev, and the Russians to help her election prospects through hefty contributions to the Clinton Foundation in return for special favors, like the sale of 20 percent of our uranium in the Uranium One deal vis-à-vis Canadian sources to the Russians, backing off any opposition to what the Russians were doing in the Ukraine and their annexation of the Crimea, Russian interference and support for Assad in Syria, and the Iranian nuclear program.

In Pres. Barack Obama's bilateral meeting with outgoing Russian President Dmitry Medvedev a few months prior to the 2012 US presidential elections, he told Medvedev, "This is my last election. After my election, I have more flexibility."

Medvedev in turn told Obama, "I understand. I transmit this to Vladimir [Putin]."

Why would a sitting president make such a promise to his Russian counterpart? I really doubt they were only discussing missile defense. When world leaders get together privately, their discussions don't typically focus on a single issue, especially when Medvedev was a key benefactor of the Russian reset put in motion in 2009 by Clinton. When Obama made the offer of greater flexibility, even if he was referring to a very contentious missile defense issue at that moment, it could easily have been interpreted by his Russian counterpart as greater flexibility on other issues as well or, perhaps worse, a lack of resolve.

When you are dealing with a very formidable adversary and former KGB officer, like Putin, that can be very dangerous. It proved to be just that when Vladimir Putin again assumed the presidency in 2012 over phony cries of foul play by Obama and Clinton over the election. Even then, they were hedging their bets and beginning to play it both ways to cover their own deception, publicly criticizing Putin while privately cutting deals with him behind the scenes to enrich themselves and relegate US national security interests and those of our allies to their own personal and political ambitions. All the red lines Obama and Secretary of State Clinton, Susan Rice, and later John Kerry drew in the sand were all ignored by Putin and the

Russians with little or no consequence. The Iranian nuclear deal, which was all part of a ploy by Obama and Putin to further enrich themselves at the expense of the US taxpayer, proved to be nothing less than extortion, was especially onerous, and benefitted the Iranian nuclear and missile development and military modernization programs, which Putin and the Russians had been deeply involved in supporting for many years.

As it stands now, it seems that former president Obama and the radical Left have also found a close but perhaps unwitting ally in the Vatican and made a major effort in cultivating Pope Francis during President Obama's last two years in office, during his visit to the Vatican in 2014 and during Pope Francis' historic visit to Cuba and the United States in September 2015, when he met with Obama in the White House. The pope also addressed a joint session of Congress, the UN General Assembly in New York, and joined the Festival of Families in Philadelphia. There is no doubt that the pope played a major role in restoring diplomatic relations between Cuba and the United States.

In his speech to Congress, he addressed the issues of poverty and the work of Doris Day, who founded the Catholic Worker Movement, and the progress that has been made and the need to keep in mind all those people around us who are trapped in that cycle of poverty (which Obama and the Democrats were/are prepared to perpetuate) and that part of this effort is the responsible creation and "distribution of wealth" (a subtle jab at capitalism and perceived inequities in a free market economy), the magnitude of the refugee crisis in Europe (created in large part by the open border policies of those European governments) and the plight of immigrants on our continent travelling north in search of a better life (a very direct appeal to open our borders and welcome them), citing the golden rule, "Do unto others as you would have them do unto you" (Matthew 7:12).

He also spoke then and speaks often about our moral responsibility to take care of Mother Earth and her resources referring to his encyclical, *Laudato si'* (May 24, 2015). He talked about eliminating the death penalty and cited the golden rule once again reminding us of our responsibility to defend and protect human life at every stage of its development. While he did not use the word, it was clear he was talking about the culture of death (promoted by the Democrats and Liberal Left). During the Extraordinary Jubilee of Mercy, which Pope Francis declared in April 2015 and which began on December 8, 2015 (the Feast of the Immaculate Conception) and ended on November 20, 2016 (the Feast of Christ the King), all priests worldwide were given the authority in the Sacrament of Penance or Reconciliation to remove censures and give absolution to anyone who had ever had or performed an abortion/abortions. The pope's position on many of these issues—abortion apparently being a major exception—seemed to dovetail nicely with President Obama's and the Democrats'.

In trying to connect the dots and put this all in the context of world politics and the realpolitik taking place in the United States, I am now more intrigued by the apparent similarities in Obama's, the pope's, and our new Democratic Socialist Party agenda and their political ideologies. Obama had an unusual hour-long meeting with the pope in the Vatican in early 2014, and the timing of the pope's visit to the United States just prior to the presidential election campaign of 2016 is noteworthy. Then there were also Pope Francis's three meetings with Russian President Putin in the Vatican while Russia invaded Georgia, the Ukraine, and ultimately invaded and annexed the Crimea. No one could have predicted when Pope John Paul II would die, not even the KGB/FSK, though they tried to hasten his demise in 1981. By 2005, they must have been convinced that their favored candidate, a relatively unknown, Cardinal Bergoglio would be elected to the papacy. It was during this same time frame that Barack Obama first showed up on anyone's political radar, a relatively unknown community organizer from Chicago. Then he became a senator from Illinois, with the support of some noteworthy radical left-wing personalities like Bill Ayers and billionaire globalist and Communist George Soros. Just think, if Chicago Bears coach and Hall of Famer Mike Ditka had run for that seat as he was encouraged to do, the grand deception would have been put on hold for at least a few more years. Obama was a total unknown to national politics then, as he is somewhat of an enigma even now, after spending eight years as the dream president of the FSK, SVR, and GRU and radical Left, who are all trying to undermine and dismantle our economy, military, healthcare system, and education system by promoting the most countercultural, anti-American, humanly debilitating and dehumanizing welfare policies ever contrived, with the support of democratic socialist senators and representatives in our Congress and judges in our courts.

During the immediate post-World War II era and into the 1950s and 1960s, many of the current lineup of more than twenty democratic candidates running for president would have been brought up for questioning by the then House Un-American Activities Committee (HUAC), which was created in 1938 to investigate alleged disloyalty and subversive activities on the part of private citizens, public and government employees, and organizations suspected of having communist ties. Unfortunately, being a subversive, a Socialist/Communist, and engaged in un-American or anti-American activities today seem to be acceptable and even praiseworthy in the Halls of Congress, if you're a Democrat or left-wing political activist. Who would have ever thought that a radical Alinsky revolutionary Hillary Clinton and a Communist, Bernie Sanders, would be vying for the Democratic Party nomination for president in 2016? Yet, if the democratic presidential candidate debates are any indication of their true political ideologies, each was trying to outdo the others to prove themselves to be the most strident radical socialist candidate using terminology out of Marx's *Communist Manifesto*, offering the most freebees to buy your votes, or promising to disarm all patriotic Americans.

Sen. Elizabeth Warren used outrageous language promising to "exterminate the monopolists" and "exterminate private health care." Cory Booker promised to track every gun owner by putting them into a federal government tracking database, not unlike the gun registries used in Stalin's Soviet Union and Hitler's Nazi Germany to disarm potential dissidents. New York Mayor Comrade de Blasio screamed at another candidate for saying something positive about private health insurance, the same guy in the 1980s who supported communist rebels in Nicaragua as part of the Soviet plan for global communist domination. Julian Castro vowed to ensure abortions on demand with taxpayer dollars to include abortions for transgender women. What is a transgender woman? How can *it* possibly bear a child to have an abortion if *it* doesn't have ovaries and a womb? Or if it's a sheman and dresses like a guy and grows a beard like a guy, why would it be engaging in sexual intercourse with another guy?

You can't make this stuff up. It's right there in plain sight, in your face, with the liberal media playing it up and their paid for audience made up of Marxists, anarchists, Communists, and socialists cheering them on. Our Founding Fathers and every patriot who made the ultimate sacrifice for our great republic and the freedoms we enjoy, and yes, Joe McCarthy, must be rolling over in their graves. Every freedom-loving, God-fearing citizen of this great nation better take note of what is happening and reelect President Trump and throw the Socialists out of Congress. It's also time to get rid of the career politicians, like Pelosi, Waters, Feinstein, Schumer, Schiff, and Nadler, along with the squad and the cowardly group of republican career politicians who have failed to support our president. They will always be part of the problem and never part of the solution regardless of the issue. Think about it.

In 1987, with President Reagan having won reelection in 1984 in the second most lopsided presidential election in modern US history and implementing sweeping new political and economic initiatives, Pelosi and Schumer were there in Congress blaming President Reagan "for all our problems." They should be impeached and censored. They are the reason we have to have term limits. Thirty-two years later, *both* are still there, trying to undermine and obstruct and denigrate President Trump's sweeping political and economic initiatives to Make America Great Again and Keep America Great.

> Jesus said to his disciples, "Beware of false prophets, who come to you in sheep's clothing, but underneath are ravenous wolves. By their fruits, you will know them. Do people pick grapes from thorn bushes, or figs from thistles? Just so, every

good tree bears good fruit and every rotten tree bears bad fruit. A good tree cannot bear bad fruit, nor can a rotten tree bear good fruit. Every tree that does not bear good fruit will be cut down and thrown into the fire. So, by their fruits you will know them." (Matthew 7:15–20)

I think we all know that the differences between a sheep and a wolf are irreconcilable unless the wolf is tamed, and that is not going to happen with this gang of ravenous desperate Democrats who are indeed wolves with no pretense about it, who even demonstrate a lack of civility with one another. You can be sure that our friendly Russian intelligence services who were licking their chops closely following the debates and will be engaged in active measures and covert influence operations to support the candidate(s) of their choice. We can also anticipate support by mega billionaires like Bloomberg, Steyer, and George Soros, who has advocated and expressed his own desire to destroy our economic system.

Unfortunately, the Russian FSK, SVR, and GRU and Putin and their democratic stooges suffered yet another setback in 2016 when Donald Trump was elected president, a most unlikely development according to all the mainstream media polls that are typically skewed to try to keep the opposition's voters away from the voting polls, a very well-known ploy by the left-wing media outlets who make themselves excellent conduits for our friendly Russian intelligence services' influence operations. As I recall, there was also some question about an estimated two million votes cast by illegals and unregistered voters that were supposed to ensure a Clinton win.

Yes, and there was voter fraud in Broward County, Florida, a critical swing state in the 2018 general election, as to who would win a critical Senate seat and the Florida governorship, where 116,798 more votes were cast than there were registered voters in Broward County and a full statewide recount was undertaken. Some Broward County officials reduced this number to just over seven thousand by magically increasing the original number of registered voters by some 109,000 and then claimed that an additional seven thousand registered in the five weeks prior to the election. Of course, all seven thousand plus of those voted for the democratic candidates without a single vote going to a republican candidate. Really? And we spend millions of taxpayer dollars and more than two years of hearings and investigations about Russian interference in our elections?

Democratic Party fraud and manipulation of local, state, and national elections has been ongoing for decades. While both parties have had their big-city bosses, none were as powerful and longstanding as the Democrats and their political machines—Richard Daly in Chicago; Carmine DeSapio, last head of the Tammany Hall machine that controlled NYC politics from its founding in 1786; James "the Kingmaker" Farley, who chaired the DNC, controlled NY State politics, and managed FDR's NY gubernatorial and presidential campaigns; or Huey Long and the Long family machine in Louisiana. The list goes on, but I believe my point has been made. While party bosses and machines aren't nearly as powerful today, fraud and corruption remains a hallmark of Democratic Party politics. It was no coincidence that the democratic supervisor of Elections in Broward County was also at the epicenter of the 2000 presidential election recount in Florida, one of the most notorious political controversies in modern American politics.

If the Russians were attempting to influence our elections in 2016, and I frankly believe they were, they were doing so on behalf of the Clintons, Obamas, and the Democrats who were already deeply indebted to Putin for their personal enrichment and he to them. Hillary was most definitely involved during her tenure as secretary of state, with the Clinton Foundation, and during the campaign. The FSK/SVR and GRU cyber and information warfare warriors not only were successful in exploiting Hillary Clinton's and the DNC's e-mail servers and conducting their covert influence operations and active measures during our 2016 election campaign but also have infiltrated our educational and religious institutions; they all but control our mainstream media through active manipulation and have even gained a foothold in our own intelligence services, FBI and DOJ. Since Clinton lost the election, they simply have operated from behind the scenes to manufacture and orchestrate a series of crises to deflect attention away from the real collusion with the DNC, Clintons, and Democrats and the high crimes and misdemeanors of Obama, Biden, and their previous administration. Their desperate and quite devious propaganda and covert influence operations campaign to discredit President Trump while conducting their groundless impeachment proceedings actually had some success. However, I believe the vast majority of Americans can see through the bogus nature of it all and are tired of the democratic-inspired charade. The American electorate should be appalled by the behavior of the Democrats and former president Obama. Obama is the first former president in our short history to set up a shadow government akin to a deposed dictator to actively and both openly and covertly attempt to discredit and subvert his successor. Conspiracy or treason? Judge for yourself.

Let's not forget that Russia, despite some economic and social reforms, is still ruled by the Communist Party and remains our number one peer competitor from both a strategic political and military perspective, with China a close second. For his part, Vladimir Putin and his Russian intelligence services would no doubt see some strategic benefits in supporting Obama's shadow or deep state government and the radical Left's efforts to unseat the president and to further polarize our domestic political environment and undermine our credibility internationally. Putin can't be trusted; he's a seasoned intelligence operative and former KGB officer and a Communist. You can take the man out of the KGB, but you can't take the KGB out of the man.

With the 2020 presidential election campaigns now in full swing, I believe Putin and the Democrats in Congress are likely to focus much more of their attention on influencing the election's outcome by any means. President Trump's approval rating remains high and has achieved new highs with blacks and Hispanic voters. If the Democrats are unable to identify a candidate capable of winning given their extreme move to the left, they will become even more desperate. Obama's endorsement of Biden who was considered damaged goods prior to the coronavirus pandemic was only made official in mid-April after Biden's only opponent; Bernie Sanders bowed out of the race after being subverted again by the DNC. Bloomberg represents the richest of the rich left-wing career politicians who had launched a big money campaign with TV ads full of misrepresentations that had audiences believing that he had been endorsed by former president Obama. Once again, the DNC also made a rule change in its requirement for candidates to meet a grassroots donor threshold to allow Bloomberg to buy his way onto the debate stage in Nevada. Several democratic candidates like Tulsi Gabbard (D-Hawaii) who were deemed ineligible based on that rule rightly complained that the DNC was changing the rules. Even MSNBC's anchor Ari Melber called out the DNC and its chairman Perez for changing its debate rules as being unfair. Once again, the Democrats and DNC make the rules and break the rules as they go along without any regard to fairness or equity. Democrats don't play by the rules. Remember, there isn't anything democratic about the Democratic Party.

While there are still some frantic calls to impeach again, the Mueller report and congressional investigations and testimony have all but ended any chance of that succeeding. What is more concerning is the possibility that one of their radical lunatic fringe supporters, antifa or a Russian intelligence surrogate or asset, attempts a more violent course of action. Political assassination has always been considered a useful tool when needed in the Russian intelligence services' active measures toolbox, and they have used it without hesitation and much more frequently than most realize. I would strongly recommend that President Trump's and Vice President Pence's Secret Service details be doubled or tripled during this election cycle. The Russian intelligence services will continue their cyber and information warfare campaign to manipulate our already politicized and partisan mainstream media, which has made itself the perfect target of Russian influence operations acting as the primary conduit for the successful implementation of this campaign. All the leaks, all the lies, all the fake news, and the spying and active measures will continue.

What is taking place before our very eyes is more than a creeping coup. It is all part of an Alinsky-inspired sociocultural-political revolution. It's not happenstance. It is organized, it is contrived, and it is planned, even if poorly so. It has been implemented over decades but is now gaining momentum and will reach a fevered pitch as we approach the 2020 elections, and it will be accompanied by increased violence promoted by antifa and other extremist groups. There are very powerful forces behind it and responsible for it, both within and outside our sovereign borders. Decades of infiltrating the institutions of American society and government, something the countercultural radicals of the 1960s weren't able to do, was and remains Alinsky's and his disciple's model for deception and revolution. And its fruits are now within the grasp of the current group of radical left-wing career politicians in Congress and their global and foreign intelligence service allies. Whether they fully realize it or not, they are all acting as agents of Putin's and the Russian intelligence services. Many of the key players in the Obama shadow government and Alinsky disciples like Obama and wannabe Hillary Clinton, along with their globalist allies, are participating willfully to promote their own lust for power, prestige, and riches. Many others may be unwitting participants but excellent conduits for Russian active measures, disinformation, and propaganda, like the mainstream media and certain members of Congress, but they are nonetheless culpable for creating a hate-filled divisive environment and making themselves targets ripe for exploitation and manipulation by the demagogues, demons, and masters of deception.

# CHAPTER 5
# The True Legacy of the Democratic Party

*It ain't so much ignorance that ails mankind as
it is knowing so much that ain't so.*
—American humorist, Josh Billings

Let's start with the basics. There is nothing democratic about the Democratic Party, historically, or as its members conduct themselves today. In fact, it is a party of elitist demagogues and demons who have perfected the art of lying and deception, even about the legacy of their own political party.

So let's set the record straight. The Democrat Party emerged when the dominant Democratic-Republican Party became fractionized around the 1824 presidential election when Andrew Jackson, military hero and statesman, was defeated by John Quincy Adams (sixth US president, 1825–1829), and Jackson and his supporters formed the modern-day Democrat Party. Jackson became the seventh president of the United States (1829–1837), winning the presidential election in 1828 by defeating Adams who ran as the National Republican Party candidate and then also defeating Henry Clay, National Republican Party candidate, in 1832.

Jackson was known as a populist president, and he and the Democrats did much to broaden the influence of the citizenry in government, that is, the white Anglo-Saxon Europeans. He dismantled corrupt banking institutions and became the only president to completely pay off the national debt, but then that achievement was quickly erased by the Panic of 1837.

Clay, Adams, and other opponents of Jackson coalesced into the Whig Party (taking its name after the Patriots or American Whigs), those colonists of the thirteen colonies who rejected British rule during the American Revolution and declared our independence in July 1776. Their political philosophy was based on republicanism, as expressed by spokesmen such as Thomas Jefferson, John Adams, and Thomas Paine, all Founding Fathers. It included many active Protestants and voiced a moralistic opposition to Jacksonian and democratic policies on slavery and forced migration of Native Americans from their ancestral homes in the Southeastern United States to lands west of the Mississippi River. The Indian Removal Act was signed by President Jackson into law on May 28, 1830, and was fully implemented by Jackson's successor democratic president Martin Van Buren (1837–1841). The forced migrations become known as the Trail of Tears because it resulted in thousands of Native American deaths from exposure, disease, and starvation.

Democratic president Jackson was also a strong supporter of slavery and gained his wealth and social foothold in Southern society on the backs of his African-American slaves, buying and selling them and using their labor to build his fortunes and even bringing them to the White House to work for him. The more land he acquired, the more slaves he bought. At one point, he owned over 150, who he beat regularly. And when they ran away, he pursued them, "putting them in chains," subjected them to public whippings, and even offered an additional $10 for every hundred lashes doled out according to newspapers of the day. He also opposed policies that would have outlawed slavery in the new western territories of the United States and opposed the abolitionist movement, which grew stronger in his second term in office.

So while Jackson is best known as the hero of the Battle of New Orleans and advocate for democracy and the common man, in the final analysis, Jacksonian democracy upon which your modern-day Democrat Party was founded was not all that democratic from it's very beginning—as it was then, it is now and always has been. I believe democratic presidential candidate Mr. Biden and all democratic candidates need to read up on their history or at least the history of the Democrat Party they represent before they start screaming at their audiences as Biden is known to do that "them [Republicans] are going to be putting you all back in chains" or accusing Republicans of being racists when the Democrats' true legacy is built on racism. To be fair and balanced, I would also suggest that President Trump's former senior strategist Steve Bannon should have done his homework before proudly comparing the president with Andrew Jackson and, as such, doing President Trump a great disservice. The only thing the two have in common is that Trump and Jackson were swept into office as populist candidates and attacked the swamp and corruption of Washington politics with great vigor and authority.

As for the Whig Party, after the election of 1852, when the democratic candidate Franklin Pierce defeated former general and Mexican-American war hero Winfield Scott, the Whig Party fell apart because of growing tensions between the proslavery Southern Whigs and the antislavery Northern Whigs and ceased to exist. Some Southern Whigs would join the Democrat Party and many Northern Whigs would help to form the new Republican Party in 1854. While President Lincoln had been a member of the Whig Party before 1854, he then became the first president under the banner of the new Republican Party.

As such, contrary to the propaganda and attempts to alter history by the Democrats who claim him as their president, he was and always will be the first Republican Party president and the Republican Party that was composed of abolitionists, the party opposed to slavery.

The Democrat Party was strongly opposed to the abolition of slavery and opposed President Lincoln's policies to abolish slavery at every opportunity. Despite these irrefutable historical facts and truths, you can find a portrait of President Lincoln hanging in the DNC headquarters, a wonderful propaganda and brainwashing tool for all their visitors, especially students, who no longer have the benefits of studying history in our public schools. "Seeing is believing" even when it isn't real.

The Emancipation Proclamation or Proclamation 95, which President Lincoln signed on September 22, 1862 (signed by President Lincoln and Secretary of State William Seward), was an executive order issued under the president's authority to suppress rebellion and not an act of Congress. He first issued a preliminary Emancipation Proclamation on September 22 as a warning to the rebellious Southern states that if the rebels did not end the fighting and rejoin the union by January 1, 1863, all slaves in the rebellious states would be free. It was then issued on January 1, 1863, as the nation entered its third year of bloody conflict, declaring, "All persons held as slaves within any State or designated part of a State...in rebellion [Confederate States of America] against the United States, shall be then, thenceforward, and forever free." Some 3.5 million of the estimated four million African-American slaves were emancipated. Of course, the Southern states in rebellion were dominated by the Democrats, and we can therefore surmise that they were staunchly opposed to the Emancipation Proclamation as they were to all abolitionist measures.

Lincoln complemented the Emancipation by ordering the Union Army to protect escaped slaves and encouraged border states (Delaware, Maryland, West Virginia, Kentucky, and Missouri) to outlaw slavery. Lincoln and his Republican Party pushed the Thirteenth Amendment to the US Constitution through Congress, which outlawed slavery across the country. It was supported by 100 percent of Republicans in the House and Senate and only 23 percent of the Democrats who were largely Northern Democrats and War Democrats.

Southern democratic senator Andrew Johnson from Tennessee was the only sitting senator from a Confederate state who did not resign his seat when he learned of his state's succession and remained firmly with the union. President Lincoln appointed him military governor of Tennessee in 1862. Johnson was a War Democrat and Southern Unionist and became President Lincoln's running mate as vice president on the National Union Party ticket (temporary name adopted by the Republican Party) for the presidential election of 1864, which Lincoln won in a landslide victory over Democrat and Union Army General George McClellan. President Lincoln was assassinated by John Wilkes Booth on Good Friday, April 14, 1865, only a month into his second term and was succeeded by Johnson. Booth was a Confederate sympathizer and was strongly opposed to the abolition of slavery. Booth was tracked down and killed twelve days later in Port Royal, Virginia, and eight other coconspirators were tried and convicted and four were hanged.

Johnson, a former slave owner, quickly reverted to his democratic roots issuing a series of presidential proclamations of his own favoring rapid measures to bring the South back into the union and allowing those states to determine the rights of former slaves and freedmen, while the republican-controlled Congress sought stronger measures to uphold the rights of African-Americans including their right to vote, whereas Johnson and the Democrat Party were strongly opposed to this.

Johnson's regressive reconstruction policies prevailed until the election of 1866, when the Republicans gained majorities in both houses of Congress. This enabled the Republicans to pass the Fourteenth Amendment giving full citizenship while federalizing and guaranteeing equal rights for the newly emancipated African-Americans. Every voting Republican in the House (128/134 with six not voting) and every voting Republican in the Senate (30/32 with two not voting) voted for the amendment, while there were no Democrats in the House or Senate who supported it. In 1866, the republican Congress also passed the Freedmen's Bureau and civil rights bills and sent them to Johnson for his signature, which he promptly vetoed. After Johnson vetoed the bills, Congress overrode his vetoes making the Civil Rights Act of 1866 the first major bill in the history of the United States to become law through an override of a presidential veto. It was also the first law passed by Congress detailing the rights of all US citizens, including the right to buy and sell property, engage in business, make contracts, and sue and give evidence in court. It was a key aspect of Congress's efforts to control reconstruction of the union and ensure the eradication of slavery.

Frustrated by Johnson's opposition to congressional reconstruction policies and veto of the Civil Rights Act, the Republicans promptly followed up the passage of the Civil Rights Act by drawing up the Fourteenth Amendment to the Constitution, which was rat-ified in 1868. It further reinforced the Civil Rights Act of 1866 and forbade any state to abridge or reduce the rights declared therein of any citizen. Congress also brought up impeachment charges against Johnson in the House, but the action failed to pass by one vote in the Senate. So Andrew Johnson became the first president to face impeachment, that is, until democratic president Bill Clinton did so in 1999. While in both cases the House voted to impeach, the Senate did not do so.

Unfortunately, all the actions taken by President Lincoln to end slavery, passage of the Thirteenth Amendment to the Constitution, Reconstruction and passage by the republican Congress of the Civil Rights Act of 1866, and ratification of the Fourteenth Amendment to the Constitution all enraged the Southern states and Democrats and led to the emergence of the Ku Klux Klan and increased acts of violence and vigilantism. It's interesting to note that the Klan was founded in Pulaski, Tennessee, in December 1865 during Pres. Andrew Johnson's term in office to oppose the Reconstruction pol-icies of the republican Congress and to maintain white supremacy in the South. Of course, Johnson was in his own dogfight with the republican Congress, working to obstruct every attempt by the Republicans to guarantee the rights of the African-Americans.

It also makes me marvel at how history does have a way of repeating itself. Johnson was the only one of the three—President Lincoln, Secretary of State Seward, and Johnson himself—all alleged targets for assassination on Good Friday, April 14, 1865, who was spared by Booth and his coconspirators. Seward, also one of Lincoln's closest advisors and an ardent abolitionist, was at home in bed recovering from a carriage accident when he was attacked by Confederate Lewis Powell and stabbed multiple times with a bowie knife. George Atzerodt, who was allegedly assigned to kill Johnson, got cold feet and never followed through on the attempt. Needless to say, all the conspirators and Johnson himself along with the vast majority of Democrats were die-hard and dyed-in-the-wool antiab-olitionists who were staunchly opposed to civil rights and equality for African-Americans. In Frederick Douglas' own words, which are worth repeating, "I am a Republican, a black, dyed-in-the-wool Republican, and I never intend to belong to any other party than the party of freedom and progress."

Pres. Woodrow Wilson was described by my very own political science professors as a model for democracy, Wilsonian democracy as it was called. The twenty-eighth president of the United States, a Democrat, a former professor and president of Princeton University, and former governor of New Jersey, he oversaw progressive legislative policies that were unparalleled until Franklin D. Roosevelt's New Deal in 1933. Wilson also led the United States into World War I in 1917. He was the first Southern Democrat to be elected president since the Civil War. Under the umbrella of his progressive New Freedom domestic agenda, he lowered tariffs, established the federal income tax and the estate tax raising it to 77 percent, and established the Federal Reserve and Federal Trade Commission. While he received strong support from African-American leaders and voters at the polls in 1912 as a result of promises he made to deal with the problem of segregation, to the disappointment of his African-American supporters, he allowed his cabinet members to segregate their departments. His record on civil rights, not only for African-Americans but also for women, was abysmal.

A new generation of African-American leaders, like W. E. B. Du Bois, Marcus Garvey, and William Monroe Trotter confronted President Wilson over his segregation policy in government offices. Du Bois was only the sixth black man admitted to Harvard and graduated with honors. Garvey was a visionary and brilliant orator and a personal and political antagonist to Du Bois and a bit of a manipulator. He founded the largest African-American organization Americans had ever known, the Universal Negro Improvement Organization, that promoted racial unity, economic independence, educational achievement, and moral reform. Trotter also attended Harvard and was the first black member of the Phi Beta Kappa Honor fraternity. Along with Du Bois and others, Trotter organized the Niagara Movement in 1905 that evolved into the National Association for the Advancement of Colored People (NAACP).

Trotter led a delegation of civil rights leaders and activists to Washington in 1914 who had supported Wilson at the polls and met with President Wilson on November 12, 1914, to protest Wilson's policy of segregation in government offices and a surge of segregation in the country. Wilson's response that "segregation [in government offices] was caused by friction between the colored and white clerks, and not done to injure or humiliate the colored clerks, but to avoid friction" infuriated Trotter. To his credit, he told President Wilson, "We are sorely disappointed that you take the position that the separation itself is not wrong, is not injurious, is not rightly offensive to you." Isn't it ironic how history tends to repeat itself and democratic presidential candidate Joe Biden is now dealing with a similar challenge from his competition about his position to oppose school busing to support desegregation? As a result of an ensuing heated discourse between Trotter and Wilson, the president lost his temper and Trotter and his delegation were shown the door, but not before Mr. Trotter got another shot across the bow of Wilson's Ship of State by posing a question to President Wilson about his economic reform program, "Have you a 'New Freedom' for white Americans and a new slavery for your Afro-American fellow citizens? God forbids!"

President Wilson declared neutrality between the Allied Powers and Central Powers (Germany, the Austro-Hungarian, and Ottoman empires/Turkey and Bulgaria) at the outbreak of World War I in 1914. He finally asked Congress to enact a declaration of war against Germany and the Central Powers on April 6, 1917, due to Germany's policy of unrestricted submarine warfare against all US ships. Congress also passed the Espionage Act on June 15, 1917, enabling the prosecution of those working with the enemy to hamper the war effort.

W. E. B. Du Bois and other African-American leaders supported America's entry into World War I, thinking that it was one more way for black Americans to gain equality and advance political reform both at home and abroad. That turned out to be wishful thinking. Over 380,000 African-Americans served in World War I according to the National Archives, and some 200,000 were sent to Europe, but more than half of those that deployed were assigned to labor and stevedore battalions building roads, bridges, and trenches for frontline battles.

One of the African-American regiments, the Harlem Hellfighters, National Guard soldiers of New York's 15th Infantry Regiment, eventually joined a decimated French 16th Division on the front lines. While their regimental number was changed to the 369th, they continued to carry their 15th regimental flag and their nickname "Black Rattlers." They got their initiation during the last German Spring offensive in 1918 at Château-Thierry and continued to fight alongside the French 162nd Regiment in the Aisne-Marne counteroffensive during the summer of 1918. The Black Rattlers would go on to distinguish themselves in operations for the duration of the war, receiving the highest French honor, the Croix de Guerre, for its unit actions and some 171 individuals were awarded the Legion of Merit for heroism.

While you might think that this would have changed some attitudes in the Wilson administration, it didn't, despite additional efforts by Du Bois and Trotter to press for more social justice in the postwar world at the peace talks in Paris in 1919. Du Bois arranged to have the French convene a Pan-African Conference and presented its findings to Wilson's inner circle and even met with Wilson's advisor, Colonel House, with no results.

Du Bois, Trotter, and Garvey continued their efforts in the fight for civil rights long after Wilson was gone. Garvey was permanently deported in 1927 after a campaign by the government and other black leaders to discredit him. Trotter was marginalized by his unwillingness to work with established groups, but his nonviolent protest was adopted by the civil rights movement of the 1950s and 1960s. Du Bois became increasingly radicalized embracing communism and spent his final years in Ghana.

Let's not forget our women and Wilson's opposition to women's suffrage, routinely referred to by them as Kaiser Wilson. We celebrated the hundredth anniversary of the passage of the Nineteenth Amendment by Congress on June 4, 1919, and ratified on August 18, 1920, granting women the right to vote. On May 21, 1919, the House of Representatives passed the amendment by a vote of 304-90, and two weeks later, the Senate passed it by a vote of 56-25. What the Democrats didn't want anyone to know is that the Republican Party supported women's voting rights since its founding in 1854, and a republican congressman first introduced the Nineteenth Amendment in 1878. The measure was reintroduced by the Republicans at every session of Congress for forty years and blocked by the Democrats, until the Republicans won such huge majorities in both Houses in the 1918 midterms, enabling the Republicans to override democratic obstructionism to deny women justice.

Even though the Democrats knew the Republicans held what we call a super majority and the Democrats could no longer prevent the passage of the amendment, many still voted against it. Republicans voted in favor of the amendment—200-19 in the House and 36-8 in the Senate, compared to the Democrats 104-71 in the House and 20-17 in the Senate. Even before the Nineteenth Amendment was passed and ratified, twelve states all with republican-controlled legislatures had given women full suffrage, while eight of the nine states that voted against ratification were democratic-controlled; twenty-six of the thirty-six states that ratified it had republican legislatures. On August 18, 1920, Tennessee became the thirty-sixth and final state to ratify the amendment, and it was certified by Secretary of State Colby on August 26, 1920, changing the face of American politics forever. In fact, Wilson did his best to take credit for the achievement with his own brand of propaganda by holding an elaborate presidential signing ceremony despite the fact that the amendment required no presidential signature. You can call it good public relations, but I call it hypocrisy and deception.

The reality and truth of the matter is that Wilson, the Democrats, and Democrat Party stubbornly opposed the passage of the Nineteenth Amendment and women's right to vote for nearly half a century much as they opposed the abolition of slavery and equality for African-Americans. It's just another blatant example of how the Democrats have attempted to deceive the public and electorate by hiding and obscuring the facts and the truth and turning reality on its head, and even revising history. Anything goes if it supports their self-serving political agenda.

I want to share another personal anecdotal story. My wife and I celebrated the seventy-fifth anniversary of women's suffrage at the Woodrow Wilson House in Washington DC in 1995 with our daughter, who was an intern there and spent much of her internship preparing for that anniversary celebration. Of course, we were proud of our daughter's contribution to the exhibit and celebration, so I was reluctant to share with her the irony that the exhibit and celebration was centered on President Wilson and held at the Woodrow Wilson House. I'm not even sure that the female curators there knew the true history of the women's suffrage fight with Kaiser Wilson and the Democrats, as I'm sure most of them were Democrats and Wilson admirers. I'm certain that my own daughter never had any US history courses in high school or college, majoring in art history and the performing arts at American University. Like many college students and graduates today, they wouldn't have a clue about Wilson's and the Democrats' decades of opposition to women's suffrage or the fact and the truth that it was the women's suffrage movements and the Republican Party, GOP, who made it a reality.

The Democrats are masters at exploiting and manipulating this lack of knowledge of history and guilefully use it very effectively against their political opponents to hide and obscure the facts and create their own reality, even if it means revising history to propagate their lies and deception to support their own political agenda—the ends always justifying the means—comforted knowing that the vast majority of the voting population won't know the difference and won't bother to seek out the facts for themselves. This is where the liberal mainstream media also offers itself up as a conduit and enabler for demagoguery and deception.

The big lie and myth about the big switch where the Republican Party of President Lincoln magically becomes the Democrat Party of Andrew Jackson and the Democrat Party becomes the Republican Party through some political and ideological metamorphosis make for a wonderful storybook tale. But it is simply just that, an old bait-and-switch attempt by current-day democratic politicians and academicians to revise history to take credit for reforms that the Democrat Party vigorously opposed while demonizing the political opposition, the Republican Party, that was historically and in reality responsible for the reforms. This applies especially to social justice and civil rights during the latter half of the nineteenth and early twentieth centuries as history has recorded.

Democrats today continue to propagate these myths by proudly pointing to the great accomplishments by democratic presidents Franklin Roosevelt and his *New Deal* and Lyndon Johnson and the *Great Society* as examples of their modern liberal heritage and civil rights achievements. During the Great Depression of the 1930s, which followed the stock market crash of September 1929, there were significant defections of African-Americans and other minorities from the Republican Party to the Democrat Party, who supported the election of Pres. Franklin Delano Roosevelt in 1932 (1933–1945). Republican president Herbert Hoover (1929–1933) was blamed for not doing enough to end the crisis, though it's doubtful that any president at the time could have brought the crisis to an end. In President Hoover's case, he was operating with democratic majorities in both the House and the Senate from the midterms in 1930 throughout his tenure in office. Indeed, the Great Depression continued (1929–1939) through President Roosevelt's first term and even into his second, despite all his campaign promises. The New Deal promised to alleviate economic desperation and joblessness, provide greater opportunities for all Americans, and restore prosperity with an increased role of the federal government in addressing the nation's economic and social problems. Work relief programs like the Civilian Conservation Corps (CCC), Works Progress Administration (WPA), and the Tennessee Valley Authority (TVA) were established to create jobs and stimulate the economy. And in 1935, the Social Security Act and unemployment insurance programs were added as safety nets. The Democrats built on the majorities they had won in the two previous midterms, providing Roosevelt with a democratic supermajority in Congress. This marked the first time since the Civil War that an incumbent president's party gained seats in a midterm election, followed by 1998, 2002, and 2018.

There is no doubt that the significant expansion of the Democrat Party's base in the early and mid-1930s was a direct result of the economic depression that prompted African-Americans and other minorities to flock to President Roosevelt and his Democrat Party based on the promises of the New Deal. As former president Obama's former White House chief of staff and former mayor of Chicago, Rahm Emanuel, put it, "never let a serious crisis go to waste." I'm sure that such thoughts were not lost on career politicians like Roosevelt in his day. Changing demographics also had an impact on democratic successes with African-Americans and other minorities living in urban environments controlled by democratic big-city bosses and democratic machines that are democratic-controlled strongholds even today. That's also why the Democrats can always find a few thousand more votes in big-city precincts than there are registered voters actually living there.

Franklin Roosevelt's top aide, Harry Hopkins, used the new relief programs of the New Deal as a device to support the machines, with precinct workers (our early democratic community organizers) trained on how to assist local families and getting on relief projects like WPA and CCC. One of the most powerful party leaders of the day was James A. Farley who was the chief dispenser of Democrat Party patronage during the Roosevelt administration's New Deal. Farley was not considered a boss because he worked under the direction of Roosevelt himself and controlled most midlevel and low-level appointments in collaboration with state and local democratic organizations. Farley's ability to build up the Democrat Party's national political machine coupled with the Solid South, the big-city bases, and the populist vote made it the most organized and powerful in American history.

The New Deal programs to relieve the Great Depression are generally regarded as a mixed success in ending unemployment. Many New Deal programs like the CCC were very popular; and the new Democratic Liberals and Republicans alike hailed them for improving the life of the common citizen, providing jobs for the unemployed (CCC/WPA), legal protection for labor unionists, modern utilities for rural America (TVA), living wages for the working poor, and price stability for the family farmer. Economic progress for minorities, however, was hindered by discrimination, an issue often avoided by the Roosevelt administration for fear of alienating their Solid South democratic voting bloc.

Another historical fact that seems to escape our guileful democratic wizards of deception is that throughout the 1930s, 1940s, 1950s, and 1960s and into the 1970s, both major American political parties, Republican and Democrat, had conservative and liberal factions. The Solid South of the Roosevelt era was basically the Solid South of the post-Civil War era, which was still with us during the Great Society of the 1960s and into the 1970s. It was controlled by the ultraconservative faction of the Democrat Party, not the Republican Party as today's Democrats would otherwise have you believe. So when did the mystical big switch occur? In my research, I encountered some studies and articles suggesting that it occurred during the progressive period of republican president Teddy Roosevelt's era, others during Wilson's New Freedom program, still others as a result of the New Deal, and finally others during the Great Society. There is no evidence to substantiate any of these claims by the Democratic Liberals for their mythical and magical transformation and metamorphosis that they would like everyone to believe had taken place, making them the party of President Lincoln or the party that has fought for civil rights.

On the contrary, during the Roosevelt administration, New Deal programs were racially segregated with blacks and whites rarely working alongside one another. The largest relief program by far was the WPA, which operated segregated units as did its youth counterpart, the National Youth Administration. Blacks were hired as supervisors in the Republican North. Of ten thousand WPA supervisors in the South, only eleven were black. In the first few weeks of operation, CCC camps in the north were integrated. By July 1935, thanks to Roosevelt's so-called liberal democratic supermajority in Congress (or wait, maybe they were racist Republicans disguised as Democrats), all the camps countrywide were segregated and blacks were strictly limited in the supervisory roles they were assigned. Roosevelt and his administration were unwilling to challenge their Southern Democrats' segregation laws carried on from Civil War Reconstruction. Like the Black Codes of the 1860s, the Jim Crow laws were state and local laws that enforced racial segregation in the Southern States. All were enacted in the late nineteenth and early twentieth centuries by white Far-Right democratic-dominated legislatures after the Reconstruction period and remained in place until the mid-1960s. Jim Crow laws mandated racial segregation in all public facilities, starting in the 1870s and 1880s, and were upheld in 1896 by the US Supreme Court's separate but equal legal doctrine and decision in the case of Plessy v Ferguson. As a body of law, Jim Crow institutionalized economic, educational, and social disadvantages for African-Americans and other people of color in the South, while racial segregation in the Northern and Western states was a matter of fact enforced in housing, bank lending practices, and employment, including labor union practices.

I have acknowledged that a mass defection and migration of African-Americans and other minorities occurred from the Republican to the New Deal and Democrat Party largely as a result of the Great Depression along with a significant change in demographics that favored and greatly expanded the political and electoral base of the Democrat Party in the 1930s and 1940s. That did not change the political identity or philosophy or ideology of the Democratic or Republican parties. It did offer Roosevelt and the Democrats a unique opportunity to lure an entirely new segment of the electorate and population to their ranks, and they exploited it as never before in the annals of American politics. It certainly appears that the Democrats and the radical Left are now trying desperately to expand the party's shrinking political base by promising their own version of the New Deal, a socialist Mecca, a mega welfare state, and a new form of slavery for all those gullible enough to buy into it.

Frankly, with the booming economy and unemployment at its lowest levels in decades, and more African-Americans and Hispanics with meaningful employment and enjoying a level of prosperity never before experienced, I would expect a larger percentage of their electorate will vote to reelect President Trump than voted for him in 2015. African-Americans and Hispanics are awakening to the lies and deception of the Democrats and are slowly but surely coming back to the Republican Party due to the increasing prosperity they are now experiencing with President Trump's Make America Great Again economic renewal. I believe the Democrats' desperation and fanaticism will only increase as we get closer to the elections. It is also very apparent that they are frantically attempting to bring the millions of illegals into their political base along with a larger percentage of millennials with their promises and guarantees of a socialist paradise. The real irony here is that the vast majority of those illegals who are invading America today are doing so to escape those failed socialist economies in Central and South America and the tyranny that accompanies socialism and communism. Let's not forget that there is also a large criminal and gang element associated with these mass migrations.

The New Deal did not end the Great Depression. World War II and the mobilization of the US economy ended the Great Depression with a significant increase in the size of the armed forces with the Selective Training and Service Act (military draft or universal conscription) and mobilization of industry to transition to produce massive amounts military equipment, ammunition, ships, and aircraft. New Deal programs ended with massive war spending bringing full employment with millions joining the wartime labor force and the military. The federal budget increased from $8.9 billion in 1939 to over $95 billion in 1945. Thanks to pressure from civil rights activists like A. Philip Randolph, who led the march on Washington in 1963, and Walter Francis White, who led the NAACP (1929–1955), Roosevelt eventually issued Executive Order 8802 to prohibit racial discrimination in the national defense industries during World War II. They were also successful in getting Pres. Harry Truman to issue Executive Order 9981 in 1948, ending segregation in the armed forces.

Liberalism in the immediate postwar years and throughout the 1950s and 1960s was the heir of Roosevelt's New Deal, but after 1945, the left-wing liberal alliance that apparently operated during the New Deal years split apart for good over the Cold War and communism. Anticommunist Liberals led by Walter Reuther and Hubert Humphrey expelled the Far Left from labor unions and the New Deal coalition and committed the Democrat Party to a strong Cold

War policy of the containment of communism, including support for the North Atlantic Treaty Organization (NATO).

Liberals became committed to a quantitative goal of economic growth and largely rejected Keynesian economics and the structural transformation dreamed of by the earlier Far-Left Liberals and Roosevelt's new economic Bill of Rights. FDR considered this Bill of Rights his tool for guaranteeing employment for veterans and others after World War II. But it was more than a mere jobs ploy; it had the potential to transform American society. It included a right to a job with fair pay and working conditions, equal access to education for all, equal access to health care and nutrition for all, and "wholesome housing for all." Our first Bill of Rights that became part of our Constitution granted freedoms from government interference and rights to freedom of speech, assembly, religion, and press. These imposed no obligation on anyone to provide the means to exercise these rights.

However, Keynes argued that capitalism was inherently unstable and would rarely provide full employment and that government planning and intervention running large deficits was needed to guarantee the right to jobs, housing, health care, and education and it was every citizen's duty to provide the revenue to support these rights. The National Resources Planning Board that FDR established in 1939 were all Keynesian disciples, who believed that taxpayers as a group had a duty to provide the revenue for all these freebies that millions of Americans would be demanding if FDR's economic Bill of Rights became law. I think all this should begin to sound very familiar, if you've paid any attention to what the radical left-wing democratic socialist candidates today are preaching. Of course, I seriously doubt based on their outlandish proposals and ideas that any have any real understanding of economics, macro or micro. Thankfully, the majority of congressmen from both parties rejected Roosevelt's Bill of Rights and instead, after vigorous debate, scrapped the bill and cut tax rates instead. American business expanded and thrived, revenues to the Treasury increased to balance the federal budget, and unemployment was held at 3.9 percent in 1946 and 1947.

The Far Left had its last stand with Henry A. Wallace who was the Left-Wing Progressive Party candidate in the 1948 presidential elections. Wallace supported additional New Deal reforms and opposed the Cold War, but his campaign was taken over by the Far-Left, and he and the party were accused of being a tool of the Communist Party; he received less that 3 percent of the vote and retired from politics. The United States and Soviet Union engaged in a Cold War and arms race with threats of nuclear annihilation by the two superpowers adopting deterrent doctrines of mutual assured destruction, which came to a head, but did not end, with the Cuban missile crisis lasting for decades through the Reagan administration and 1990s.

While FDR, Churchill, and other world leaders were eagerly preparing to bring the war to a just conclusion, Joseph Stalin and the Soviets were already well on their way to occupy Eastern Europe. The Soviets then as the Russians now remain masters of deception. World leaders like FDR and their confidants also used deception to hide illnesses and vulnerabilities, whether unwittingly or intentionally out of necessity. In FDR's case, he confronted his paralysis from the waist-down head-on and with unbelievable courage, but the general public was never aware of how debilitating his condition was. Secret Service details prevented photography of FDR in his wheelchair or on crutches, with all of his public appearances carefully choreographed to depict a "healthy," vigorous president. Even his personal physician, Admiral Dr. Ross McIntire, US Navy Medical Center in Bethesda, Maryland, announced to the nation during FDR's campaign for a fourth term in May 1944 that the president "was enjoying excellent health." Even his vice presidential running mate Harry Truman and wife Eleanor Roosevelt voiced concern about his unhealthy appearance. President Roosevelt was diagnosed with diastolic hypertension in 1939 and systolic hypertension in 1941, but they were disguised under various aliases, F. David Rolph and Mr. John Cash.

During his last year in office and during that campaign for a fourth term, he was a dead man walking and, given the intelligence advantages of Joseph Stalin and the Soviets already discussed, put him at even a greater disadvantage in negotiations at both the Tehran and

Yalta Conferences hosted by Stalin. Even the location of the conferences and accommodations were ultimately made by Stalin and the People's Commissariat of Internal Affairs (NKVD) [predecessor of KGB] to maximize their advantage; like all deceptions, the deceiver always has the advantage. In order to get to Yalta in the Crimea, in his rapidly declining state of health, Roosevelt had to sail, fly, and ride over rough road to get to Yalta, which had been left in ruins by the Nazis, with Stalin and entourage conveniently arriving a day later. While American and British accommodations were surveilled 24/7, according to the Mitrokhin Archives, Moscow felt that good intelligence provided by all the Cambridge Five, no longer suspected of being double agents for the Soviets, and Alger Hiss (who was in the American delegation at Yalta) had contributed to Stalin's success at Yalta. Hiss and his whole group were awarded Soviet decorations. Hiss was there to conduct negotiations with the Soviets for the formation of the United Nations and was appointed by the Big Three acting secretary-general of the United Nations organizing conference in San Francisco (yet another irony of history). In retrospect, not only were the vast disparity of intelligence and Roosevelt's health key factors in the outcome of those two conferences, but also the gullibility of Roosevelt and Churchill in dealing with the leader of one totalitarian regime, to defeat another, and not consider Stalin's record of tyranny, is hard to imagine.

A year before his death, Eleanor Roosevelt, seeking a second opinion from Dr. Ross McIntire's reports, had a young navy cardiologist Dr. Bruen assigned who found FDR to be cyanotic, breathless with rales in his lungs, left ventricular enlargement, a booming aortic sound, a blowing apical systolic murmur, and blood pressure (BP) of 186/108 mm Hg. His BP had not been checked since February 1941 when it was 188/105. He was diagnosed with hypertensive heart disease, congestive heart failure, and acute bronchitis. He was prescribed digitalis, bed rest, curtailing his cigarette smoking, codeine for cough control, and general sedation. A week later, his BP was 210/110 mm Hg. Regardless of your politics, a man or woman in this condition should never again be permitted to run for the office of president. Whether it was pride, his Democrat Party cohorts' desires, or the belief that he could not pass on the torch of leadership before he saw the war come to its final conclusion, he should not have been permitted to run for a fourth term. Yes, I know, it's history. Let it go. The real problem and issue is that all of this was hidden from the American people and electorate, when he was reelected to an unprecedented fourth term in November 1944. Despite severe chest pains and hypertension, he went to Yalta in February 1945, and there still smoking and under heavy sedation, his BP was 260/150 mm Hg, enough to blow the top of your skull off and pulsus alternans noted for the first time. Eight weeks later, he had a massive cerebral hemorrhage with BP that morning of 300/190 mm Hg. This was not shared with the public, even after his death. In fact, there was some evidence that Dr. McIntire may have destroyed FDR's medical records.

Concessions agreed by Roosevelt and Churchill at Tehran and Yalta and the deception of communist dictator Joseph Stalin and the Soviets ushered in forty years of slavery, fear, and abject poverty for hundreds of millions of Russians and Eastern Europeans trapped behind what became known as the Iron Curtain. Millions died of starvation and millions more who dared to question or challenge authorities were executed or exiled to the gulags, Soviet forced labor camps, set up by Vladimir Lenin and reached their peak during Stalin's rule from the early 1930s to the early 1950s. Historians estimate the number of deaths in Russia during Stalin's Great Purge or Great Terror in 1936–1938 alone reaching over a million and included summary executions, massacres, mass murders, and ethnic cleaning of political opponents, Red Army leadership, Trotskyites, and ethnic minorities. Most of those were carried out by the NKVD, one of the precursors of the Committee for State Security or KGB (1954–1991), responsible for internal security, foreign intelligence, and the secret police. It's also difficult to believe that Roosevelt and Churchill were not aware of this Soviet holocaust.

Upon Roosevelt's death on April 12, 1945, Vice President Truman became president and the man who had to make that awesome and horrific decision to end the war with Japan by employing the first atomic and nuclear weapons with the bombing of Nagasaki and Hiroshima. Historians estimate that a million or more American lives were probably saved by avoiding an invasion of the Japanese mainland against a stubborn Japanese protagonist. The decision also successfully brought the war to a decisive end. As for the Russians declaring war on Japan, another clever deceptive move by Stalin to regain territories lost during the Russo-Japanese War without so much as firing a shot before the Japanese agreed to an unconditional surrender. However, Stalin and the Soviet Communists weren't going to settle for the spoils of World War II and Yalta in Eastern Europe or be satisfied with reclaiming territories in the Far East. Instead, they armed and supported the Soviet puppet, Kim Il-sung, and the North Korean Communists in the invasion of South Korea on June 25, 1950. This undeclared war and the victory of Mao Zedong with the support of the Soviet Union in 1949 became the hallmark of communist imperialism and expansionism in the Far East, which President Truman had to deal with following his election in 1948.

It's no wonder that the far-left democratic forces who controlled Congress during the Roosevelt administration, which was in fact heavily infiltrated by American and Soviet agents, were rejected by the American electorate and that these events gave rise to a second Red Scare and McCarthyism. The perception was that American and Russian communist agents and sympathizers were infiltrating and subverting US society and the federal government and that perception was built on some very convincing evidence. The first Red Scare followed the Bolshevik Russian Revolution of 1917 and during an intense patriotic period during World War I as anarchists' bombings and left-wing social agitation aggravated national, social, and political tensions, mounting fear and anxiety that a Bolshevik revolution in America was imminent, a revolution that would change church, home, marriage, civility, and the American way of life.

I think there is a growing segment of the population in America today who have legitimate concerns about the resurgence of the radical Left and Democrat Party's radical socialist agenda—their lack of civility, daily attacks on our president, efforts to denigrate the traditional bonds of marriage and the American family, and attempts to abridge our religious freedoms and take God out of every facet of our lives all this while calling for and encouraging violence against anyone who dares to oppose them. Not only are they the party of deception, but also they are the party of violence calling on their radical left-wing militant supporters (antifa) to use all means available to intimidate the opposition. Activists involved in the antifa movement tend to be anticapitalists, anti-American, anarchists, Communists, and Socialists along with some Liberals and social Democrats. The fact and truth of the matter is that there is very little difference, as far as political ideologies go, between right-wing and left-wing extremists, between fascism, Nazism, and communism and socialism. All are grounded in hate, racism, tyranny, repression persecution, and intolerance and there is no place in America for any of them. The fact that the most violent, countercultural, and lawless of the groups are radical left-wing vigilantes of the Democrat Party shouldn't surprise anyone. Let's not forget the Klu Klux Klan was an organization that grew out of the white supremacist, antiabolitionist, and racist policies of the Democrat Party, not the Republican Party, which was staunchly abolitionist.

It might also be worth looking more into the history of communist, socialist, and fascist regimes like the Soviet Union, Cuba, Nazi Germany, Fascist Italy, Argentina, and more recently Venezuela and the tyranny that accompanied them. I had a very bright university political science professor in 1966 who suggested that it makes more sense to compare political ideologies on a circle rather than linearly on a straight line. He argued quite convincingly that at the top of the circle are the moderates both Liberal and Conservative, and as you slide down each side of the circle, you find the center left Liberals and center right Conservatives until you approach the very bottom of the circle where you will find the extremists, radical/ultra Left and reactionary/ultra Right. The fact is there are more similarities than differences between the two, and no good has ever been achieved by either; they have only ever evoked feelings of hate, fear, and bigotry and are always accompanied by evil, violence, repression, and persecution.

Two more very important pieces of civil rights legislation were passed during republican president Dwight Eisenhower's administration, which you hear very little about and they were the Civil Rights Act of 1957 and the Civil Rights Act of 1960. The Civil Rights Act of 1957, which sought to protect the voting rights of black Americans, was the first piece of civil rights *legislation* passed since the republican-controlled Congress passed the Nineteenth Amendment in 1919. The Civil Rights Act of 1957 passed the House in a 286-126 vote. Only 51 percent of Democrats or 119/235 members voted for the bill, while 84 percent of Republicans or 167/199 members voted in favor. The bill then went to the Senate, where Southern Democrat Strom Thurmond, an ardent opponent of integration, filibustered the bill for twenty-four hours and eighteen minutes, the longest individual filibuster in history. After the filibuster and some changes were made to the bill, it passed the Senate with a vote of 72-18. The bill received 43/46 or 93 percent of republican votes and only 29/59 or 59 percent of democratic votes. The bill had to be sent back to the House after being amended and was approved in a 279-97 vote, 75 percent of Republicans voting in favor and 55 percent of Democrats. Republican president Eisenhower signed the bill into law on September 9, 1957. The Civil Rights Act of 1960 also addressed the voting rights of black Americans establishing penalties for those who would try to prevent people from voting. The bill passed the House with a vote of 311-109 with the support from both parties, 87 percent of Republicans and 64 percent of Democrats. In the Senate, it was amended and received similar levels of support, with 83 percent of Republicans and 65 percent of Democrats supporting it. It passed with the final vote in the House 288-95, once again with a larger percentage of Republicans, 81 percent voting in favor than Democrats, 59 percent supporting it.

I have already discussed President Kennedy's handling of the Bay of Pigs and Cuban missile crisis, his assassination, and the Soviet's and KGB active measures, which targeted his presidency during his short time in office (January 20, 1961, to November 22, 1963). President Kennedy's legislative record was the best of any president since Roosevelt's first term in office (1934–1938) and included the landmark Civil Rights Act and Labor Law of 1964, which President Kennedy, not President Johnson, originally proposed in 1963, outlawing discrimination based on race, color, religion, sex, or national origin. It prohibits unequal application of voter registration requirements and ended segregation in schools and public places and made discrimination in employment practices illegal. The bill was enacted into law on July 2, 1964; and once again, contrary to the lies and deception of the Democrats, the Bill received more support from the Republicans and Republican Party, the GOP of President Lincoln than the Democrats and the Democrat Party, despite the fact that the Democrats held majorities in both the House and Senate. The House passed the bill after two and a half months of public debate and testimony in a 290-130 vote. Around 78 percent or 138 Republicans voted in favor, while only 60 percent or 152 Democrats voted in favor. In the Senate, the bill faced very strong and organized opposition from Southern Democrats, Richard Russell, Strom Thurmond, Robert Byrd, William Fulbright, and Sam Ervin, who joined to launch a fifty-seven-day filibuster with President Johnson, who apparently used every card he had to play and every chip he had to cash in with his old cronies, cheering them on from the White House. When some changes were made to mollify the senate Democrats, it passed the Senate 73-27, with 82 percent of the Republicans in favor and 69 percent of the Democrats voting in favor. The amended Senate bill passed the House with 76 percent support from the Republicans and 60 percent support from the Democrats. Congress also passed the Civil Rights Act of 1968, also known as the Fair Housing Act. And once again the vast majority of Republicans, 87 percent in the House and 81 percent in the Senate, voted in favor, compared to 68 percent of the Democrats in the House and 66 percent in the Senate with the Democrats controlling majorities in both houses.

One final detail that deserves mentioning—there is some credible evidence that when President Johnson realized his cronies could not prevent the passage of the Civil Rights Act and he would have to sign or veto and the votes were there, in both the House and Senate, to override his veto, he jumped on the bandwagon and made a real spectacle of his support for the bill. This was followed by some very revealing commentary on Johnson's reaction to the passage by Congress of the Civil Rights Act of 1964. One sentence often attributed to President Johnson, which went viral on the Internet at one time, was, "I'll have those [African-Americans, N-word deleted] voting Democrat for 200 years." The source of the two-hundred-year quote is Kessler's 1995 book, *Inside the White House*. Kessler got the quote from Robert MacMillan, an Air Force One steward and African-American, who said LBJ made the comment—using the N-word—to two governors during a conversation on the Civil Rights Act of 1964 before he was forced to sign it. Kessler's source is historically sound and LBJ's fondness of the use of the N-word is well documented. It also falls in line with Doris Kearns Goodwin's biography of LBJ, *Lyndon Johnson and the American Dream*, where he is quoted,

> These Negroes, they're getting pretty uppity these days and that's a problem for us since they've got something now they never had before, the political pull to backup their uppityness. Now we've got to do something about this, we've got to give them a little something, just enough to quiet them down, not enough to make a difference.

Be your own judge. The lies and propaganda and deception have continued to this day. Recently deceased democratic representative Elijah Cummings was either ignorant of the facts of history and the history of his own party or maybe just grandstanding when he claimed in his speech at the Democratic National Convention in 2016 that Democrats gave blacks the right to vote. I've already clearly revealed the facts and truth about this issue. It doesn't matter if you're talking about the Thirteenth, Fourteenth, Fifteenth, or Nineteenth Amendment to the Constitution or any of the Civil Rights Acts passed since 1878. The Republican Party and Republicans have done more to promote the civil rights and freedoms of all Americans— blacks, women, and other minorities—than the Democrats could ever dream of doing, so they lie, deceive, and create their own version of reality and history.

It's time that all Americans and the American electorate recognize and accept the truth and reject the big lie and propaganda that the Democrats have promoted for decades. I would hope that our African-American brethren in particular reject the lies and hollow, self-serving promises of the party of bigotry, demagoguery, and deception, the party of socialism and the welfare state, that will never allow anyone to escape the bonds of perpetual poverty, slavery, and despair. They'll say and do anything to hold onto the African-American, women, and Hispanic vote. It's all deception, showing and declaring the fake and hiding and obscuring the real.

# Chapter 6
## The Church in Crisis

*Nothing can do men of good will more harm than apparent compromises with parties that subscribe to antimoral and antidemocratic and anti-God forces. We must have the courage to detach our support from men who are doing evil. We must bear them no hatred, but we must break with them.*
—Bishop Fulton J. Sheen

Just when many of us were beginning to feel that the healing process in the Catholic Church was progressing and the issue of sexual harassment and abuse was being justly and adequately addressed, the bombshell eleven-page letter issued in August 2018 by former Vatican apostolic nuncio to the United States Archbishop Carlo Maria Viganò created a firestorm of renewed accusations that the leadership of the church, particularly Pope Francis, was wavering in their commitment to make amends and redress the problem. The letter described a series of warnings to the Vatican regarding Cardinal Theodore McCarrick, who had allegedly abused a minor and multiple adult seminarians. As a result, he was removed as a cardinal and was forbidden by Pope Francis from leaving the grounds where he was residing and from celebrating mass in public in July 2018, pending the results of a canonical trial. Viganò also claimed that he had written a memo concerning McCarrick's abuse while Viganò was Vatican Official Secretariat of State in 2007. This led Pope Benedict XVI, sometime in 2009 and 2010, to place severe restrictions on McCarrick's movements and public ministry. Viganò insisted that

Pope Francis knew about McCarrick's alleged abuse shortly after he became pope in 2013 but removed the sanctions placed on McCarrick by Pope Benedict XVI and made McCarrick his trusted counselor. In the letter containing these allegations, Viganò called on Pope Francis and all others who covered up McCarrick's conduct to resign. Viganò also accused three consecutive Vatican secretaries of State of knowing about McCarrick's behavior but doing nothing about it.

Cardinal Daniel DiNardo, president of the US Conference of Catholic Bishops, released a statement declaring that regardless of what you may think Viganò's reasons for writing the letter, Viganò's letter raised questions that "deserve answers that are conclusive and based on evidence. Without those answers, innocent men may be tainted by false accusations and the guilty may be left to repeat the sins of the past."

I couldn't agree more with Cardinal DiNardo's comment. Once again, it's all about seeking the truth and trying to determine how much of this crisis is based on the fake and what is real. I'm concerned that there is a critical element in this crisis that no one in the church or media have seriously considered, the likelihood of infiltration and subversion, active measures, and covert influence operations by our friendly Russian foreign intelligence services. If they have considered it, they have failed to express it in any meaningful way. After praying on it, I was inspired by the Holy Spirit to break out my discussion lost in chapter 4 on Russian active measures against the Catholic Church to address it more fully and thoughtfully on its own. Please understand I am not trying to downplay the seriousness of the abuse or the suffering of the victims of that abuse. I am interested in sharing my analysis of another potential piece of the puzzle that may explain why this crisis just seems to have taken on a life of its own and will never really go away. I will argue that anti-Catholicism has been around for centuries, and Christianity and the Catholic Church are under attack by socialists, militant secularists, progressives, and their increasingly hostile attempts to take away our religious freedoms.

The Pennsylvania Grand Jury report that was also issued in August 2018 at the same time Viganò's letter was released to the press regarding sexual abuse in Catholic dioceses in Pennsylvania that identified priests who were accused of sexual abuse received little or no media coverage. I propose that it wasn't newsworthy, because the report was not sufficiently negative. It was factual, thorough, and objective. If the results from that report are combined with the two other dioceses in Pennsylvania that had already been subjects of investigation, the results showed that 8 percent of five thousand priests who served in Pennsylvania during the seventy-year period covered by the report was credibly accused of abuse. It also alleges that bishops systematically covered up incidents of abuse. While the report provides a scathing indictment of the history of abuse in the church, it also clearly suggests that the zero tolerance policies and reforms and procedures for reporting abuse have significantly reduced the occurrence of abuse in the past decade. The report also indicated that only two priests were involved in abuse during the ten-year period (2008–2018) and those were reported by the dioceses. Why isn't this newsworthy? Because there is an anti-Catholic cultural bias that runs strong and deep and is played up by a mainstream media controlled by non-Catholic, politically progressive, and militant secularist moguls.

However, the firestorm created by Viganò's letter has apparently had its intended effect and has created a very divisive impact on the Catholic Church here in the United States and has intensified tensions between ideological Conservatives and Liberals within and outside the Catholic Church. Many Conservatives and more doctrinal Catholics have pointed to the alleged role of homosexuality in clergy sex abuse and have expressed concerns that Pope Francis has not been sufficiently strict in enforcing doctrinal orthodoxy. On the other hand, many Catholic Liberals have blamed the sex abuse on what they perceive to be excessively strict and inflexible dogmatism and have called for the church to be more flexible, welcoming, and inclusive of homosexuals and same-sex marriage.

Conservatives have been willing to accept at least some of Viganò's accusations, while Liberals are very critical of the letter and Viganò's motives for attacking their liberal pope. Unfortunately, Pope Francis's response to a journalist who asked him to comment on the letter was rather noncommittal stating, "Read the statement carefully and make your own judgement. I will not say a single word about this. I believe the statement speaks for itself... But I would like your professional maturity to do the work for you. It will be good for you." Veteran Vatican journalist, John Allen, suggested that the clear suggestion from the pope was that "if they [journalists] did so, the charges would crumble under their own weight." Others saw the pope's silence and Viganò's insistence that documents related to the case be made public as an indication that Viganò was probably telling the truth, or at least believed himself that he was telling the truth.

"As a matter of honor, one man owes it to another to manifest the truth" (Saint Thomas Aquinas).

In the meantime, going back for a moment to Cardinal DiNardo's comment, Cardinal George Pell, former archbishop of Melbourne and Sydney, Australia, and later the Vatican's chief financial officer was brought to Rome by Pope Francis to clean up Vatican finance. He was in the midst of investigating some really serious corruption involving hundreds of millions of euros when charges of abuse dating back to the 1990s were laid on him. Cardinal Pell did not legally have to return to Australia to confront his solitary accuser, but he chose to do so to defend himself knowing that he was innocent of the charges brought forth by that one man. He now sits in jail in Melbourne because he dared to defend himself in an atmosphere of anti-Catholicism, which has been a staple of Australian culture for decades. Corruption in policing and law enforcement in Victoria is also well documented as is the local media's bias and misrepresentation of Cardinal Pell.

The cardinal's first trial ended in a hung jury with ten of twelve jurors voting for acquittal. In the retrial, the defense again demonstrated that it would have been physically impossible for the alleged abuse to have occurred since the cardinal and the individual who alleged the abuse were physically in two different places when the alleged abuse occurred. The retrial jury took days to reach a verdict, and after a juror asked the trial judge for guidance on how evidence should be considered, the overwhelming vote at the first trial for acquittal was flipped for a unanimous vote for conviction. Aggressive secularists couldn't forgive him for his robust Catholicism, and most

Catholic progressives couldn't abide by his orthodoxy. But some of his enemies had the integrity to dismiss the charges against him as ludicrous, and some said afterward that his conviction was and is a travesty. There was never any corroborating evidence presented by the prosecution that the abuse ever took place, only the word of one individual who the prosecution claimed was a truthful person.

Then there is also the timing of the charges filed and Cardinal Pell's investigation into the shadowy world of global finance and the Vatican. I can't help but recall that a certain Bishop Viganò was exiled by Cardinal Tarcisio Bertone to become the apostolic nuncio to the United States after confronting Bertone with allegations of corruption in Vatican finances while Viganò was secretary general of the Vatican City Governorate where he was also engaged in cleaning up Vatican finances. Coincidence or contrived, you be the judge.

I would also like to suggest some alternative explanations for the crisis we are dealing with in the Catholic Church today, by boldly going where no one else has gone by considering the history of anti-Catholicism and decades of Soviet active measures directed at infiltrating and subverting the Russian Orthodox and Catholic churches. These active measures included covert influence operations, propaganda, and infiltrating seminaries and were often accompanied by arrests, imprisonment, and murdering clergy and defacing and closing churches and campaigns to eliminate and subvert religious institutions. Let's not forget the Soviet state was the first to attempt to eradicate God.

Lenin's denunciation of religion was particularly venomous, stating, "Every religious act, every idea of God...is unutterable vileness, vileness of the most dangerous kind...millions of filthy deeds, acts of violence and physical contagions are far less dangerous, than the subtle, spiritual idea of God." Any of this sound familiar?

During the 1930s, most priests were arrested and condemned to the gulag from which few returned. Most churches, with their religious symbols removed or defaced, were turned into barns, garages and cinemas or turned over for other secular purposes. After two decades of brutal persecution, the Russian Orthodox Church was revived by Stalin for its support during World War II but was forced to cooperate with the NKVD and its successor KGB to ensure subservience of church to state and the Communist Party of the Soviet Union. The top two patriarchs in the Orthodox hierarchy joined the World Peace Council, a Soviet front organization founded in 1949, and were highly valued by the KGB as agents of influence. The Orthodox Church also took a prominent role in establishing another front organization, the Christian Peace Conference (CPC), in 1958 with its headquarters in Prague in order to mobilize worldwide support for Soviet peace policies. At the second conference of the CPC in 1960, delegates from the rest of the world, unaware of its orchestration by Moscow and the KGB, outnumbered those from the Soviet Bloc. In 1961, the CPC joined the World Council of Churches with the blessing of the KGB.

Khrushchev, however, was in the midst of a ferocious antireligious campaign that closed down many of the reopened churches, seminaries, and monasteries and disbanded half of the Orthodox parishes. According to a secret KGB directive of 1961, to strengthen their influence and stranglehold on the churches and institutions that remained open, they infiltrated their agents among the students of these ecclesiastical training establishments to influence the state of affairs within the Russian Orthodox Church and exert influence on the believers. In 1962, the head of the second chief directorate of the KGB, internal security and counterintelligence, Gen. Oleg Gribanov, reported that during the previous two years, the KGB had infiltrated reliable agents into the leading positions of the Moscow Patriarchate, the Catholic dioceses, the Armenian Gregorian Church, and other religious groups. These would make it easier, he believed, to remove remaining "reactionary church and sectarian authorities" from their posts.

Fast-forward to October 16, 1978, when Cardinal Karol Wojtyla, archbishop of Krakow, becomes Pope John Paul II, the Polish pope, the real Polish crisis for the Soviets begins. According to the Mitrokhin Archives, the day after his election as pope, the head of the KGB mission in Warsaw, Vadim Pavlov, sent Moscow an assessment of him by the SB, the KGBs Polish equivalent.

> Wojtyla holds extreme anti-Communist views and has criticized the Socialist system and the way the state agencies of the Polish People's Republic function, making accusations about restrictions of basic human rights, unacceptable exploitation of workers, restrictions on the activities of the Catholic Church, and that Catholics are treated as second class citizens. In Wojtyla's view, the idea of a one-party state "meant depriving people of its sovereignty." "Collectivization," he believes, "led to the destruction of the individual and his personality."

In 1979, following Pope John Paul II's historic visit to Poland and prior to the creation of the Polish Solidarity trade union, communist leadership in Poland became increasingly concerned about domestic instability. A multifaceted campaign was launched by Polish communist authorities including propaganda and suppression of religious activities while internationally attempting to label the Vatican and newly elected pope as belligerents against peace. As in Lithuania and Romania and other Soviet Bloc states, the KGB attempted to sow divisions between the Catholic Church hierarchy and Conservatives on one side and liberal Catholics on the other.

I hope the reader at this point is beginning to understand why I'm going into such great detail to document Soviet, KGB, active measures against the church. It's always been a key element inherent in socialism and communism and militant secularism. Yet, as we know, all attempts to quell resistance of the Catholic Church in Poland proved futile. There was also reference to a Politburo document that concluded that the Vatican had embarked on an "ideological struggle against socialist countries." In November 1979, the Central Committee secretariat approved a six-point "Decision to Work Against the Policies of the Vatican in Relation with Socialist

States," prepared by a subcommittee that included Yuri Andropov, chairman, and Viktor Chebrikov, vice chairman of the KGB, further emphasizing how important it was to the Soviets and KGB to subvert the Vatican and the pope.

One of the chief priorities of the Polish SB foreign operations department, Poland's KGB counterpart, was to build up an agent network among the Poles in Rome and in the Vatican. As early as June 1980, the KGB reported to the center, the Kremlin, "Our friends [the SB] have serious operational positions [agents] at their disposal in the Vatican, and these enable them to have direct access to the Pope and to the Roman congregation. Apart from experienced agents…our friends have agent assets among the leaders of Catholic students who are in constant contact with Vatican circles and have possibilities in Radio Vatican and the Pope's Secretariat."

In Poland, Lech Wałęsa, chairman of the Solidarity movement (1980–1990), Poland's first independent trade union, and later president of Poland (1990–1995), summed up the contrasting Polish view of the Soviets and communism and of religion, specifically Catholicism, this way,

> If you choose the example of what we Poles have in our pockets and in our shops, then…communism has done very little for us. But if you choose the example of what is in our souls, I answer that communism has done very much for us. In fact, our souls contain exactly the opposite of what they wanted. They wanted us not to believe in God, and our churches are full. They wanted us to be materialistic and incapable of sacrifice. They wanted us to be afraid of the tanks, of the guns, and instead, we don't fear them at all.

Thus, it is pretty clear that the Polish nationalists linked their struggle against the Soviet Union with the struggle against atheism and tyranny in concert with their Polish Pope John Paul II. Of course, it is also very clear that the Soviets and the KGB considered

Pope John Paul II a very serious threat to communism and the Soviet system, not only in Poland but also throughout all the Slavic states in Eastern Europe. KGB reporting emphasized during Pope John Paul's visit to Poland that in his homilies, he frequently called himself not only the Polish pope but also the Slav pope, recalling one by one the baptism of the peoples of all of Eastern Europe.

Given this background, it should be clear to all that the Catholic Church and the Vatican have been priority targets for Soviet and KGB active measures for decades but, more accurately, since the Russian or Bolshevik Revolution of 1917. Perhaps the most daring and diabolical of all Russian active measures and influence operations in recent history were those conducted against the Catholic Church, the Vatican, and Papacy and specifically Pope John Paul II and Pope Benedict XVI. Remember, the Soviet intelligence services—the KGB and its successors—don't play by our rules, and assassination is an acceptable and useful tool when considered necessary.

Pres. Ronald Reagan, a victim of an assassination attempt himself by John Hinckley Jr. on March 30, 1981, had referred to the Soviet Union in a speech to the national association of Evangelicals in 1983 as the evil empire and as the "focus of evil in the modern world." Once again, I am looking at this as an intelligence analyst in the context of strategic world events and simply trying to connect the dots based on historical and circumstantial evidence and my knowledge and experience.

It's not just a coincidence that both President Reagan and Pope John Paul II, who had supported Solidarity and Poland's breakaway from the Soviet Union, had a major role in bringing down the Wall or the Iron Curtain and bringing about the collapse of the Soviet Union. Full diplomatic relations were reestablished between the United States and Vatican following President Reagan's visit in 1982, ending more than a hundred-year hiatus in formal diplomatic relations. While not surprising given their personal relationship, it was a union of political will and faith by both to bring an end to the slavery and death brought on by communism and the tyranny that always accompanies it. Some papal historians have even suggested a kind of holy alliance between the pope and President Reagan. In some ways, it was just that, because they both recognized that socialism and communism want to kill both the body and the soul by denying and eliminating God. It is precisely what the militant secularists and radical left-wing Democrats are attempting to do here and now in America. Of course, the alliance between the pope and President Reagan then must have been a very chilling and unwelcomed development for Brezhnev and those Soviet leaders who followed including Mikhail Gorbachev who oversaw the collapse.

As a result, there is little doubt that Pope John Paul II was a priority target of the KGB, much as President Kennedy was in 1963, following the Bay of Pigs and Cuban missile crisis. This is why the KGB and the East German Stasi (East German Intelligence Service) reportedly attempted to assassinate Pope John Paul II. While it was an unemployed thirty-seven-year-old Lech Wałęsa who ostensibly was the leader of the Solidarity movement, the strikers all carried the Pontiff's photograph on their banners. In August 1980, the pope told a crowd in St. Peter's Square, "We, now present in Rome, are united with our compatriots in the motherland." In January 1981, Wałęsa and members of Solidarity met with the pope in the Vatican. At that point, there was no doubt that the pope was involved and fully in charge and meant trouble for communism and the Soviet Bloc.

On May 13, 1981, the Feast Day of Our Lady of Fatima, a Turk, Mehmet Ali Ağca, who was trained in Syria for two years, shot and critically wounded the pope. Mehmet was a Marxist, member of the Popular Front for the Liberation of Palestine, and an agent of the KGB, contrary to what was reported by the media at the time who tagged him a lone gunman, right-wing extremist, and gang member. The Italian security and intelligence services had it right and always insisted that the KGB was behind both attempts on the Pontiff's life.

A CIA study titled "Ağca's Attempt to Kill the Pope: The Case for Soviet Involvement" was issued in April 1985, after CIA director William Casey had expressed his personal conviction that Ağca was an assassin employed by the Bulgarian security services at the behest of the KGB. According to Pope John Paul II's biography written by Tad Szulc, for its part, the NSA was picking up cable traffic between the Bulgarian embassy in Sofia and Rome for weeks prior with references to teams, safe house, points of entry, travel documents, money transfer routings, and following the assassination attempt with inquiries about the "exfiltration of the team." Of course, no firm conclusions were ever drawn by the IC or law enforcement agencies, but firm conclusions are rarely achieved by the IC on any issues, and anyone who dared to challenge the lone gunman theory was quickly labeled a conspiracy theorist. This was also the case with the assassinations of President Kennedy, Robert Kennedy, and Martin Luther King, Jr. Why? Because it's always easier to rely on the lone gunman explanation and cover-up when it really is a conspiracy and attempt to misdirect, discredit, and shut down all other potential explanations—like Benghazi and the YouTube video and the gang who were just out looking to kill a few Americans that fateful night or the manufactured whistleblower claims to initiate the groundless impeachment proceedings against the president to draw attention away from the true origins of Russiagate and Obama administration corruption. Easy-peasy.

It's no secret that the KGB and its successor (FSK/SVR), a reincarnation of the KGB on steroids, have had a long-term objective of infiltrating the Catholic Church and undermining her powerful, worldwide appeal, and basic doctrine, which has always stood in stark contrast to communist totalitarianism and social engineering, which is now reflected in much of the Democratic Socialist Party and radical left-wing agenda to demonize America and all the Judeo-Christian values our country is built on. Their constant attacks on and attempts to curb our religious freedoms and take God out of every facet of our daily lives have always been a key objective of their strategy of deception to "promote social change" and fundamentally transform America. This has always been and remains one of the top priority missions of the Soviet KGB and their successor Russian intelligence services. It's difficult to determine or positively identify just how many agents or assets of the Russian intelligence services are directly engaged in this effort. Regardless, the fact is that the increasingly radical political platform and agenda of today's Democratic Socialist Party are more closely aligned with and are working to the advantage of Putin and the Russian intelligence services than anyone could ever imagine.

Now, fast-forward to 2005 and Pope John Paul II's death, and the FSK/SVR are at it again—only they don't rely on covert action or assassination, because they have already infiltrated the College of Cardinals and the papal conclave and probably believed they had the votes locked up for the election of Jorge Mario Bergoglio.

Cardinal Bergoglio, a relatively unknown, a Jesuit, and first to eventually become pope, is the first non-European since Gregory III (eighth century) and first from the Americas/Argentina. However, Putin, Moscow, and the Russian intelligence services knew they had a great deal at stake in who would be selected as Pope John Paul II's successor and would have carefully assessed the potential candidates. I seriously doubt that Cardinal Bergoglio would have had any idea that he might be Moscow's favored candidate for pope or ever even thought about it. However, the facts suggest, based on what we know now, that ideologically Pope Francis is much more favorably disposed toward a liberal and broad-minded approach to church doctrine than either Pope John Paul II or his immediate successor, Pope Benedict XVI. Having spent decades infiltrating the Catholic Church and the Vatican, the Russian intelligence services must have thought they would finally achieve their long sought-after objective with the election of a pope, not only sympathetic to but also apparently a more ardent supporter of socialism than anyone else cares to or wants to think or say. Or is all of this just a coincidence and I am a paranoid conspiracy theorist? I'm saying that I believe that Pope Francis was a favored candidate of the Russians. While not an eager or active or even a witting participant, Jorge's politics and ideology made him the perfect candidate for Russian influence operations, which were actively seeking to support his election as pope. This would not be all that much different than conducting active measures to influence elections in the United States or anywhere Moscow might believe their own best interests were at stake.

In any case, the results of all four ballots had the dean of the College of Cardinals, Cardinal Joseph Ratzinger (Pope Benedict XVI), receiving the highest number of votes and Cardinal Jorge

Mario Bergoglio receiving the second highest number of votes. The voting was apparently close enough on the first two days of the conclave to force a fourth ballot on day 3, which resulted in the election of Cardinal Joseph Ratzinger from Germany who became Pope Benedict XVI. So the FSK, GRU, and SVR suffered yet another setback, and Putin and the Russian intelligence services would have to wait a few more years for Jorge Mario Bergoglio's ascendancy as pope and bishop of Rome. But Putin and the GRU and FSK/SVR are not a patient lot, and although Cardinal Joseph Ratzinger is elected pope, he becomes the first Pontiff in over eight hundred years (Celestine V in 1284) to resign on "his own initiative" in 2013.

To say the decision was unexpected is an understatement. It was dramatic and there was a lot of speculation and still is as to why he did so. E-mails disclosed in 2016 by WikiLeaks (which were never intended to be made public) revealed an apparent plot in Soros-Clinton-Podesta e-mails in 2011 that Podesta and other left-wing activists were planning to create a Catholic Spring revolution in the Catholic Church—a sardonic reference to the disastrous Arab Spring coups that Obama administration policies promoted to bring radical Islamic regimes to power and give rise to ISIS. To the contrary, the Catholic Spring revolution was to bring an end to what Podesta and other radical progressives referred to as the Middle Ages dictatorship in the Catholic Church. While I'm reluctant to accept this at face value, Podesta has been in the middle of a great deal of controversy and alleged corruption during both the Clinton and Obama administrations, while Soros is akin to Satan himself. In addition, a respected group of Catholic lay leaders sent a letter to President Trump in January 2017 requesting an official investigation into the matter. In light of this and other evidence and the timing of these events, I'm convinced that there was a covert effort to subvert Pope Benedict. I'm not buying old age and poor health. He was one of the five oldest popes when elected at seventy-eight and was eighty-six when he resigned. However, he's ninety-five and still with us, and while appearing frail, his mind is as sharp as ever, as his position and letter that was juxtaposed against Pope Francis's position on sexual abuse clearly demonstrated. It also reflects the thoughts of a man of great moral courage and conviction.

Let me propose that the FSK/SVR were also fully engaged in covert influence operations, and while they had misjudged the effectiveness of those operations and their foothold in the College of Cardinals eight years earlier, their ace in the hole was the Roman Curia, the church's civil service, and the Vatican Secretariat, where they were already stirring the pot to undermine Pope Benedict's papacy.

What was Vati-Leaks all about? We've had our Watergates and WikiLeaks and Russiagate. Pope Benedict's butler reportedly photo-copied numerous documents that reflected great tension and turmoil within the Vatican and provided them to a journalist. The documents also reflected alleged blackmailing of homosexual clergy from outside the Vatican.

Apparently, there were letters written to the pope and Secretary of State Cardinal Tarcisio Bertone by Archbishop Carlo Maria Viganò in 2011, the same now retired Archbishop Viganò who wrote the bombshell letter in August 2018. Viganò wrote these letters while he was the secretary general of the Vatican City Governorate, complaining of corruption in Vatican finances. Viganò, formerly the second-ranked administrator to the pope, requested not to be transferred for having exposed alleged corruption that cost the Holy See millions in inflated contract prices. It was Viganò in 2009 who centralized accounting procedures and accountability in the Vatican and turned a $10.5 million deficit for the city-state into a surplus of $44 million in one year. However, Viganò later allegedly recommended that the Vatican drop out of the euro currency agreement, which required adherence to stricter European banking regulations than the Vatican chose to adhere to. Former president of the Vatican Bank, Ettore Tedeschi, was appointed in 2009 by Pope Benedict to reform the bank and bring it back to international standards of transparency. However, in 2010, Tedeschi became the subject of a money-laundering investigation, and he contended later that he was removed from his position in 2012 by the Vatican Bank board of directors as a result of his intentions to make radical reforms. During that period,

Tedeschi claimed that he feared for his life. He also indicated that he had "discovered something scary" and was engaged in a struggle against the Vatican secretary of state, Cardinal Bertone, the same Cardinal Bertone who had Archbishop Viganò exiled to the United States in 2011. Oddly enough, the inquiry was dismissed following Pope Benedict's resignation.

Cardinal Bertone had Viganò transferred to the United States over his strong objections, and Viganò became the apostolic nuncio to the United States (August 2011 to April 2016) developing a close and friendly relationship with Barack Obama. You can check out the photo of him and Obama in Wikipedia. Cardinal Bertone, who had squashed the financial corruption investigation and reforms, then served as cardinal secretary of state (2006–2013) and concurrently as Camerlengo of the Holy Catholic Church (2007–2014). The latter is an office of the papal household made up of dignitaries who administer the property and revenues of the Vatican, placing Bertone, in my analysis, right at the epicenter of corruption and cronyism in Vatican finances and also making him a major figure in the cover-ups of complaints and warnings about sexual abuse.

Oddly enough, I wouldn't think that Viganò and Obama would have much in common—Obama a radical Liberal and Viganò extremely conservative Catholic. Could Mario Viganò, whose tenure as nuncio overlapped very nicely with Obama's, in part out of retaliation for Bertone's action, or unwittingly, have spilled the beans and shared what he knew about alleged corruption in the Vatican with Obama, Clinton, Podesta, or others in the radical Left's inner sanctum? The dates of the meetings between Obama and Pope Benedict XVI at the Vatican in 2009 shortly after being elected and in 2011 at the White House curiously overlap with much of Viganò's accusations. If you're trying to connect the dots, dates, and actors, it's pretty easy to conclude that Pope Benedict's resignation amounted to a coup orchestrated by forces within the Vatican hierarchy and outside the Vatican. It's also a fact, but not common knowledge, that in 2012, an anonymous letter made the headlines in Italy for its warnings of a death threat against Pope Benedict. There is plenty of evidence that I've already addressed that suggests that this may also have been complemented or reinforced with threats of black-mail and intimidation by the Obama administration and globalist allies and financiers like George Soros to force Pope Benedict to step down. Even Deutsche Bank reportedly had been induced to block all ATMs in Vatican City due to the alleged lack of transparency by the Vatican Bank but were reactivated immediately following the pope's resignation. I would propose that Pope Benedict was deceived and betrayed by those around him and abdicated to save the church any further embarrassment caused by all the spying, lying, and political infighting in his midst. It was also quite revealing that just prior to his resignation, Pope Benedict described the Curia as "the leprosy of the Papacy" and considered them "narcissistic" and "self-referential."

It was a crowning success for Obama, Putin, and the Russian intelligence services because his resignation opened the door, finally, for the candidate of their choice, Cardinal Jorge Mario Bergoglio, to become vicar, Pontiff, world leader, head of the Catholic Church, one of the most powerful organizations in the world. Not only does the pope have influence over 1.2 billion Catholics around the world, but also he is the spiritual leader for a large portion of the American elec-torate, estimated today at more than fifty million Catholics. There is little doubt that former president Obama, former secretary of state Hillary Clinton, and globalists like Soros or Cardinal Danneels's mafia would have celebrated such a change in Vatican leadership.

Not surprisingly, President Obama wasted little time in trying to curry favor and support from Pope Francis, meeting with him on a laundry list of his more radical policies from homosexuality, abortion, climate change, his welfare state, and even hot button national security issues like open borders and immigration and the Iran nuclear deal. While the Pontiff does not seem to be going so far as to change church doctrine, he certainly has taken a markedly more liberal stance on issues like abortion, same-sex marriage, and the environment than any of his predecessors. He also seems more willing to express his political views and offer spiritual guidance on such issues, which has had Liberals praising him and more conserva-tive Catholics questioning his intentions.

He has been especially outspoken on what he considers the ills of capitalism, poverty, climate change, and gay rights, which seem to reflect some of Obama's own more radical policies to transform America. President Trump has rightly attempted to modify or reverse those policies, but not without criticism from this pope. Whether Pope Francis ever intended to profess support for Obama's more radical socialist policies or not, his comments certainly can be interpreted as such. I would hope that Pope Francis would never support the creation of the kind of welfare state that President Obama and the Democrats seek to create by placing 44 percent of Americans on welfare with job creation practically nonexistent during his eight years in office. It represented nothing less than a new form of slavery and the total dependence of millions of Americans, especially blacks and Hispanics, on the government for their needs, accompanied by despair and a lack of self-worth.

Of course, this is a key element of the Democratic Party's agenda and a despicable and evil one at that, representing nothing less than human bondage for millions. For their part, the Democrats and their mainstream media propaganda machine will characterize such policies in their deceptive political platform as just and caring when the real truth is they are simply harvesting potential voters. But then again, slavery is a large part of their legacy. The Democrats' idea is that the more Americans on welfare and dependent on big government to include the millions of illegal immigrants still streaming across our southern border and camping out in many of our large democratic-controlled sanctuary cities, the larger the democrat's voter pool. This is all part of their grand deception to promise them everything and make them think that the Democrats really care about their welfare, when the truth is that once they are captives, they are forever captive to a cycle of poverty and dependence.

As already documented, you need only look at Nancy Pelosi's or Maxine Waters's congressional districts in San Francisco and Los Angeles that contain the largest homeless populations in California, while they live in their mansions outside their congressional districts. They're not alone, for hypocrites abound in the Democrat Party. Another fact and truth that I hope our good pope is aware is that an America that can do no better than that for its own people, with Obama declaring during his tenure that 1 percent growth in our GNP would be the new norm, clearly would never be in a position on the world stage to continue to be the most charitable nation on the planet, bar none. The United States provides more foreign aid to the poorest of the poor nations of the world than all the others combined. Nor would there be a United Nations or the thousands of charitable organizations in the United States that provide billions in assistance. In addition, our US military allocates billions annually to support humanitarian assistance, nation-building, and disaster relief operations worldwide and in many cases in conflict zones and places where no other assistance is possible. I really don't think that Pope Francis would want to see an America that would no longer have the economic capacity, capability, or political will to continue to provide such aid and support to the less fortunate, poorest of the poor, and otherwise forgotten peoples of this world. So I ask myself and everyone who might pick up and read this book, especially every Christian and Catholic, what is Pope Francis really trying to achieve?

I would like to see and hear Pope Francis support President Trump's efforts and policies to Make America Great Again and Keep America Great so that this great nation can continue to be a beacon of hope for all the less fortunate of the world and that includes those who want to immigrate to the United States and become American citizens. I'm not sure if Pope Francis realizes that his political rhetoric and negative commentary about President Trump only serves the radical Left and those disciples of the antichrist, who are seeking to undermine our president and destroy America and replace it with their socialist-/communist-style government-controlled political/economic system to serve their own selfish purposes, the lust for more power and wealth. Certainly, Pope Francis, a true man of God, mercy and divine discernment should be able to see through the lies and deceit. As I pointed out in my "Introduction," the differences in political ideologies and agendas between the Republicans and Democrats have never been starker—freedom versus tyranny, jobs and self-respect versus welfare and despair, culture of life versus culture of death, God and family first versus godless and me too first, spirit of Christ versus spirit of the antichrist, rule of law versus lawlessness, less government versus more intrusive big government, light versus darkness, American exceptionalism versus American mediocrity, truth versus deception, capitalism and free markets versus socialism/communism and a government-controlled economy, and sovereignty and security versus open borders, gangs, drugs, and violence. I pray for the pope every day and ask the Holy Spirit to enlighten him. If Pope Francis really understood American politics, he would see and discern that Obama, the Clintons, and Democrats really stand for darkness and a culture of death, not light and a culture of life. I also pray that Pope Francis will be more equitable in his comments and pronouncements about President Trump and conservative American Catholics. Where there is faith, there is hope.

Pope Francis has now met with Russian President Putin a third time in the Vatican, coincidentally on July 4, 2019, which may well have been a subtle form of the pope's own attempt at influence operations and messaging of his continued displeasure with President Trump and America and American Catholics in particular, by holding the meeting while we celebrated our very own Independence Day—maybe a stretch, unless you contrast how cordial the pope has been in his meetings with former president Obama and even the president of Communist Russia and former KGB officer, Vladimir Putin, with his rather tepid treatment of President Trump and the First Lady. Certainly, Pope Francis knows that Putin served as a senior KGB officer in the former Soviet Union, where millions of Catholics were and are still being persecuted and dying at the hands of their tyrannical masters. I have to ask myself, Could this pope be unaware of the decades-long attempts by the Soviet Communists, KGB, and Russian intelligence services to infiltrate and subvert the Catholic Church or so gullible and naive as to make himself a soft target and vulnerable to the wiles of the self-serving progressive secularists and Socialists in his midst in the College of Cardinals, his Secretariat, and the Roman Curia who are covertly and overtly bombarding him with their own active measures and influence operations? It's possible that he was so insulated from the corruption and tension within the Vatican during most of his time in Argentina that he was unaware of the true nature and scope of that tension. Yet while I want to give him the benefit of the doubt, I believe his actions and his words reveal a much shrewder, determined, and radical pope.

He has lashed out at President Trump for building the border wall to protect our sovereign borders and compared it to the Berlin Wall, an absurd comparison. Everyone should realize that the former is strictly intended to keep illegals, drugs, and criminal gangs engaged in human trafficking and other violent crimes from entering the United States, while the latter was built by Moscow and Soviet Communists to enslave the people of East Germany and all of Eastern Europe and deter and prevent any escaping to freedom at the risk of execution. To underscore his position, he had reportedly provided $500,000 through Catholic charities to help thousands of Central American migrants reach the United States. It's ironic that most of these illegals are being forced to leave their homeland or escape the tyranny and failed economies brought on by socialism and communism and the tyranny that accompanies them. It doesn't appear that Pope Francis really grasps the nature of the crisis in Central and South America, when he equates it to the seriousness of the migration crisis in Europe brought on by the ravages of war and violence and chaos in Syria, the Middle East, and North Africa. The threat that it has posed to European governments, economies, and communities that opened their borders has been staggering and has been accompanied by increased crime and violence. Most governments have since closed their borders or placed strict limits on any additional migration.

Most of Latin America is not suffering from conflict or religious persecution that we see in other parts of the world. However, there are examples of more subtle types of persecution. This persecution and repression are usually at the hands of the old militant secularists—authoritarians steeped in the antifaith, secular, materialistic dogma of the twentieth century's hard Left. Today, for example, in Mexico, some of this is an ongoing legacy of the secularist policies of the long-ruling Institutional Revolutionary Party (PRI) and socialist Party of Democratic Revolution (PRD) parties. According to one contemporary report, Mexico is the most dangerous place in the world for Catholic priests and laity because many are targeted by drug cartels for taking a stand against violence and corruption. In Cuba, onerous legal restrictions are designed to put religious people in jeopardy of breaking the law, being fined and jailed. According to the US State Department, the Cuban Communist Party uses threats, international and domestic travel restrictions, detention, and violence against religious leaders and their followers, while the government continues to harass or detain members of religious groups whether Catholic or Protestant.

It also appears that the pope is conducting his own quiet purge of more traditional and conservative clergy by sidelining conservative cardinals, installing like-minded allies in key positions, and taking personal control of the Knights of Malta for defying him and has chastised conservative Catholics in the United States accusing them of joining Evangelical Protestants and voting for and supporting President Trump's MAGA agenda. One of his more recent accusations that President Trump and those of us who support him are bad Christians is to say the least, un-popelike. Those statements sound like they could have been taken out of a page of Hillary Clinton's deplorables speech in September 2016.

As recently as June 2019, he dressed down and demanded obedience from his Vatican ambassadors telling them that while they may have reservations about papal policy, they don't represent themselves and can't "criticize the Pope behind his back, have blogs or join groups hostile to him." The dressing down came after claims by several envoys that Pope Francis had ignored warnings that he denied he had received in 2013 about now defrocked former Cardinal McCarrick's sexual encounters with seminarians. Even Pope Emeritus Benedict XVI has broken his silence in a lengthy letter on the subject. He contradicted Pope Francis emphasizing the retreat of religious belief and firm church teaching and the rise of secularism and cultural changes inside and outside the church that he argued began in the 1960s with the rise of "all-out sexual freedom" and that Catholic moral theology "suffered a collapse." "Ultimately," he stated, "the reason [for the abuse] is the absence of God." Meanwhile, Francis has simply attributed it to the corrupted power of the clergy, calling it a crime and acknowledging and apologizing for the church's practice of protecting its own, which has led to cover-ups.

Another indicator of this pope's unorthodox style has been revealed in the October 2019 Amazon synod. Pope Francis convened the synod ostensibly to discuss ecological issues and the pastoral care of indigenous peoples. However, there was some legitimate concern that this synod would be more than an internal affair dealing with strictly pastoral matters, but rather a platform for radical environmentalism and ecological activism that, in the Vatican's own words, would present a new social, economic, and political paradigm for Western civilization to imitate. Those and even some unspoken concerns expressed by several cardinals, groups of bishops, priests, and laity about the Amazon synod's working document were proven to be more than justified.

The lack of transparency itself is disturbing, with the final document on the synod, which has significant implications for the Universal Church not just the Amazon region, officially released by Pope Francis and the Vatican only in Spanish. I obtained my copy of the translated English version from LifeSiteNews, dated November 5, 2019.

The participation and attendance at this synod were also largely restricted to bishops from the region and other like-minded clergy and laity handpicked by the Vatican, making it much more like a by invitation only event. As such, the convocation was steeped in liberation theology, which has its origins in Latin America and the writings of Dominican father Gustavo Gutiérrez, whose seminal work *A Theology of Liberation* gave the movement its name. The controversy surrounding liberation theology rests largely with its use of Marxist economic theory applying it to the gospel and often calling for reorganization of social, governmental, and economic structures so that the poor are not merely cared for but guaranteed all the necessities of life. Of course, we have heard Pope Francis speaking about economic injustice, denouncing capitalism, and trickle-down economics and even advocating the redistribution of wealth including property rights. Gutierrez was invited by Pope Francis and visited the Vatican in February 2014 and reportedly received a hero's welcome. Obama's ideology and the radical Democrats' agenda are closely linked to these policies.

The final document actually opens the way for even more radical changes in church doctrine than promoted by the liberation theologians who created the preparatory documents, which were denounced by many cardinals and bishops for threatening to undermine the Catholic faith. It apparently opens the way to a married priesthood and women in clerical orders. In the section on "New paths for ecclesial ministry" (paragraphs 93–133), there were proposals for new lay ministries (paragraphs 93–96), official ministries for women (paragraph 102), encouragement for the work of the "Study Commission on the Women's Diaconate" (women becoming deacons of the church; paragraph 103), a broader understanding of the permanent diaconate (paragraph 104), and the admittance to the priesthood of married men already deacons (paragraph 111).

The synod fathers also placed great emphasis on Pope Francis's agenda of decentralized synodal churches that would allow each region to make its own rules and doctrine. The words synodal and synodality appear forty-one times in the final document. There are also proposals for a synodal structure for the Amazon (paragraphs 112–115) that would allow it to develop its own form of Catholicism and incorporate its native traditions into its religious practices. The document exalts indigenous cultures and traditions, characterizing them in very positive terms without mentioning the facts that they are inspired by paganism and a pantheistic worship of nature or that some of these traditions involve pedophilia, incest, or rampant forms of superstition and idolatry. Rather it blames the deep moral collapse of the region on capitalist economic development and urbanization (paragraph 10). Yet contrary to the extremist ecology-mongers and population eugenicists that the Vatican now consults (Joachim Schellenberg, Naomi Klein, and Jeffrey Sachs) or the media-orchestrated campaigns, like the troubled left-wing-manufactured psychotic, traumatized Swedish schoolgirl Greta Thunberg, current forms of development actually save lives, offer people greater freedom and dignity, and are gradually eliminating age-old scourges like famine, plagues, resource wars, and early mortality.

As such, it seems that in terms of process, participation, and end-game, Pope Francis and the Vatican were dealing from a stacked deck not much unlike the 2016 Democrat Party Presidential Primaries where the process, delegate participation, and the endgame were rigged by Debbie Wasserman Schultz and the DNC and the media to guarantee Hillary Clinton's nomination at the expense of Bernie Sanders and all other potential democratic candidates. In the case of the Amazon synod, the final document indicates that Pope Francis and the Latin American liberation theologians got what they wanted with many liberal like-minded clergy and laity indoctrinated and well versed in liberation theology participating in the convocation with the exclusion of others.

It's not surprising then that earlier this year, Pope Francis replaced the archbishop of Lima, Peru, with Father Carlos Castillo Mattasoglio, a university professor and parish priest known for his affinity with liberation theologians and his personal opposition to his doctrinally sound predecessor, Cardinal Juan Luis Cipriani Thorne. It's reminiscent of how the pope handled the replacement of Archbishop Hector Aguer of La Plata, Argentina, a traditionalist known for his conservative positions and "obsession with sexual morality," with Pope Francis's ghostwriter of *Amoris laetitia* and close confidant Bishop Víctor Manuel "Tucho" Fernández. In both cases, staunch defenders of Catholic doctrine and life have been replaced by tenants of the theology of the people. In Aguer's case, he was ordered by the pope to leave the archdiocese immediately and was not allowed to retire there.

Perhaps the most recent and telling of Pope Francis's doctrinal leanings occurred in August 2019 when he endorsed the refounding of the Pope John Paul II Institute on Marriage and the Family with its focus on the theology of marriage and the family. Pope Francis ostensibly expanded the curriculum to study the family from the perspective of the social sciences. Monsignor Livio Melina, president of the institute and professor of moral theology, and Father José Noriega, who taught specialized courses in moral theology, were fired, while the remainder of the faculty were "temporarily" suspended. It all seems more like a purge and elimination or reversal of what Pope John Paul II intended when founding the institute with a heavy emphasis on moral theology than a simple expansion of the curriculum. The church has been slow to accept findings of modern science and the so-called social sciences, because of suspicions that what's being offered as scientific truth conceals false assumptions, philosophical presuppositions, or ideology masquerading as the latest and greatest research findings. Oftentimes, this is the case. We have been told by the new Pope John Paul II Institute administrators that the new and improved Pope John Paul II Institute is deepening and continuing the late Pope John Paul II's legacy, when in fact and truth, it's clearly doing just the opposite.

A similar misinformation campaign is being conducted by Cardinal Cupich, ninth archbishop of the Archdiocese of Chicago and a member of the Roman Curia's Congregation for Bishops, regarding Cardinal John Henry Newman, who was supposed to be canonized during the Amazon synod. Cardinal Newman was a stalwart opponent of the way most people view or understand conscience. Over a century ago, Newman warned that people were regarding conscience (much like free will in my words) as a license to decide and do whatever they want. The Catholic view has always been that conscience (like free will) is the "aboriginal voice of God," to choose between good and evil, as is the case with free will, to do God's will in choosing between good and evil, not what's convenient or feels good. Contrary to the philosophy of moral relativism, Pope John Paul II taught that moral law is universal across people of varying cultures and is in fact rooted in the human condition. Apparently, this has not stopped Cupich and others in the Vatican hierarchy like all good Liberals from turning Cardinal Newman's and Pope John Paul II's teachings on their heads. Moves such as we've seen at the Pope John Paul II Institute will try to misrepresent Newman and others in the tradition. That fakeness and bad faith embrace of social science may not last forever, but it will certainly delay and sideline the real renewal we now desperately need into the Catholic tradition to offset the materialism, moral relativism, social secularism, and superficiality of the world around us.

> America, it is said, is suffering from intolerance—it is not. It is suffering from tolerance. Tolerance of right and wrong, truth and error, virtue and evil, Christ and chaos. Our country is not nearly so overrun with the bigoted as it is overrun with the broadminded. (Bishop Fulton J. Sheen, 1967)

I will close this chapter with a prayer for our Pope Emeritus, Pope Benedict XVI, "*Vade retro Santana, nunquam suade mihi vana, sunt mala quae Libas, ipse vinena bibas*" ("Begone, Satan, do not tempt me with your lies. You offer me an evil cup; drink your own poison").

This is one of the many prayers of Saint Benedict who was betrayed by the very monks who had asked him to be their abbot. He and they didn't mesh, so they eventually tried to kill Benedict, with a poisoned cup and poisoned bread. Benedict always prayed over his intended meal, and as the story goes, at that moment, the cup shattered and a raven flew down and snatched the bread away. Our good Pope Emeritus, Benedict XVI, also seems to have been betrayed by those surrounding him in the Vatican and was no doubt the victim of some sort of attempted coup or at a minimum foul play arranged by his liberal protagonists, both within and outside the Vatican with support from our friendly Russian intelligence services relying on decades of infiltration, subversion, and covert influence operations.

We also pray for Pope Francis every day that the Holy Spirit will give him the discernment and courage to do God's will and not that of those around him, who are attempting to influence him and impose their will to push for what appears to be a radical shift in the church's theological and moral teachings and doctrine.

# CHAPTER 7
# The American Family under Siege

*Woe to those who call evil good, and good evil, who put darkness for light, and light for darkness, who put bitter for sweet, and sweet for bitter.*
—Isaiah 5:20

Secularism, socialism and the welfare state, the sexual revolution of the 1960s, technology, social media, and political correctness have all led to the gradual disintegration of the traditional American nuclear family. Yet this process has never been more pronounced or menacing than we are experiencing today. The American family is now under siege and being buried in a tsunami of radical left-wing progressive programs and policies built on lies, demagoguery, and deception. Obviously, the Democrats and their progressive and increasingly radicalized agenda have been and are continuing to promote the upside-down thinking and their radical socialist and godless ideology to create the very kind of society that the passage from Isaiah warns us of and condemns. G. K. Chesterton, the great Catholic writer of the early twentieth century, once said that only dead bodies go with the current, and it takes live ones to swim against it. It's so much easier to go along with the crowd and let group think take over than seek and speak the truth.

"I am the way, the Truth and the Life, no one comes to the Father except through me" (John 14:6).

In his apostolic exhortation, *Amoris laetitia* (*the Joy of Love*), Pope Francis addresses the pastoral care of families, where he calls for a "broader vision and renewed awareness of the importance of marriage and the family." The pope considers the contemporary realities of family life, acknowledging the unique challenges faced at the present time, including phenomena like migration, lack of housing, inattention to persons with disabilities, lack of respect for the elderly, and "the ideological denial of differences between the sexes." He speaks both of the importance of the nuclear family and of the importance of understanding the family as operating within a much wider network of relationships. Present-day progressivism is in reality more of an ideology of regressivism, negativism, and narcissism with several very specific radical cultural and societal objectives, all of which have and continue to impact negatively on the family structure and core values.

In his apostolic response to the World Synod on the Family at the Vatican nearly forty years ago, Pope John Paul II stated, "The future of the world and the church passes through the family" (Pope John Paul II, *Familiaris Consortio* [On the Family] [1980]).

We also need to reflect on the words of Pope John Paul II's Great social encyclical, *Centesimus annus* (*the Hundredth Year*), published in 1991, recognizing the anniversary of Pope Leo XIII's encyclical, *Rerum novarum* (*Of the New Things*), written in 1891, addressing the condition of the working classes and challenges that the industrial revolution of his day created for families and the family's importance as a refuge. Pope John Paul II wrote, "It is necessary to go back to seeing the family as the sanctuary of life. The family is indeed sacred: it is the place in which life—the gift of God—can be properly welcomed and protected against the many attacks to which it is exposed and can develop in accordance with what constitutes authentic human growth. In the face of the culture of death, the family is the heart of the culture of life" (*Centesimus annus*).

The most damaging of those radical progressive objectives of our time has been an unyielding attack on Christianity, the Christianity of the New Testament, a more orthodox and disciplined moral theology, and the Christianity that is shared by conservative Catholics and Evangelical Protestants. Unfortunately, but not surprisingly, the Christianity and Catholicism of more conservative Catholics and

Evangelical Christians have been criticized by our more liberal Pope Francis. Progressives—I hate to even use the term because it is a blatant misnomer—don't seem to express much opposition to liberal Christianity, which is a kind of ambivalent relativistic Christianity that has actually been inspired by progressivism. The chief weapons that progressivism has used against Christianity and the family have been the sexual revolution and radical feminist movement, both outgrowths of the political turmoil of the 1960s.

The sexual revolution promoted the idea of sexual freedom and persuaded the American public that there is nothing morally objectionable in sexual promiscuity, fornication/adultery, unmarried cohabitation, out of wedlock childbirth, *abortion*, homosexual conduct, same-sex marriage, or prostitution and pornography. Let's face it, once they get rid of Christian morality, most barriers to the final dismantling of the doctrinal foundations of that morality and the cohesion of the family disappear.

As a result of this assault, many Americans seem to have turned away from God and retreated into purely personal, self-help, and even narcissistic preoccupations. While possessing a sense of uniqueness and importance is part of our human nature, we seem to be suffering from an epidemic of a "me too," "me first," and the onslaught of entitlement-driven moochers who have little regard for those around them. In fact, like so many other disorders of the day, the medical and psychological professions have labeled it, in its extreme cases, as narcissistic personality disorder (NPD). There is no doubt that the pharmaceutical giants have already come up with any number of new drugs to deal with the disorder, but the truth is that there is no simple cure for selfishness and self-centeredness. Many people have convinced themselves that what matters most is psychic self-improvement, getting in touch with their feelings, dieting, taking ballet or guitar lessons, jogging, immersing themselves in the wisdom of the East, and overcoming the fear of pleasure. We are now also dealing with the concepts of trigger warnings and safe zones in schools and on college campuses, which actually allow and encourage young adults to avoid interpersonal relations or communications with others who may make them feel uncomfortable. Some are even permitted to excuse themselves from discussions or class assignments that might stress or bruise their mental health. What's truly unfortunate about all this pandering and self-indulgent pitiful behavior is that when these students graduate and leave the womb of the university safe spaces and trigger warnings, many are incapable of functioning in the real world, where there are few bubbles to hide in—that is, until the Progressives impose their radical minority views on this much too passive majority. I believe a very well-known twentieth-century poet, D. H. Lawrence, captured the essence of self-pity in his little-known poem.

> Self-pity
> I never saw a wild thing
> Sorry for itself.
> A small bird will drop frozen from a bough
> Without ever having felt sorry for itself.

Self-pity is what the poet described as a pansy like the flower, which also took on a somewhat derogatory and more colloquial meaning in the later twentieth century, which the poet never intended, that of an individual who can't or won't defend themselves against verbal or physical attack, a wuss or coward. The poem is written in free verse but focuses on the words "sorry for itself" both in the second line and again at the conclusion, suggesting the way self-pity is self-consuming and ultimately self-destructive.

There is an alternative. Prayer and placing your trust in God and his only begotten Son, our Lord Jesus Christ, who came into this world humbling himself in the image of a man to suffer and die an ignominious death to free us from our sins and offering through his resurrection the promise of eternal life for all who believe. Jesus said, "Peace is what I leave with you. It is my own peace I give to you. I do not give it as the world does. Do not be afraid and upset. Do not be afraid" (John 14:27).

Instead of seeking the true source of security, joy, and fulfillment in their lives—our Lord and Savior Jesus Christ—they have turned to the self-help gurus and self-possessed maniacs, where social media, high-tech cell phones, and video games allow certain personalities to live in an isolated virtual world of self-deception and smoke and mirrors, reflecting their own egotistical impulses and behavior. As such, I'm not sure why we should be surprised that the Progressives and political correctness police have been able to convince so many that truth and reality itself must be made to conform to the private feelings of so few individuals and groups. After all, when you refuse to recognize anyone or anything outside or above, self is all you have left. That can be a very lonely and frightening world indeed, where God and family are marginalized or altogether abandoned.

The Judge Kavanaugh hearings were a direct reflection of how radically anti-Catholic and anti-Christian the Left and the Democrat Party have become, along with many Obama-appointed radical judicial activists handing down judgments and supporting abortion on demand, no prayer in public schools, no Bible reading in public schools, and no religious symbols on public display and rejecting marriage as a covenant between God, a man, and a woman and supporting attempts to force Catholics and other Christians to violate their consciences to enforce compliance with radically more offensive secularism and political correctness. It's very apparent that an important part of the Progressives long-term agenda is to get rid of Christianity and replace it with what will become their new religion going back to the days of John Dewey and for some Karl Marx. This new religion is radical, secular progressivism, which is atheism with a fake and deceptive umbrella of egalitarianism. Their models are the likes of the former Soviet Union, Cuba, Venezuela, and every other failed socialist and communist totalitarian state. In 2012, Cardinal Timothy Dolan, while president of the US Conference of Bishops, stated succinctly that Obama's White House and the Liberal Lefts' attack on religious liberty "is strangling" the Catholic Church. Cardinal Dolan's comment reinforces what I have already described as a conspiracy by the Obama administration with the witting or unwitting participation of Bishop Viganò to promote and prolong the crisis in the church, undermine Pope Benedict, and instigate their Catholic Spring to bring an end to what Podesta, Soros, and Obama saw as a middle ages dictatorship in the Catholic Church.

While it's not a slam dunk, there certainly is enough circumstantial evidence to suggest that it is more than just speculation on my part.

"Beloved: Who is the liar? Whoever denies that Jesus is the Christ. Whoever denies the Father and the Son, this is the antichrist" (1 John 2:22).

God gave us all free will, but that free will doesn't entitle us do whatever we please or to do whatever feels good. It entitles us to do God's will, to choose between good and evil, right and wrong. The liberal mind-set will always argue that there is no good or evil, right or wrong, and that everything is relative and situational and based on personal choice. That is precisely how they create their own reality and have attempted to persuade their followers and others that their ideology and policies are good and progressive and those who oppose them are evil and that they are right and everyone else is wrong. This is especially the case if it means denying Christ and if it means rewriting history to hide their real demonic identity and replace it with a more wholesome attractive but fake identity. Satan does it so well, but he and they are the liars.

One of the most evil manifestations of this radical liberal ideology is abortion and the demagoguery and deception surrounding Planned Parenthood, prochoice, and Roe v Wade, which has brought us abortion on demand and now a battle over the very right to life itself with the passage of the Reproductive Health Care Act in New York and elsewhere, a culture of death versus a culture of life, good versus evil, family and God first versus me too first.

One of the naked truths and ironies of abortion is that the first human being to recognize our Lord Jesus Christ was an unborn baby. When Elizabeth heard Mary's greeting, *the infant (Jesus's second cousin, John the Baptist) leaped in her womb*; and Elizabeth filled with the Holy Spirit, cried out in a loud voice, and said, "Most blessed are you among women, and blessed is the fruit of your womb. And how does this happen to me, that the mother of my 'Lord should come to me? For at the moment the sound of your greeting reached my ears, *the infant in my womb leaped for joy*'" (Luke 1: 41–44).

The advocacy for continued funding of organizations like Planned Parenthood demeans and eradicates the concept of natural rights and denies the right to life to the most vulnerable in our society, the unborn child. However, it won't end there if we allow this cancer on our society, culture, families, and core values to grow. If the powerful and outspoken and overbearing minority can impose its will to deny the unborn child its natural, self-evident right to life, then what is to prevent them from denying certain other humans—the elderly, infirmed, crippled, or indigent—their right to life?

"Why are those who are notoriously undisciplined and immoral also most contemptuous of religion and morality? They are trying to solace their own unhappy lives by pulling the happy and moral down to their own abysmal depths" (Bishop Fulton J. Sheen, *Seven Words of Jesus and Mary: Lessons from Cana and Calvary*).

Never has there been a more evil and sinister deception imposed upon the American family and the American people in our short history as a nation. Planned Parenthood is a fraud and a hoax and was created to murder the innocent and unborn and continues today slaughtering the unborn and even those children that survive the abortion. Let's not forget the origin of Planned Parenthood and the true purpose of that organization, which as everything else liberal has been distorted and turned upside down to appear not only benign but also caring and pure and good.

Let's talk about the founder of Planned Parenthood and the truth about Margaret Sanger and her true intentions and the real consequences of her programs.

"The most merciful thing a large family can do to one of its infant members is to kill it" (Margaret Sanger, *Women and the New Rage*).

If that doesn't get your attention, maybe this will, "Colored people are like human weeds and need to be exterminated." Margaret Sanger

Margaret Sanger at some point in her life may have become a theosophist, and her eugenic policies and birth control programs are products of occult beliefs. However, she was one of eleven children (September 14, 1879, to September 6, 1966). Her mother and father were both Irish immigrants, her mother Catholic and father a *freethinker*, whatever that was. She married an architect, left her nursing training, had three children, and then moved to New York City where she became involved in a circle of feminists and Socialists. Some of her earliest articles were written for the Socialist Party newspaper, *the Call*. As a eugenicist, she believed in racial purification, targeted poorer communities made up of black and Hispanic populations, and believed that a "stern and rigid policy of sterilization and segregation should be applied to that grade of population whose prodigy is tainted, or whose inheritance is such that objectionable traits might be transmitted to offspring."

Fast-forward to 1973 and Roe v Wade, and thirteen million black children have now been killed before their birth, according to Rev. John J. Raphael of Howard University. Around 40 percent of black pregnancies end in abortion. The New York City Summary of Vital Statistics in 2012 indicated that of all abortions performed, 42.4 percent were of black children and 31 percent Hispanic children. According to the Alan Guttmacher Institute, 30 percent of abortions are performed on black women and 25 percent on Hispanic women in the rest of the country.

The tragic passage of the Liberal Lefts' Reproductive Health Care Act in New York and similar bills in Vermont and Virginia and the outrageous statements by radical left-wing Virginia governor Northam (a pediatrician by profession) demonstrate that these radicals are not satisfied with killing children in the womb. They also want to murder them if they survive the abortion. North Carolina governor Roy Cooper recently vetoed legislation passed by the republican-controlled House and Senate in North Carolina, the Born Alive Abortion Survivors Protection Act, that would require abortion providers to keep babies alive if they survived the procedure. It is no surprise that Cooper receives campaign support from Planned Parenthood, a very good example of the tyranny of the minority. This should be an outrage to every American family, the American people, and all of humanity.

> You are of your father the devil, and your will is
> to do your father's desires. He was a murderer
> from the beginning, and has nothing to do with
> the truth, because there is no truth in him. When
> he lies, he speaks according to his own nature, for
> he is a liar and the father of lies. (John 8:44)

There have been many countries in this world that the United Nations and the United States have sanctioned for lesser human rights violations. And the United Nations, NATO, and the United States have sent our military to intervene to prevent such violations on many occasions, yet here we are, the most advanced democratic republic in the world with Planned Parenthood alone slaughtering humans at a rate of 911 per day. These figures are based on their own annual report for fiscal year (FY) 2017 with a total of 332,757 abortions committed, an increase of over 11,000 from FY 2016.

Abortion is an intrinsically evil act, the intentional taking of innocent human life. Statistics from the Guttmacher Institute that contacts abortion clinics in all fifty states are believed to be most reliable, though there may be as much as a 5 percent undercount in its most recent figures. According to Guttmacher's numbers, there have been at least 60,942,033 total abortions since the Supreme Court of the United States Roe v Wade decision in 1973; Planned Parenthood performed approximately twenty-one million or roughly 35 percent of all abortions in the United States during that same period. This is genocide. There isn't anything relative or progressive about it. This is pure evil and one of the biggest liberal lies and malicious deceptions ever propagated by the Democrats on the American family and people. It fits nicely, however, with their attempt to turn history on its head and take credit for all the civil rights legislation ever passed in America since the Emancipation Proclamation and the passage of the Thirteenth, Fourteenth, Fifteenth, and Nineteenth Amendments, when in fact they opposed them all and every one since, as I have pointed out in the previous chapter, "the True Legacy of the Democratic Party." Isn't it ironic that the Democrat Party has claimed through lies, deception, and demagoguery to be the party that cares so much about equality, civil rights, and human suffering yet in truth has practiced and represents just the opposite, a culture of death and promises of a new form of slavery in a radical socialist welfare system?

So I ask you, who are the real racists, Nazis, and Fascists? The Democrats with Roe v Wade and their beloved Planned Parenthood have murdered more than sixty million children over a forty-five-year period, an entire generation—repeat, an entire generation—of human beings, of Americans, and most of them African-American and Hispanic. This is a fact that should get the attention of every African-American and black community leader and organizer, including the race-baiters like Al Sharpton, compliments of the Democrat Party and Planned Parenthood. The current black population in the United States is roughly thirty-six million with as many as thirteen to nineteen million black babies aborted since 1973 (thirteen million based on the Howard University study and nineteen million based on a study by protectingblacklife.org). The missing thirteen to nineteen million human beings represent an enormous loss for the American black community, which would now number between forty-nine 49 and fifty-five million without abortion. Abortion has swept through the black community like a scythe, cutting down every fourth member.

By comparison, the Nazis murdered and exterminated at least six million Jews and eleven million others during their ethnic cleansing campaigns referred to as the Final Solution or Holocaust during World War II. During the Rwandan Civil War in 1994, over a million Tutsis and political opponents of the majority Hutus were slaughtered in a gruesome hundred-day ethnic cleansing campaign. It was condemned as genocide by the United Nations, which intervened with an international peacekeeping force to stop the slaughter, but to no avail. The United States and Clinton administration stood idly by providing no assistance to stop the slaughter. However, in its aftermath, my colleagues and I received a snowflake from our management in the IC, directing us not to use the "g" word (genocide) to describe the situation, probably in deference to the president and the embarrassment he had already experienced.

Following the collapse of the Soviet Union, the Socialist Federal Republic of Yugoslavia broke up into independent republics and war ensued between the Bosnian Serbs and Bosnian Muslims or Bosniaks. In 1992, Serbian strongman and dictator Slobodan Milošević set out to support the Bosnian Serbs, secure ethnic Serb territory, and ethnically cleanse Bosnian territory by systematically removing all Bosnian Muslims. Taking a page out of Hitler's Final Solution, many Bosniaks were driven into concentration camps, where women and girls were systematically gang-raped and other civilians tortured, starved, and murdered. In July 1995, the Serbs committed the largest massacre in Europe since World War II. In what was supposed to be designated a UN-declared and UN-secured safe area, 23,000 women, children, and elderly were put on buses and sent to Muslim-controlled territory, while eight thousand battle-age men and boys were detained and slaughtered. The safe area fell without a single shot fired by UN peacekeepers.

So you may be asking why I am presenting these examples of genocide and ethnic cleansing. Because I worked these problems as an intelligence analyst and briefing officer for the Office of the Secretary of Defense in the Pentagon at the time (August 1992 to June 1996). And as most readers are probably aware, many of the individuals engaged in these atrocities were hunted down, tried as war criminals, and imprisoned or executed. I would argue that intentionally killing more than sixty million human beings is not only genocide but also an atrocity committed against humanity and must be stopped. I would also argue that Margaret Sanger's legacy and program of racial purification lives on.

A 2015 policy report submitted to Congress by the Center for Urban Renewal and Education on "the Effects of Abortion on the Black Community" indicates that disproportionally, the leading consumer of the abortionist's services are black women, who have the highest abortion rate in the country with 474 abortions per a thousand births. Percentages at these levels suggest that as many as nineteen million black babies have been aborted since 1973, higher numbers than those reported by Howard University or the Guttmacher Institute. According to a study by protectingblacklife.org, the slaughter goes on with 79 percent of Planned Parenthood surgical abortion facilities located in black and Hispanic minority neighborhoods and only 21 percent located in other neighborhoods.

Sadly, and pathetically, blacks have been the victims of deception and a not so hidden racist agenda by Democrats and all those liberal legislators who support abortion and birth control organizations. They have sold the big lie to minorities by portraying them as supporting a new civil right, the right of choice. Even members of the congressional black caucus have teamed up with the prochoice caucus on Capitol Hill to urge their constituents to challenge the prolife position, obviously being so steeped in their own partisan political agendas that it has blinded them to the fact that abortion has and will continue to destroy their own future constituencies.

I would urge all Catholic and Christian voters and Americans of all colors and creeds, regardless of your party affiliation, not vote for any candidate who supports abortion or anything like abortion. It is and those who perform abortions, the killing of innocent babies in the womb, are intrinsically evil.

While I would never characterize the feminist movement of the 1960s and 1970s as necessarily evil, it has had a profound impact on weakening family bonds by placing self ahead of God and family. I would also call it all misguided. Betty Friedan and her book published in February 1963, *the Feminine Mystique*, are often credited with sparking the second-wave feminist movement in the United States in the early 1960s. Based on a very small sample of housewives across the United States, she argued that women who were housewives were universally unhappy despite living in material comfort and being married with children. She concludes, "We can no longer ignore that voice within women that says: I want something more than my husband, and my children and my home." Is this real?

Germaine Greer, an Australian writer, is also considered one of the major voices of the second-wave feminist movement in the late 1960s and early 1970s, a more radical women's liberation advocate who argues that the struggle is for freedom of women to "define their own values, order their own priorities and decide their own fate." In her international bestseller and important text in the feminist movement, *the Female Eunuch*, she argues that the traditional suburban, consumerist, nuclear family *represses* women sexually and this "devitalizes" them, rendering them eunuchs.

As such, it's very apparent that the feminist movements represented another key element of radical progressive secularism's contribution to the undoing of the traditional American family and core values of love, marriage, commitment, and child-rearing.

While such radical women's liberation ideas may have been popular with the more inhibited and frustrated women's libbers, there was sufficient blowback from women who didn't require such sophistries and battering rams to achieve both true happiness and fulfillment with their God-centered family life, husband, children, and professional endeavors. Thank God for my wife of fifty-two years, Sherry, who is an elementary school teacher for forty years, the mother of my two children, who are now loving parents themselves and have given us five precious grandchildren. And we have remained one very blessed family.

Unfortunately, there is a new challenge, somewhat of an unintended consequence of the more radical feminist ideas promoted by Germaine Greer and the concept of the female eunuch and the LGBT(Q) movement and those politically correctness Nazis who have captured the imagination of some very misguided millennials and a new generation of parents. The trend toward a society that embraces bisexual, transgender, and questioning or queer, the latter describing the Q in LGBTQ, the new and upcoming connotation for those who might be any one of the LGBT community or not know where they belong. Either is an acceptable description according to Fred Sainz, a spokesman (yes, he is a spoke[man]) for an organization that lobbies for LGBT rights.

The newest trend is for parents, no doubt millennial parents, to raise their children as "theybies," neither boy nor girl. As the "theybe" grows, they will determine their own gender, chose it when the baby wants, and live that way; and the parents will go along for the ride.

The problem with this is manyfold. First it is a perversion and represents the highest form of parental neglect and ignorance that I can imagine. The idea that sex is innate and something given by God along with the blessed child but gender is a societal determination is fabricated entirely by a progressive—no, a regressive and perverted—mind-set that wishes to eradicate gender and the existence of God. Once again, this mind-set even turns science on its head and defies the laws of nature and the beauty of the God-given child. Denying this biological reality and easily observable fact and truth is cruel and disingenuous, especially when imposed upon a toddler. This is utterly reprehensible. So now these young parents are adopting a new approach to child-rearing by turning their gift from God into eunuchs at birth, neither male nor female, who will become part of the Q generation. If you don't know what a eunuch is, it's a male who has been emasculated with testicles and penis removed (literally, but in this case, it can also be psychologically) through child-rearing by parents who are more interested in going with the flow and the dictates of the politically correct police and radical secularists than doing what is morally right.

> When a child is given to his parents [by God], a crown is made for that child in heaven, and woe to the parents who raise a child without consciousness of that eternal crown. (Bishop Fulton J. Sheen, *Life Is Worth Living*)

> He called a little child to Him, and placed the little child among them. And He said, "Truly I tell you, unless you change and become like little children, you will never enter the kingdom of heaven…and whoever welcomes one such child in my name welcomes me. If anyone causes one of these little ones, who believe in me, to stumble, it would be better for them to have a large milestone hung around their neck and to be drowned in the depths of the sea." (Matthew 18:2–6)

205

If you think this is just all a short-lived fad, there are already cases of it being enforced in our schools. During the first week of school in September 2019 in Duval County, Florida, two teachers were called to the principal's office, one for failing to call one of his transgender students by her preferred pronoun (instead of by name) and another disciplined for scolding students for refusing to stand for the national anthem. Both cases reflect yet another aspect of the radical Left's progressive agenda, which is their attack on America and American exceptionalism. It's apparent that demonizing or criticizing our own history permeates our educational institutions and impacts directly, and in a most insidious way, not only on the formal education of our children but also on their emotions and values. Our public schools and universities have become battlegrounds in recent years, consumed by a radical brand of identity politics, pushing aggressively enforced speech codes, and brainwashing our children and grandchildren with distorted and demeaning anti-American propaganda while imposing near-total suppression of contrary thoughts or opinions.

This is what President McKinley prophetically referred to as the tyranny of the minority. First, they took away school prayer and then the Pledge of Allegiance and now free speech, which is only permitted by those who are properly indoctrinated and conform to progressive speak.

In August 2018, mobs at the University of North Carolina threw a noose around the neck of a century-old statue known as Silent Sam, a bronze statue of a Confederate soldier, stomping and spitting on it, armed with bats and clubs to silent any dissent. At the University of Notre Dame, a Congregation of Holy Cross institution, responding to complaints by some students, 134-year-old portraits of Christopher Columbus were shrouded or removed. The University of Pennsylvania English Department removed portraits of a dead white male, William Shakespeare, hanging in the department's hallway and replaced it with a photograph of Audre Lorde, a black feminist writer. High schools across the country remove masterpieces like *Huckleberry Finn* from their libraries because they contain ideas or words that offend the few. A high school outside Philadelphia,

Lansdowne Penn Wood High School, earlier in 2019 sponsored a drag show during school hours featuring a video about the history of drag along with runway performances. The high school also sponsored a daily gay pride parade show in the hallways of the school, which was described by some as disruptive. The majority of the community, including a 15–20 percent Muslim population, opposed the program, and many have had to pull their children out of the school and place them in parochial or Christian schools at their own expense while continuing to pay taxes to support public education. School administrators have reportedly offered little pushback to the demands of the minority and are even offering scholarships to attract more LGBTQ students.

Anthony Kronman, a former dean and professor of Yale Law School, himself a proclaimed progressive who cut his teeth as a political radical in the 1960s, argues in his article in *Imprimis* that "the politicization of academic life has put a cloud over the notions of truth and objectivity, what are normally our academic values" and has compromised the very thing our schools are supposed to be about. In his new book *the Assault on American Excellence* (Free Press), he tries to coax academia back from the precipice, rooting his argument in 2,500 years of philosophical tradition, to convince his colleagues to abandon politics and reclaim their role as protectors of independent thought and the free search of truth. What really motivates the left-wing Progressives attempting to enforce their new regime of political correctness? I personally see it as a very effective form of intimidation.

Politically correct speech codes and the refusal to tolerate opposing ideas are obvious insults to conversational ideals, making free debate and open discussion impossible. The verbal whiplashing that the Democrats and the radical Progressives use to beat down and insult the opposition with their constant name calling and accusations of racism really underscores the fact that they have nothing of substance to offer the American people. The most recent democratic debate in Nevada was a savage demonstration of hate, frustration, and demagoguery. It seems that everything these self-serving Democrats and radical Bolsheviks say and do has become increasingly more negative. They act like adolescent bullies, who out of frustration and their inability to compete have to run around beating on the smart kids with Harry Potter glasses and the opposing party and the president who have all the right answers for the American people and they have none. The slavish devotion to progressive politics and the notion of group identity and the dogma of diversity have also had a negative effect on the search for truth and objectivity and have stifled our freedom of speech and expression. Our public educational institutions and universities have become factories producing zombies brainwashed in the dictums and fake tolerance of progressive group think. They have no interest in seeking the truth, but rather theirs is the politics of deception and demagoguery, to hide and obscure the truth and the real and to proliferate the false and the fake.

Marxist Herbert Marcuse wrote an essay in 1965, called "Repressive Tolerance." It's a totalitarian classic in which he distinguishes between two types of tolerance. What he calls bad or false tolerance is what most of us would call true tolerance, the kind of behavior our parents and Jesus encouraged, "Do unto others as you would have them do unto you." The second type of tolerance is what he calls liberating tolerance, which he defines as "intolerance against movements from the right and tolerance of movements from the left." It would seem that the Democrats and Progressives have taken a page right out of Marcuse's essay.

Another great example of this upside down or what I will call deceptive or false tolerance is the democrat's position on the mass migration of more than eleven million undocumented, unauthorized illegals into the United States from Mexico and South and Central America who are not interested in becoming American citizens or assimilating into our culture, the most diverse on the planet. The United States has more immigrants than any other country in the world. According to Pew Research, unauthorized illegals now make up nearly a quarter of all the US foreign-born population. There are 35.2 million lawful immigrants, 45 percent of those are naturalized citizens, and 12.3 million lawful permanent residents and 2.2 million lawful temporary residents. The crisis is one of mass migration, not immigration. This is not our first rodeo with mass migrations from failed socialist states. That is the real irony for those radical left-wing Democrats who have embraced and preached the goodness of socialism. It's mass migration prompted by third-world dictators like Venezuela's Hugo Chavez and "Nicki" Maduro and Fidel and Raul Castro in Cuba before them—all former president Obama's good buddies who drove their countries and citizens into the ground with failed socialist and communist economic systems, corruption, economic mismanagement, and failed governance. The vast majority of the 390,000 illegals apprehended at our southern border in the first eight months of FY 2019 were children and parents or family members. Nevertheless, many of these migrations/caravans are made up of not only the poorest of the poor and a very small percentage of asylum seekers but also hardened criminals, gang members, drug dealers, and human traffickers.

In the case of the mass migrations from Cuba, in response to the US open arms policy during the Carter administration, Castro called for the deportation of convicted criminals, the mentally ill, homosexuals, and prostitutes. While as many as 125,000 Cuban refugees emigrated to the United States as a result of the Mariel migration, which resulted from an agreement with the Cuban government, based on a 1985 *Sun Sentinel* magazine article, Castro still managed to empty his jails and send us some sixteen to twenty thousand criminals.

The Democrats insist on treating this unlawful invasion and the current crisis as an immigration issue, calling for everything from open borders and blanket amnesty to free health care and education to placing the eleven million new arrivals on the welfare rolls. While it is truly a tragedy and humanitarian crisis, the Democrats' true motivation and virtuous polemics and demagoguery have nothing to do with contributing to help relieve the suffering or resolve the crisis. Rather it is all part of another left-wing democratic deception to further exacerbate the crisis as a cover for a massive campaign using community organizers to mobilize and expand the rolls of welfare recipients and expand their political base in time for the 2020 presidential election and beyond. This will all be accomplished on the backs of American citizens and taxpayers under the guise of helping and caring for the thousands of poor, unskilled migrants who have entered the United States illegally. Their needs for health care, education, housing, food, clothing, and other basic needs and preventing the separation of parents from children are obviously, as President Trump has pointed out repeatedly, more important to the Democrats than taking care of the needs of the American family. The Democrats exposed their true intentions under Obama, who had the absolute worst record for unemployment in decades with the numbers on welfare and food stamps soaring to all-time highs for all Americans, with blacks and Hispanics suffering most.

I believe this was by design. As it was during Roosevelt's New Deal and Johnson's Great Society, they were pure programs of deception to take advantage of the crises of their times, the Great Depression and World War II and the chaos and turmoil of the 1960s, to expand their political base with little sincere regard for the suffering families.

An excellent example of this insincerity and true disregard for immigrants and the contribution that they and diversity have made to building this great nation comes from New York's very own Comrade Mayor de Blasio. The She Built NYC project began in the summer of 2018 as an attempt by de Blasio's wife Chirlane McCray to balance the male-female mix of statues of eminent New Yorkers in the city. More than 1,800 suggestions were received in a public poll to honor seven women, none of whom McCray selected from the poll. Mother Frances Xavier Cabrini received more votes than any of the other women in the process. Mother Cabrini was America's first saint and the patroness of immigrants. She was herself an Italian immigrant, who became a naturalized US citizen, and did more than any woman of her day to help the immigrant community in the United States. McCray and former deputy mayor Alicia Glenn ignored the public poll and chose seven women they wanted to honor, none of whom were among the top seven in the poll. Instead, they selected abortion rights activist Dr. Helen Rodríguez Trías and drag queens Sylvia Rivera and Marsha P. Johnson, among others. Sickening, yes, but representative of exactly where this nation is headed if our electorate follows this blue wave of left-wing democratic infidels and socialist progressive fanatics.

It shouldn't surprise anyone that with all the wailing and gnashing of teeth and hate speech that the Democrats have engaged in since President Trump's election and failure to manufacture even a modicum of evidence to impeach, they are already posturing themselves and their community organizers to try to steal the next presidential election. Only the Democrats, after engaging in decades of political corruption and deception, could find yet another novel way to stuff the ballot box and steal an election after election day. It's called ballot harvesting, which is the collecting and submitting of absentee and mail in ballots by volunteers or workers (anyone) and is illegal in many states. A Ninth Circuit Court judge upheld the ban on ballot harvesting in Arizona in 2018, and individuals have been prosecuted for the practice in Texas.

However, ballot harvesting is one of the latest rages in the sanctuary state of California along with tent cities, illegal immigrants, and crime. Ballot harvesting, a surge in illegal migrants from the southern border, and Middle Eastern refugees resettled by Obama in Orange County and other formerly conservative strongholds, for example, contributed to the loss of seven of fourteen House seats by Republicans after election day in the 2018 midterm elections. Thanks to changes to a California State Assembly Bill by far-left governor Jerry Brown in 2016, harvesting is legal, and the number of mail-in ballots harvested by volunteers and counted in Orange County alone was unprecedented with some 250,000 ballots produced and counted weeks after the election. Large last-minute submissions of votes delayed results and altered the outcomes of several elections with republican candidates leading, swinging the results of all those elections to Democrats. The actual likelihood is improbable, but then we are dealing with the politics of deception and democratic politicians who are so desperate at this time to save their party from extinction that they are literally operating in an alternative universe, totally out of touch with the American electorate with nothing positive or substantive to offer our families, communities, and nation, but rancor, hate, discord, and division.

> You are aware indeed that the goal of this iniquitous plot is to drive people to overthrow the entire order of human affairs and to draw them

over to the wicked theories of socialism and communism, by confusing them with perverted teachings. (Pope Pius IX, *Nostis et nobiscum* [December 8, 1849])

We speak of that sect of men who, under various and almost barbarous names, are called socialists, communists, nihilists, and who spread over all the world and bound together by the closest ties in a wicked confederacy, no longer seek the shelter of secret meetings, but openly and boldly marching forth in the light of day, strive to bring to a head what they have long been planning—the overthrow of all civil society whatsoever.

Surely, these are they who, as the sacred scriptures testify, "Defile the flesh, despise dominion and blaspheme majesty" (Jud. 8). (Pope Leo XIII, *Quod apostolici muneris* [December 28, 1878, 1])

# CHAPTER 8

# God Is Watching Us

*My sheep hear my voice, says the Lord; I*
*know them, and they follow me.*
                                        —John 10:27

We are at war for the heart and soul of our nation and republic, and our God and Savior is watching us. He has created each of us in his image with a free will not to do as we please, but to do what is morally right and just, following God's will.

> Modern prophets [politicians] say that our economics have failed us. No, it is not our economics that have failed; it is man who has failed man, who has forgotten God. Hence no manner of economic or political readjustment can possibly save our Civilization [and nation]; we can be saved only by a renovation of the inner man, only by a purging of our hearts and souls; for only by seeking first the Kingdom of God and His Justice will these other things be given unto us. (Bishop Fulton J. Sheen, *Go to Heaven: A Spiritual Road Map to Eternity*, [Ignatius Press])

This is not the end of the story, as Paul Harvey, the conservative radio broadcaster (September 4, 1918, to February 28, 2009), used to say in *the Rest of the Story* segments of his program that he made famous. From 1952 to 2008, his broadcasts reached more than twenty-four million people a week, 1, 200 radio stations, and four hundred armed forces network stations and were carried in three hundred newspapers. He received the Presidential Medal of Freedom in 2005.

Now, I'm going to give you the rest of the story with some help from Mr. Paul Harvey and Bishop Fulton J. Sheen (May 8, 1895–December 9, 1979), another iconic figure and true disciple of Christ. My parents, first-generation children of German (maternal) and Italian (paternal) immigrants of the mid to late nineteenth century, and my older brother and I all admired both for their integrity, faith, and abiding love for God and country that they shared every day with their viewers and listeners. They both had a sense of humor and could tell a story like no one else that I knew. Their discernment and warnings about America and the necessity for us to choose the right path to fight for and preserve our freedoms as "one nation under God, indivisible, with liberty and justice for all," or end up in the junk heap of nations gone south in the annals of history, were prophetic and sometimes chilling. They both warned that our love of self and lust for wealth and power, all while abandoning the love of God and neighbor, would eventually mark our downfall. I'm afraid that we are rapidly approaching that moment in our history where we are at a tipping point and crossroads that in the words of the Grail Knight in *Indiana Jones and the Last Crusade*, seeking the holy grail, the cup that Jesus Christ and his apostles drank from at the Last Supper, "But choose wisely, for while the true grail will bring you life, the false grail will take it from you."

In Hillary Clinton's world and the world of the militant progressives and secularists who want to trample on the Constitution and Christian moral teachings, it is perfectly acceptable and in fact honorable for a judge to declare that "the goal is never to shut down a business because they refused to compromise their religious beliefs to support what they viewed as immoral, but to rehabilitate," as if Christian moral teachings are a mental illness, when in fact those with the mental illness are those militant secularists. Hillary Clinton stated in April 2015 that "deep seated religious beliefs have to be changed." What else would you expect from a megalomaniac and schizophrenic who is living in her own Alinsky alternative world of self-aggrandizement and lust for power? She is not and never was interested in serving the people but only to be served and never interested in providing for the common good, but only herself and her radical secularist agenda.

Isn't it ironic and true today that not only are our own personal futures but also those of our children, grandchildren, and nation dependent on us making the right choices, choosing the right path to follow, professionally, spiritually, politically, and socially? It all comes down to all those choices that I mentioned in my "Introduction" that come full circle to confront us again and again and again, and more so now than ever. However, seeking the real and the truth and sorting out the false and the fake is no easy task when politicians, political parties, and the media deliberately obscure the truth and promote the fake and the big lie with their propaganda, demagoguery, and deception.

Trying to sort it all out seems like a monumental task for today's young adults and parents, but the answer is simple and direct—the truth and joy are found in our Lord Jesus Christ. One immutable truth and fact of life is that we will all have to face death since we are mortals and we are all going to die. The choices we make will determine whether we die in Christ and enjoy the rewards of eternal life and salvation promised by him through his life, death, and resurrection or die with total disregard and disbelief and suffer eternal damnation. The choice is ours, and we can't take Yogi Berra's advice, "When you come to a fork in the road, take it."

Jesus said to his apostles,

> When the son of Man comes in his glory and all his angels with him, he will sit upon his glorious throne and all the nations will be assembled before him. And he will separate them one from another, as the shepherd separates the sheep from the goats. He will place the sheep on his right and the goats on his left. Then the king will say

to those on his right, "Come you who are blessed by my Father, inherit the kingdom prepared for you from the foundation of the world. For I was hungry and you gave me food, I was thirsty and you gave me drink, a stranger and you welcomed me, naked and you clothed me, ill and you cared for me, in prison and you visited me..." Amen.

"I say to you, whatever you did for one of these least brothers of mine, you did for Me."

Then he will say to those on his left, "Depart from me you accursed, into the eternal fire prepared for the devil and his angels... What you did not do for one of these least ones you did not do for me. And these will go off to eternal punishment, but the righteous to eternal life." (Matthew 25:31–46)

It's also refreshing to know that Paul Harvey always seemed to have a way with identifying and elucidating those choices in a very direct and rational manner. There's little doubt that Paul Harvey was one of the most popular conservative radio talk show hosts in broadcasting in my lifetime. He was a devout Christian who was deeply concerned about the many misguided paths and choices that he saw America taking and Americans making in the turbulent 1960s. His essay, "If I were the Devil" was broadcast in 1965 and can be found on YouTube today, in which he warns of attacks against marriage, the family, sexual promiscuity, pornography, socialism, communism, drug abuse, and gambling, among other ills and evils. He updated it and broadcast it over the years in a variety of media, concluding that if he were Satan, he would just continue to do the things he was doing and capture the greatest prize of all, America. His warnings were prophetic and are every bit as relevant and perhaps even more so today than they were in the 1960s. I found the oldest genuine version of Paul Harvey's essay with the help of Snopes in his newspaper column in 1964; however, the following is an updated 1996 newspaper version:

> If I were the prince of darkness, I would want to engulf the whole world in darkness. I'd have a third of its real estate and four-fifths of its population, but I would not be happy until I had seized the ripest apple on the tree—thee.
>
> So, I would set about however necessary to take over the United States. I'd subvert the churches first, and I would begin with a campaign of whispers. With the wisdom of a serpent, I would whisper to you as I whispered to Eve: "Do as you please."
>
> To the young, I would whisper that the Bible is a myth. I would convince the children that man created God instead of the other way around. I'd confide that what's bad is good and what's good is square. And the old, I would teach to pray after me, "Our Father, which are in Washington..." Then, I'd get organized, I'd educate authors in how to make lurid literature exciting so that anything else would appear dull and uninteresting.
>
> I'd peddle narcotics to whom I could. I'd sell alcohol to ladies and gentlemen of distinction. I'd tranquilize the rest with pills. If I were the devil, I'd soon have families at war with themselves, churches at war with themselves and nations at war with themselves until each, in its turn, was consumed. And with promises of higher ratings, I'd have mesmerizing media fanning the flames.
>
> If I were the devil, I would encourage schools to refine young intellect but neglect to discipline emotions. I'd tell teachers to let those students run wild. And before you knew it, you'd

have drug-sniffing dogs and metal detectors at every schoolhouse door. Within a decade, I'd have prisons overflowing and judges promoting pornography. Soon, I would evict God from the courthouse and the schoolhouse and then from the houses of Congress.

In his own churches, I would substitute psychology for religion and deify science. I'd lure priests and pastors into misusing boys and girls and church money. If I were the devil, I'd take from those who have and give to those who wanted until I had killed the incentive of the ambitious.

What'll you bet I couldn't get whole states to promote gambling as the way to get rich? I'd convince the young that marriage is old-fashioned, that swinging is more fun and that what you see on television is the way to be. And thus, I could undress you in public and lure you into bed with diseases for which there are no cures. In other words, if I were the devil, I'd just keep right on doing what he's doing. (Paul Harvey Aurandt, "If I were the Devil," 1996 version [September 4, 1918–February 28, 2009])

May God bless him and all the souls of the faithful departed.

Let me propose that our great Civil War and the Reconstruction that followed was only the *first act* in a Shakespearean tragedy brought to us courtesy of the Jacksonian and antiabolitionist proslavery Democrats of the time along with their black codes and their Ku Klux Klan warriors of the Reconstruction. God was there and got us through it, with President Lincoln and a Republican Party able to issue the Emancipation Proclamation and pass the Thirteenth, Fourteenth, and Fifteenth Amendments to our Constitution during Lincoln's first term against staunch democratic opposition, before he was assassinated by a crazed antiabolitionist, John Wilkes Booth.

*Act 2, stage left*—tragedy of World War I, the "war to end all wars," brought to us and our totally unprepared and unequipped doughboys by isolationist and broken promises democratic president Woodrow Wilson along with his democratic antisuffragist proponents. God was there with the Blessed Virgin Mary appearing in Fátima, Portugal, on May 13, June, July, and monthly through October 13, 1917. She promised through her intercession to end the war if certain conditions were met, and they were, and the war ended, and Armistice signed on November 11, 1918.

God must have also been there for the women suffragettes who were given the patience and tenacity to continue their just fight for voting rights and passage of the Nineteenth Amendment with strong support from the Republican Party that controlled both houses of Congress with large majorities as a result of midterm elections in 1918. The Republicans first introduced the amendment in 1878, and the Democrats fought and opposed it for forty years—just another example of democratic deceit and deception, revising history and turning reality on its head.

With the truth now known, and if it's also true that "hell hath no fury like a woman scorned," then Democrats and the Democrat Party should rightly be in the doghouse today for their legacy of opposing women's rights. Hopefully, more women have been and will be enlightened by the truth and true legacy of the Democrat Party and opposition to minority and women's rights, yet it's hard to counter the lies and deception that the Democrats have honed into a fine art.

Maybe the fact and reality that women have benefitted significantly from President Trump's economic policies and booming economy will have some positive impact. According to the Bureau of Labor Statistics, the number of women working now is the highest it's ever been, at more than seventy-five million, while black and Hispanic unemployment rates are at all-time lows. The Labor Department job report in January 2020 showed that there have never been more black and Hispanic Americans in the workforce.

*Act 3, stage left*—the Great Depression (1929–1945), democratic isolationist policies toward Nazism, the war in Europe, and contrary to popular pop culture and democratic and media propaganda, the New Deal was not such a good deal for blacks and minorities. However, democratic president Franklin D. Roosevelt's administration did prove to be a very good deal and provided a very favorable environment for Socialists and Communists alike, who infiltrated every key branch of his administration. Pope Pius XI (1922–1939) argued in his encyclical (*Quadragesimo anno*, May 15, 1931, no. 111) that socialism cannot be reconciled with Catholic doctrine.

The deception surrounding FDR's true state of health and the arrogance and self-serving political partisanship of his closest democratic advisors, some of whom were Communist operatives, ended with him giving away half of Germany and Berlin and all of Eastern Europe at Yalta to Stalin and the Communists. While he claimed, "Victory in Europe," his decisions also ushered in a forty-year Cold War with the Soviet Union that threatened humanity with nuclear annihilation and enslaved an entire generation of millions of Europeans in East Germany and Eastern Europe behind the Iron Curtain.

God was watching us, and he was with us at the height of the Cold War to provide us leaders with great discernment and moral courage to stem the tide of Communism in the third world and confront the brutal Stalinist dictatorship and evil empire, the Soviet Union, with the election and Pontificate of Pope John Paul II in 1978 and election of Pres. Ronald Reagan in 1982.

However, not before *Act 4, stage left*, and the turbulent 1960s and 1970s brought about by a lot of bad choices and selfish and derisive politics of the Vietnam War era. The countercultural sexual revolution with its excessive drug abuse, potheads, and promiscuity along with militant feminist movements and legalization of abortion were all accompanied by frontal attacks on Christianity, the family, and morality. God was there watching and waiting for us to make the right choices, but we didn't, and chaos ensued, and darkness prevailed.

In that darkness, we experienced the Cuban missile crisis, the closest America has ever come to nuclear annihilation. We grieved over the assassinations and loss of our beloved Pres. John F. Kennedy, first and only Catholic elected to that office, and his brother Robert, the attorney general, and a remarkable civil rights leader, Martin Luther King, Jr., all of whom set in motion the legislative agenda for the Civil Rights Act of 1964.

Despite democratic and revisionist historian claims to the contrary, this was accomplished against determined opposition from the Democrat Party that led a fifty-seven-day filibuster to kill the bill and a reluctant democratic president and successor to Pres. John F. Kennedy, Lyndon Baines Johnson (LBJ). God was there with a larger percentage of Republicans than Democrats in both houses of Congress voting for the bill, even though Democrats controlled and held majorities in both houses. Of course, reminiscent of Wilson's eleventh-hour support for passage of the Nineteenth Amendment (after the fact), once Johnson realized the bill would pass with or without his support and a veto would be political suicide, he and Senate Majority leader Mike Mansfield threw their full weight and support behind the bill and the Great Society was born.

Johnson was a shrewd and politically astute politician long before he became Kennedy's vice president, and his motivations on civil rights were certainly not altruistic. His was more likely a well-orchestrated and choreographed personal and partisan effort to make sure he and the Democrat Party got all the credit for passage of the bill. Thanks to decades of propaganda and efforts to obscure the truth and revise history, the Democrats have been very successful in maintaining that myth and convincing the uninformed they are the party of civil rights. With God's help and inspiration from the Holy Spirit, I'm hoping that this book will help set the record straight once and for all on that and other issues that I've addressed.

The fact the enemies of God must face is that modern civilization has conquered the world, but in doing so has lost its heart and soul. And in losing its heart and soul, it will lose the very world it thinks it gained. The secularization of our culture in America and the embrace by the Democrat Party and far left of socialism, if not checked, threaten to eliminate even those remaining pockets of individual freedom, which are preserved only because religion and God have remained in their hearts and souls. And as religion and God are turned away by the militant secularists and Progressives, so also will freedom fade, for only where we find the spirit of God is there true freedom and liberty. Freedom does not give us the right to do whatever we please, but rather to do what is right and just and make choices that we believe God would want us to make. The right to do whatever we please reduces freedom to a physical power and ignores the fact that freedom is a moral power granted by God.

> Beloved, we love God because He first loved us. If anyone says, "I love God," but hates his brother, he is a liar; for whoever does not love a brother whom he has seen cannot love God whom he has not seen. This is the commandment we have from Him: Whoever loves God must also love his brother. Everyone who believes that Jesus is the Christ is begotten by God, and everyone who loves the Father loves also the one begotten by Him... For the love of God is this, that we keep His commandments. And his commandments are not burdensome, for whoever is begotten by God conquers the world. And the victory that conquers the world is our Faith. (1 John 4:19–5:4)

*Act 5, stage right*—two world leaders and disciples of Christ who were brought together at a critical crossroads in our history and that of the world, Pope John Paul II and Pres. Ronald Reagan. I've spoken in detail about their relationship earlier, but I need to underscore the fact that it was their mutual faith in God and love and concern for humanity and the grace of God that enabled them to work in concert to bring about the collapse of the Soviet Union. God was there, and through the intercession once again of the Blessed Virgin Mary, Pope John Paul II survived the attack of a KGB-sponsored assassination attempt on May 13, 1981, the Feast Day of Our Lady of Fatima, in St. Peter's Square. The gunman, Ağca, fired four shots at point-blank range with a 9 mm Browning high-powered semiautomatic pistol critically wounding the pope. But while all four bullets hit the pope, miraculously, no vital organs were hit.

Pope John Paul II always attributed his survival to the protection by the Blessed Virgin Mary. There is little doubt that if Pope John Paul II had not survived, it would have been a much different Europe and a much different world for generations to follow. The collapse of the Soviet Union meant freedom for millions of Europeans from the evil and slavery imposed by the most ignominious totalitarian communist system the Western world has ever known, and as President Reagan so aptly referred to it, "the evil empire."

"When we do not profess Jesus Christ," Pope Francis says, "we profess the worldliness of the devil, a demonic worldliness."

As Bishop Fulton J. Sheen once pronounced in one of his many radio and TV broadcasts, "Very few people believe in the devil these days, which suits the devil very well. He is always circulating the news of his own death. The essence of God is existence, and he [God] has defined himself from the beginning of time as: 'I am Who am.' The essence of the devil is the lie, and he defines himself as, 'I am who am not.' Satan has very little trouble with those who don't believe in him; they are already on his side."

Yes, Virginia, there is evil in this world and there is also good, and the distinctions are clear and constant and not situational. There are also clear distinctions between what's true and what's false, despite all the propaganda and brainwashing of an overbearing minority of progressive secularists (more accurately regressive secularists) and political correctness Nazis who no longer even attempt to hide the fact that they will promote evil and perverse lifestyles and behavior and call it good while condemning all that is good and righteous in God's eyes as bad, passé, old fashioned. God's will, morality, civility, and doing what is right have been rejected and abandoned by the Democrats and the radical Left. The anger, hate, and vilifying comments by the candidates about our president, the American electorate, and one another in the Democrat Party presidential debates are a true spectacle of liberalism gone amok. One of the many things that they all have in common is their modus operandi, the ends always justify the means. One of the most disturbing aspects of their godless agenda is their unbridled determination to impose their will and that agenda on the American people and America at all cost. Attempts to eliminate God and restrict our religious freedoms while attacking traditional Christian and family values have been at the core of their hateful speech and behavior, along with the demonization and contempt expressed not only for our duly elected president but also for all those who support him and dare to oppose their radical socialist and secularist ideology and agenda.

In his encyclical, *Veritatis splendor* (*the Splendor of the Truth*), Pope John Paul II states emphatically that moral truth is knowable, that the choice of good or evil has a profound effect on one's relationship with God, and that there is no real contradiction between freedom and following the good. He asserts that there are indeed absolute truths accessible to all persons. Contrary to the philosophy of moral relativism, the encyclical argues that moral law is universal across all peoples, in varying cultures, and is rooted in the human condition. Therefore, in the depths of our hearts, there always remains a search for absolute truth and the "splendor of truth shines forth deep within the human spirit."

"Moral principles do not depend on a majority vote. Wrong is wrong, even if everybody is wrong. Right is right, even if nobody is right" (Bishop Fulton J. Sheen).

So if we are all endowed with the spirit of goodness by our Creator and our God is a kind, gentle, and merciful God, why is there so much evil, hate, and division in this country and in this world of ours? Maybe it's because so many are nonbelievers and so many believers have abandoned God and their faith altogether or are just going through the motions and placing their relationship with God on an as available or as necessary basis. Maybe it's because more of us are following our own worldly desires and making all the wrong choices and those that oppose the good. Maybe it's because so many of those career politicians in Washington fit that mold and are ignoring God's will and the common good. Rather they are making all the wrong choices by following their own and the will of special interests' insatiable self-serving desire for more power, riches, and prestige. Where there is no God, there is no faith, and where there is no faith, there is no hope.

"Faith is the realization of what is hoped for and evidence of things not seen" (Hebrews 11:1).

I can't help believing that we have entered another period in our short history of darkness and chaos, where idolatry reigns supreme—love of money, material possessions, lust for power, prestige, and putting self-first—with little regard for those around us or for the common good.

"Do not be anxious about anything, but in every situation, by prayer and petition, with thanksgiving, make your requests known to God. Then the peace of God that surpasses all understanding will guard your hearts and minds in Christ Jesus" (Philippians 4:6,7).

The hate speech and bitterness and division being sewn by a vocal minority of radical career politicians in Congress and a government bureaucracy that has been tainted by sixteen years of corruption, scandals, and influence peddling during Clinton's and Obama's tenures set the stage for the final act of this Shakespearean play, which has turned out to be both tragedy and farce. But before I proceed with the rest of my story, I want to propose a question to all who read this book. Does our God of infinite love, mercy, and compassion who sent his only begotten Son, Jesus Christ, to die for us on the cross in expiation of our sin and through his life, death, and resurrection offer all the gift of eternal life to those who believe have the capacity to hate? God is love, and those who love are with God and God with them. I'm afraid that many of us believe that our freedom and our free will give us the license to do whatever we please. Wrong answer. God hates sin, not those who sin. We all sin, and we are all sinners, even the saints among us. I can assure you that while there aren't any career politicians or lawyers among the saintly candidates, there are not many on this planet today in any case.

I believe Solomon answers the question best in the book of Proverbs, "These six things the Lord hates, and seven are an abomination to Him: a proud look, a lying tongue, hands that shed innocent blood, a heart that devises wicked plans, feet that are swift in running to evil, a false witness who speaks lies, and one who sows discord among brethren" (Proverbs 6:16–19).

*The tragedy, the final act*—the two democratic presidents created more than their fair share of darkness and chaos during their White House years. The Clintons enriched themselves through the Clinton Foundation, collecting millions in pandering for Chinese special interests and favors and, of course, the many mistresses and perverted sexual endeavors of Pres. Bill Clinton, the most notable White House intern Monica Lewinsky. But there were also, Gennifer Flowers, Paula Jones, Eleanor Mondale, and a host of others that came out of the woodwork, some claiming they were mistresses and victims of sexual harassment and even rape. In his book, *Crisis of Character*, Gary Byrne notes that President Clinton "had difficulty managing where he saw his many mistresses...we [the Secret Service detail] wondered how he got any work done, and joked that he would be better running a brothel...than the White House." There's little doubt that some of his most notable accomplishments were overshadowed by the Lewinsky affair and his impeachment by the House of Representatives for lying under oath and obstruction of justice. There seemed to be no limit to what Bill and Hillary were capable of when it came to deception, lying, and influence peddling to get what they wanted while destroying those who got in their way. Just when we thought the list of Clinton associates who died mysteriously or committed suicide had come to an end, we have the stunning reports of pedophile, pervert, and very close friend of Bill Clinton's hanging himself in his jail cell while under close surveillance following at least one attempt on his life.

Flight logs show that Bill made at least twenty-seven trips on Epstein's *Lolita Express* with underage girls along with reports of Clinton on Epstein's private island, referred to as Orgy Island. Of course, all suggestions that the Clintons were involved or culpable in any of the more than fifty individual associates who died mysterious deaths are all dubbed conspiracy theories, when in fact the conspirators, Bill and Hillary, are staring us right in the face in plain sight. I thought the trail had ended in July 2016 just prior to the 2016 Democratic National Convention with the murder of Seth Rich, a DC staffer who WikiLeaks founder Julian Assange reported had information on the Clinton DNC e-mail scandal. While Rich wasn't around to testify, the leaks clearly indicated a DNC deal with Hillary to ensure her nomination while undermining her closest competitor, Bernie Sanders. So we see the trail of dead bodies of those who might dare get in the way of the Clintons and their lust for wealth, power, prestige, and, yes, sexual perversion continues to march on.

In his book, Byrne described Hillary as a lady who operated best in the darkness and used the example of how she brought Dick Morris into the White House at night as a political advisor without the knowledge of the president's chief of staff, Leon Panetta. I have to say, as an aside, that when Leon Panetta became the CIA director in 2009, some of my more conservative colleagues and I were skeptical about his intentions as a former Clinton chief of staff. However, Leon Panetta proved to be a breath of fresh air and quickly assimilated himself into the CIA's operational and analytic world. He visited many of our field stations in conflict zones and quickly became one of our biggest fans and expressed his views in trip reports that I was personally privy to as an intelligence educator. Leon Panetta was an exceptional leader and quickly gained an appreciation for CIA's resources and capabilities that he employed judiciously and effectively in tracking down Osama bin Laden and his lieutenants and always recognized the contributions and sacrifices of CIA officers. I was proud to work for a man of his character and integrity, regardless of the fact that he was a Democrat and former Clinton chief of staff.

Former president and Alinsky disciple Obama also presided over some of the worst scandals of any president, save perhaps Bill Clinton, and perhaps one of the worst pieces of legislation ever passed. Again, I don't use hyperbole when I say that Obama, then Speaker of the House Pelosi, and the Democrats also seem to work best in the darkness as they did by passing the infamous Affordable Care Act (ACA) in the middle of the night without a single republican vote. The Obama administration's pandering to sell America to the highest bidder—Russians, third-world dictators, and globalists alike—and his decision to operate from the spider hole of a shadow government to subvert his democratically elected successor have proven to be even more outrageous. It's interesting that both Pelosi and Hillary Clinton work best in the darkness, like Satan's prostitutes selling their souls in exchange for their lust for power while demonizing the innocent through false testimony, lies, and deception. They are the devil's disciples along with their cronies, the Pharisees and scribes of the twenty-first century.

Then secretary of state and coconspirator Hillary Clinton did her part by using a private unsecured e-mail account to conduct official State Department business involving the transmission of highly classified national security information and knowingly compromised American national security interests to potential adversaries and terrorists alike. She then removed, hid, or destroyed many of the e-mails to deliberately obstruct an FBI counterintelligence investigation into the e-mail scandal with some of her e-mails subsequently found in the Executive Office of President Obama. This was conduct that would have resulted in the prosecution and jail time for any intelligence professional but in her case proved to be inconsequential to FBI and DOJ officials who we now know were part of the shadow government.

In his congressional testimony in October 2018 before the House Judiciary and Oversight Committees regarding Russiagate, former FBI director James Comey claimed "he can't remember," "can't recall," or "doesn't know" 245 times when asked key questions about the FBI's counterintelligence investigation of President Trump and his campaign. Comey claimed ignorance about the facts in the case of the FBI spying on candidate and President Trump and his campaign, who paid for the manufactured Steele dossier, the roles played by the Clinton campaign, Mr. Obama, Biden, the Russians, Ukrainians, and the DNC. Then Comey suddenly remembered everything according to the Obama and Democrats' narrative and wrote a book. Ladies and gentlemen, that is what the two-and-half-year, multimillion-dollar Mueller investigation was all about, misdirection and cover-up to promote the fake and hide the real source of the scandal—the Clintons, Obamas, and democratic Trump-hating moles in the FBI, CIA, and DOJ.

Events leading up to and surrounding the Benghazi incident that resulted in the deaths of four Americans including US Ambassador Stevens were also addressed in some of those "lost," "misplaced," and destroyed Clinton e-mails. That debacle resulted in the abandonment by Obama and his State Department of those Americans to a well-trained and heavily armed, well-organized attack by radical Islamic terrorists on September 11, 2012. There was some reporting that indicated that some of those weapons, specifically Stinger missiles, may have been provided to the terrorist group Ansar al-Sharia, responsible for the Benghazi attacks, by the Obama State Department while Hillary was secretary of state. Some unsubstantiated reporting indicated that Ambassador Stevens and his security detail may have been sent to Benghazi to negotiate and "retrieve the weapons." If you consider the character of the actors, this is a very plausible explanation.

General Petraeus, CIA director at that time (September 6, 2011–November 9, 2012), apparently had refused to approve the arms transfer out of concern that the missiles might be used against civilian airlines; and we know what happened to General Petraeus, or do we? You may recall that in 2007 and 2008, there was quite an outpouring of support for General Petraeus to run for president. There were articles and even some media hype about a possible McCain/Petraeus ticket, which must have unnerved Barack Obama and the Democrats. But the very well-educated and highly decorated good general decided not to run for public office. In 2010, Obama nominated Petraeus to succeed General McChrystal as the commanding general of the International Security Assistance Force in Afghanistan. This was a step down from his previous position as commander, US Central Command, responsible for military operations in Afghanistan, Pakistan, Central Asia, the Arabian Peninsula, and Egypt.

While CIA Director General Petraeus was being pressured to testify before both Senate and House intelligence committees about Benghazi before and after, he was forced to resign. While the FBI found classified material at his alleged biographer Broadwell's home and on her computer, she was never charged because in President

Obama's own words, "there was no evidence that the material contained secrets crucial to the country's national security." She was a reservist and an intelligence officer and allegedly lost her security clearance because of her blatant security violations. I make no excuses for the general's wrongdoing. He was punished and accepted the consequences of his actions, which paled when compared to the revelations of the Clinton e-mail scandal and her security violations. Of course, this was all part of the liberal left-wing democratic double standard when it comes to meting out justice. The general did have an extramarital affair with his biographer Paula Broadwell, and he mishandled classified information and resigned at the urging of DNI Jim Clapper who wasted little time in reporting the matter to President Obama. For his part, the general eventually pleaded guilty to one misdemeanor charge of mishandling classified information and was sentenced to two years' probation and fined $100,000, though some Obama administration officials wanted more serious charges and punishment meted out. Why?

There is still some question about Paula Broadwell and how she managed to come out of obscurity to coauthor General Petraeus's biography with Vernon Loeb of *the Washington Post*. She and Loeb were then and now credited with that biography at General Petraeus's expense. Why is it that she would quickly retain the services of former Clinton Press Secretary Dee Myers and a public relations firm, the Glover Park Group, which was founded by former Clinton White House officials and served with the presidential campaign of former Vice President Al Gore, following FBI questioning and the revelations about her accessing the general's e-mail accounts and her extramarital affair? This was not a coincidence, but another classic Clinton and Obama deception and attempt at misdirection to create a monumental crisis out of a mole hill to cover up their own misdeeds with Benghazi and to eliminate General Petraeus as a credible witness concerning Benghazi or any future political threat he might eventually pose to Obama, Clinton, and the Democrats. They were using Broadwell as their mole and honeypot to finish him off. She gets what she wants, coauthorship of his biography and a lot of media hype for the book and her new business venture, Broad

Horizons, and they get what they want, Petraeus gone. Connect the dots, hiding the real, projecting the fake.

A very important and elucidating rest of the story is that none other than John O. Brennan, possibly the Obama and Russian third mole, then succeeded General Petraeus as CIA director in November 2012. That third mole is one who Brian Kelley and others knew existed in addition to Ames and Hanssen, but always eluded our counterintelligence. Could it have been Brennan who voted for Gus Hall in 1976, showed up as a CIA career trainee in 1980 along with Howard and Nicholson and others who spied for the Soviets and Russians, and made a career of it? Coincidence? Maybe. Maybe not. Certainly, the timing of Brennan's appointment as CIA director was probably intended to help buttress the false Benghazi narrative, cover Joe Biden's illicit financial dealings with the Ukrainians, and lay the groundwork to ensure Hillary's coronation in 2016. It also presented Putin and the Russian intelligence services with a softer target and more receptive environment for their covert influence operations, which included the promotion of the fake Steele dossier to undermine the Trump campaign. Problem is that it didn't work; God was there, and sixty-three million Americans made the right choice, and Trump was elected despite the elaborate deception campaign to prevent his election. This is not speculation or conspiracy theory; it's just good retrospective analysis. Get your head out of the sand and connect the dots.

Not surprisingly, Obama and Clinton attributed the attack in Benghazi to hateful American intolerance expressed in a manufactured YouTube video that they claimed prompted spontaneous riots throughout the Muslim world. It was just another Obama and Clinton deception set in motion to perpetuate their phony narrative and cover-up at the United Nations, with Congress and the American people, while apologizing to the Muslim world as Obama did on so many occasions. Imagine, the resident and commander in chief not only refusing to accept responsibility and make amends to the family members of those killed but also had the temerity to blame America and the American people for the tragedy. The mishandling of the incident and failure to act to protect American lives and property and the pathetic attempts to cover up and hide the Truth were in my judgment an act of cowardice and classic example of the politics of deception.

Of course, it shouldn't have been a surprise to anyone even the casual observer coming within a couple of months of the 2012 presidential elections, and getting rid of Petraeus was a necessary part of the cover-up. Remember Alinsky disciple President Obama blamed all his problems and failings on President Bush for the entirety of his first term in office, four years of zero accomplishments, and all because of the failed policies of his predecessor. Yet while Obama spent all his spare time minimizing the radical Islamic terrorist threat and kowtowing to his radical Muslim brethren, Pres. George Bush had the monumental task of dealing with that threat and the aftermath of the 9/11 radical Muslim terrorist attacks on the US homeland that killed 2,977 Americans, more than those killed at Pearl Harbor.

President Bush could have pointed fingers at President Clinton for failing to respond more vigorously to a series of terrorist attacks against the United States, at home and abroad, during his presidency, which were harbingers of another major attack on the US homeland—1993 truck bombing of the World Trade Center that killed six and injured a thousand; 1995 bombing in Saudi Arabia that killed five Americans and 1996 bombing of Khobar Towers in Saudi Arabia that killed nineteen and injured two hundred US military personnel; 1998 bombings of US embassies in Kenya and Tanzania, killing 257 and injuring five thousand; and the 2000 waterborne attack on the USS Cole in port in Yemen that killed seventeen US sailors. There was no finger-pointing or whining about what could have been done or should have been done during Clinton's presidency to deter the radical al-Qaeda Islamic terrorists, because God was there with President Bush and America and President Bush was making all the right choices by calling on the Lord to give us all the strength and courage to pull ourselves up out the pain and rubble. I offer just a couple paragraphs of his address to America,

> A great people has been moved to defend a great nation. Terrorist attacks can shake the foundations of our biggest buildings, but they cannot touch the foundation of America… America was targeted for attack because we're the brightest beacon for freedom and opportunity in the world. Today our nation saw evil—the very worst of human nature—and we responded with the best of America… Tonight, I ask for your prayers for all those who grieve, for the children whose worlds have been shattered, for all whose sense of security and safety has been threatened. And I pray that they will be comforted by a power greater than any of us, spoken through the ages in Psalm 23:
> "Even though I walk through the valley of the shadow of death, I fear no evil for you are with me."
> This is a day when all Americans from every walk of life unite in our resolve for justice and peace. America has stood down enemies before and we will do so this time.

America's prayers were answered when President Bush declared a global war on terrorism, we took the fight to the enemy, and Americans came together once again to rebuild and serve and care for one another as "one nation under God." George Bush was a leader, America's president, and a commander in chief who had worn the uniform and served and loved his country and his Maker. He surrounded himself with strong leaders and experienced and patriotic men and women of faith like Dick Cheney, Condoleezza Rice, Colin Powell, Karl Rove, John Bolton, Donald Rumsfeld, and Bob Gates. You can compare that leadership team any day of the week with what preceded Bush and what followed, and the Bush administration comes out on top every time.

While we have deterred and avoided any terrorist attacks on America since, we now find ourselves engaged in a conflict, an uncivil and unholy war, with enemies from both within and outside America who represent an equally brazen threat to our nation, our sovereignty, and the principles and freedoms set forth in our Constitution and Bill of Rights.

"For we do not wrestle against flesh and blood but against principalities, against powers, against the rulers of darkness of this world, against spiritual wickedness in high places" (Ephesians 6:12).

Everyone remembers where they were on 9/11. I was in the Pentagon assigned as the Deputy Defense Intelligence officer for Global Trends and Projections (room 2D541), one corridor over from the devastation of the terrorist attack that killed seven of my colleagues. We had a staff meeting planned for 9:00 a.m. in the new army chief of staff's conference room located on the third floor of the newly renovated section of the Pentagon, but were bumped and rescheduled for 11:00 a.m. No one in that conference room located directly in the path of American Airlines Flight 77 that morning survived. God was with us and the Holy Spirit was with me.

Barack Hussein Obama was a forty-year-old lawyer, professor, and Illinois State senator on his way to a policy wonk meeting in downtown Chicago. In eight years, he would be president, and promising to forever change America, in his words, during the final days of his presidential campaign, "We are five days away from transforming America." What he set in motion when elected in 2008 to transform America was never good for America or Americans, but rather a political ploy and Alinsky-inspired diabolical deception to significantly expand entitlements and create a permanent underclass and constituency wholly dependent on government handouts that would come from the Democrat Party, Congress, and apparatus. The Democrat Party leadership is trying to keep Obama's deception alive and are now attempting to add some fifteen to twenty million illegals to that constituency.

And where was race-baiter and Trump-beater Maxine Waters on 9/11 who makes her living bashing President Trump every day with some of the most psychotic attacks imaginable? She was probably at home in her multimillion-dollar California mansion or somewhere on Capitol Hill, where she has spent more than twenty-eight years (fifteen terms) as a congresswoman with Nancy Pelosi, who has served thirty-two years (sixteen terms), both poster 'octogenarians' for why there should be term limits.

Waters has represented the 43$^{rd}$ Congressional District in Los Angeles since 2013 and has been described by many as a cesspool and the worst in Los Angeles. Of course, she resides in her mansion outside the district, but her constituents keep voting for her and wonder why the garbage doesn't get picked up and their plight just doesn't get any better when the rest of the country outside the democratic-controlled big cities basks in a thriving economy and the economic renewal of the Trump administration. The same can be said for multimillionaires Pelosi who has turned her 12$^{th}$ Congressional District in San Francisco into another third-world tent city, second only to Los Angeles with her and Waters sharing bragging rights along with their fellow California Democrats and former four-term sixteen-year (1975–1983 and 2011–2019) governor Jerry Moonbeam Brown for having the largest homeless population in the country. According to the US Interagency Council on Homelessness, on any given day/night in 2018, there were 130,000 human beings on the streets statewide (sixty thousand in LA County and ten thousand in San Francisco) with Comrade Cuomo's and Comrade de Blasio's beloved state of New York a distant second with some 92,000 homeless. These are statistics that they can be proud of and are themselves wholly responsible for and accountable. These are undeniable facts and something they can't blame on anyone else.

I'll just add one more factoid about Democrats and the Liberal Left. The top ten most dangerous cities in America (violent crimes/100,000) all have democratic mayors and have all been controlled by the Democrats for decades—Detroit, Los Angeles, Baltimore, San Francisco, St. Louis, Memphis, New Orleans,

Milwaukee, Cleveland, and Indianapolis and the list of thirty-three goes on.

President Trump actually won 3,084 of 3,141 counties in the United States by landslide victories in 2016 and Hillary Clinton won just fifty-seven (all in urban areas). Yet through election fraud, gerrymandering, ballot harvesting, and intimidation, she magically ended up with a larger number of "popular" votes. Trump legitimately won the hearts and minds of the American people and 304 electoral votes to Clinton's 227, but Clinton and the demons of deception, the Democrats, actually claimed that Trump stole the election. No, the American people made the right choice and chose wisely. So you probably are wondering, How can so few in such a small segment of America, the inner cities, have so much influence on such important matters as electing our president? How is this possible? Can't the residents and voters in these fair cities understand their plight and recognize the demagoguery and deceit of the politicians they continue to put into office? Has God abandoned them and left them to fend for themselves against the princes and princesses of darkness and wiles of the devil and demons of the Democrat Party? Absolutely not.

As Albert Einstein stated, "Two things are infinite, the universe and human stupidity." I offer an alternative view that three things are infinite, the love God has for all of us, God's mercy, and the frailty of humanity. When the democratic bosses and community organizers in urban areas are offering you a monthly "paycheck" for your vote and your soul and nothing else, are you going to take the bribe or not? Unless you put your trust in our Lord and Savior Jesus Christ and reject Satan's handiwork, you will accept the bribe as the vast majority do.

Then there are the brash and insulting members of the so-called squad of radical left-wing socialist junior congresswomen who frankly stand for all that is wrong with the Democrat Party and its radical agenda. Ilhan Omar (D-MN), a Somali-born naturalized US citizen, and Rashida Tlaib (D-MI) (with areas of Detroit in her district), a Palestinian American, are the first two Muslim women to serve in Congress. Omar has recently been criticized by both Republicans and Democrats for statements made minimizing the significance of the 9/11 attacks and attributing the attacks to "some people that did something." Omar, who was twenty years old and a student at North Dakota State University when the attacks occurred and fortunate enough to emigrate and enjoy the freedom and opportunities of being in America, should have the courage to call out Islamic terrorists for who they are and what they are. She obviously is not smart enough or informed enough to know that terrorists don't discriminate and there were also innocent Muslims who died and were injured as a result of the attacks. Omar is no Muslim princess and has been accused of perjury, immigration fraud, state and federal tax fraud, federal student loan fraud, and incest for marrying her brother. Her current husband has filed for divorce as a result of her affair with a DC political consultant—a perfect foundation for a democratic career politician.

Tliab has labeled herself as a racist with her anti-Semitic diatribes and demands that the United States abandon its support and aid to Israel. She would also probably deny like her radical Palestinian terrorist brethren that there was ever a holocaust.

Another member of the squad Ayanna Pressley (D-MA) is a self-impressed and repressed female eunuch who is out fanning the flames to have Justice Brett Kavanaugh impeached even now almost three years after all the lies and false accusations by Feinstein and paid liberal feminist activists have been thoroughly debunked. Pressley's resolution to impeach Kavanaugh not surprisingly has been endorsed by the other three but is nothing more than another vain attempt to try to defend and protect Roe v Wade, Planned Parenthood, the Pro-Choice feminist fanatics and their Socialist Democrats' culture of death. There is a psychopathology at work here with all four of the junior radical left-wing congresswomen and with the octogenarian princesses Waters and Pelosi.

Tlaib and Alexandria Ocasio-Cortez (AOC) (D-NY) are both members of the Democratic Socialists of America that has its roots in the Socialist Party of America (SPA), a coalition of former members of Socialist and Communist parties of the Old Left or pre-1960s Marxist movements. Eugene Debs (1855–1926), Socialist, political activist, and trade unionist, was one of the founding members of the Industrial Workers of the World and Socialist Party and five-time presidential candidate for the SPA. This is not a movement of reformers; this is an ideology and movement that intends to destroy the America that we know and try to recast it in their own radical progressive socialist agenda and impose their will and the tyranny of their vocal and overbearing minority ideology on America, much like what Obama and the Democrats did when attempting to take over America's healthcare system.

Obama's only accomplishment in his first term was to ramrod healthcare legislation through Congress in the middle of the night, without a single republican vote, the so-called Affordable Care Act (ACA) or better known as Obamacare, which proved to be neither affordable nor workable. It was without a doubt one of the worst pieces of legislation ever to come out of the Halls of Congress, with then Speaker Pelosi and Senate Majority leader Harry "Hitler" Reid out in front of the pack unwilling to compromise or consider even the slightest adjustments to the bill by Republicans. Pelosi told America, "We'll find out what's in it after it's passed."

Yes, we certainly did. And the $515+ million taxpayer dollars paid to the Canadian firm, CGI Federal, a US-based subsidiary to build the error-plagued national Web site for Obamacare, healthcare.gov, proved to be equally costly and unworkable. Questions still abound concerning the exorbitant price tag to set up a simple Web site to buy health insurance and the fact that a Princeton classmate of Michelle Obama's was a senior vice president in the company and political donor at the time the contract was let. ACA continues to limp along. However, it was supposed to provide care for some more than thirty million Americans who didn't have it, but the price tag for its healthcare plans have continued to rise and the number of Americans signing up for new plans is decreasing with only just over eight million in 2019, down slightly from 2018. Meanwhile with the stroke of his pen and Executive action early this year, President Trump helped thirteen million Americans gain access to more affordable healthcare plans according to the White House Council of Economic Advisors (CEA). The CEA said that short-term plans, for up to 364 days and renewable for three years, would be half as expensive as the Obamacare compliant plans. And that didn't cost American taxpayers anything.

Other scandals included Operation Fast and Furious, with the Obama DOJ and Attorney General Eric Holder losing track of thousands of guns that were passed on to suspected smugglers in an attempt to "trace them to Mexican drug cartels." Really? Whose idiotic idea was that? As a result, a US Border Guard was murdered with one of those guns and Attorney General Holder was held in contempt of Congress for failing to turn over documents about the operation.

One of the least publicized scandals because of a compliant mainstream media involved an inspector general's report concerning the "misplacing" by Obama's Department of Housing and Urban Development (HUD) of $500+ billion—yes, $500 billion, not millions, of taxpayer dollars. This was reported by the OIG in 2017, based on an audit of HUD's 2015–2016 consolidated financial statements just before Obama left office. According to the OIG, "pervasive material errors" amounted to nearly $520 billion. Even after they were sent back and rereleased, the OIG report stated that they were still filled with material errors of "enormous magnitude." What happened to the $500 billion? Maybe those taxpayer dollars are being used right now to support Obama's shadow government and fund the new generation of radical left-wing socialist and communist candidates the Democrats are endorsing in congressional races and vote harvesting across the country.

As ugly as this all seems, perhaps the most illicit of the Obama administration scandals was Uranium One that resulted in the sale of 20 percent of all US uranium reserves to Russia and Mr. Putin by way of the sale of the Uranium One company. This was approved by former secretary of state Hillary Clinton and the Obama administration that resulted in an estimated $145 million from foreign investors finding its way back into the Clinton Foundation. All of those investors were linked to the Uranium One deal, including Canadian billionaire Frank Giustra, friend and benefactor of former president Clinton. Mr. John Podesta and his brother Tony also seem to be in the middle of many of the scandals. For background purposes,

John Podesta was Bill Clinton's White House chief of staff, joined the Obama administration in 2014 as senior counsel, and went on to become Hillary Clinton's presidential campaign manager.

While John was running Hillary Clinton's presidential campaign in 2016, the Podesta Group was paid to lobby for the sanctioned Russian Sberbank to have US sanctions lifted. Sberbank was the lead financial institution involved in the Uranium One transaction. Podesta's firm also represented Uranium One before the State Department in 2012 and 2015. According to Politico, the Podesta Group accepted $900,000 in payments from "pro-Russian Ukrainian politicians" for the purpose of conducting influence operations against Congress and federal agencies on behalf of the pro-Putin politicians. As part of the Obama/Clinton reset with Russia, Secretary Clinton traveled to Russia in March 2010 and met with Putin and President Medvedev, Putin's temporary stand-in. Soon thereafter, former president Bill Clinton traveled to Moscow and was paid $500,000 to "speak" by a Kremlin-backed bank, Sberbank, known to be the major promoter of Russia's energy giant Rosatom, that ended up with the controlling interest in Uranium One and control of 20 percent of US annual uranium production. Coincidence, conspiracy, or just plain old-fashioned democratic-style fraud and get rich quick corruption schemes? According to a Hill report, the FBI uncovered "substantial evidence that Russian nuclear industry officials were engaged in bribery, kickbacks, extortion and money laundering" and that millions of those dollars were routed to the Clinton Foundation.

It's also an interesting coincidence that the second largest Ukrainian energy company and natural gas producer Burisma had Hunter Biden on its board while that company was under investigation for corruption and money laundering. Obama's point man for relations with the Ukrainians was VP Joe Biden who threatened to withhold $1 billion in loans unless the prosecutor was fired and the investigation tanked, and Biden bragged about it. This was clearly the real quid pro quo and abuse of power that they conveniently projected onto President Trump. This democratic fraud needs to be further investigated. Keeping track of all the corruption and collusion with the Russians and Ukrainians that both the Clinton and Obama administrations were and still are engaged in is overwhelming.

The tragedy is that despite all the scandals, the greed, lust for power, abuse of public office, violation of the public trust, perjury, obstruction of justice, corruption, and deception to hide the truth, whatever it took, lies, cover-ups, contempt of Congress, destroying evidence, with no transparency, no accountability, there were no indictments issued in either administration. The moral of the story is that the rule of law doesn't apply to the corrupt and self-serving democratic career politicians, because they make the laws for the rest of us to follow and they are privileged and immune, or so they think.

"Evil will have its hour, but God will have his day" (Bishop Fulton J. Sheen).

*And now the farce continues, but does not end.* God was there with the midterm elections of 2014 to slow the socialist juggernaut and attacks on Christianity and America and again with the election of Donald Trump in 2016 to put an end to more than sixteen years of chaos and darkness, interrupted by only a short period of light when America renewed its faith in God and we came together to rebuild lives out of the ashes and rubble and sheer terror of 9/11. I remember the uplifting bumper stickers and lapel pins and the solemn ceremonies at Ground Zero and the Pentagon, where I attended the first of many ceremonies, honoring our brave and fallen. There were the heroes of United Flight 93 in Shanksville, Pennsylvania, where there was little more than an empty field, marking the graves of the heroes and passengers who prevented those terrorists from reaching their target. All of those sites are adorned with national memorials and rightly so, while most of us remember where we were on that fateful day.

Yet that day, like Pearl Harbor Day, is little more than a fading memory to most. A day, as FDR claimed, should "live in infamy" as one of history's greatest infamies, when America was attacked first by the aggressive imperialist Japanese Empire that led us into World War II and then sixty years later by a vanguard of Muslim extremists and terrorists. Yet I seriously doubt that either are ever mentioned in the schoolhouses of today where the progressive political correctness police have taken over our schools and curriculums to ensure such events and our nation's history are never addressed lest they injure the delicate mental health of one of the students. Yes, the Liberals have the answer—toss the wreaths and bow your head in a moment of silence if you must but never in the classroom and move on. Like everything else they do, they carried it to extremes with their left-wing media allies this year, denouncing and attacking President Trump before and after giving his 9/11 remembrance speech at the Pentagon.

Here's a quote I never thought I'd include in my book by a very prominent Democratic Liberal and former First Lady, "We are going to have to change our conversation. We're going to have to change our traditions, our history. We're going to have to move into a different place as a nation." Or in Hillary Clinton's words, "Laws have to be backed up with resources and political will. And deep-seated religious beliefs have to be changed" (April 23, 2015).

Changing our history? How do you change history, if not through lies and propaganda? Changing conversation with Liberals who are unwilling to compromise simply means the rest of us give up our values and principles and accept their godless secularist values. Of course they want to change our traditions and abandon our religious beliefs, and they want to eliminate them and replace them with their godless socialist agenda. As for changing our history, they are already well on their way to try to erase the sinful past and American exceptionalism by leveling the playing field, not only domestically by creating their mega socialist welfare state but also internationally to benefit their globalist allies and place America and move our nation—our national, political, economic, and military stature—more in line with other third-world socialist states. This was and remains the Obama model for America's future.

As such, it's not surprising that President Trump, with a far different vision of America's future and not one of the Washington rhinos or bourgeoisie career politicians, has been the victim of more negative, phony, and manufactured fake media coverage than any president in recent history from the moment he was elected. But don't be deceived. They just aren't after Donald Trump; they are after us and America and our liberties and freedoms. President Trump is only the guardian who stands in their way and must be eliminated. While their attacks have been unrelenting, he has stood his ground and remained faithful to the values, principles, and platform that he was elected on to Make America Great Again (MAGA) and to put America and American citizens first. This was the mandate that sixty-three million Americans supported, and I am certain that there will be many more supporting his reelection in 2020. This reality is driving the do-nothing Democrats insane.

While I wanted to end this chapter and this book on a conciliatory note and positive quote, I'm afraid my final message, or the rest of the story, is neither, largely because the Democrats and the media have now carried their farce and their bold-faced lies and deception to the extreme and are fanning the flames of sedition and violence as I write. I only wish that we could prosecute the media for maleficence, libel, slander, high crimes, and misdemeanors because there has been plenty of it.

First it was the illegal spying on candidate Trump and duly elected President Trump contrived by Obama and his minions in the IC, FBI, and DOJ with CIA Director Brennan at the pointy end of the spear with McCabe, Clapper, Comey, Strzok, Page, and other anti-Trumpers violating the law and Executive Order 12333, which we intelligence officers are trained to avoid violating under the threat of legal action by the DOJ. It was all a preplanned deception campaign to deflect and misdirect the real source of the collusion with the Clinton campaign onto President Trump whose victory shocked them all into a state of denial and disbelief and psychotic and irrational behavior from which they still suffer.

They perjured themselves before Congress and lied to a FISA court judge to get approval to spy on a political opponent and the president of the United States under false pretenses. The Democrats along with the conspirators and coconspirators called for an investigation into allegations by Brennan and his Trump-hating cronies of collusion with the Russians to influence the campaign in his favor. The Democrats, Brennan, and coconspirators called for a counterintelligence investigation of the allegations by an independent special counsel and a team of investigators, largely hostile to the president, including Strzok who had the lead until his anti-Trump e-mail exchanges with his mistress were discovered and he was dismissed. In both criminal collusion and obstruction of justice, Special Counsel former FBI director Bob Mueller, after twenty-three months and $25+ million in taxpayer dollars spent, there was no evidence of the obviously bogus allegations.

However, the formal impeachment inquiry based on the bogus and inaccurate anti-Trump whistleblower allegations concerning the president's July 25 phone conversation with Ukrainian president Zelensky is the latest and most desperate attempt to date by the Democrats to hijack the presidency of Donald Trump. The allegations are all part of a left-wing media campaign that has relied on hearsay, third- and fourth-hand accounts, and a whistleblower who was described by the IC inspector general who received the complaints as showing signs of political bias in favor of a rival candidate.

Trump offered no deal or even mentioned US aid or promised anything and there was no quid pro quo—release of US aid in return for a political favor—as claimed by the rabid left-wing media. Ukrainian president Zelensky himself denied that there was any such quid pro quo or pressure. The fact is that as VP Joe Biden and son Hunter were engaged with a Ukrainian energy company that was under investigation by the Ukrainians and paying Hunter $50,000 per month to sit on their board. Biden bragged about threatening the Ukrainian president at that time to withhold $1 billion in loan guarantees unless the prosecutor conducting the investigation was fired and he was based on that quid pro quo. President Trump had good reason and every right to ask President Zelensky to look into the matter as part of the counterintelligence investigation to determine the original source of Russian interference in the 2016 elections. I'm willing to bet that Obama and Biden as his point man were in on it, and therefore something had to be done to either preempt the investigation or discredit it. Preempt was the answer as it usually is with deceivers and deception.

It's also very revealing that Pelosi announced the official inquiry even before the transcript was released. The Pelosi and Schiff impeachment inquiry and Biden's public call for Trump's impeachment are the strongest indications that Biden and son Hunter are the guilty parties here, and this is another vain attempt to cover up Biden's abuse of power and his office to extort and bribe a foreign leader/government for personal gain.

What we have witnessed is another farce and charade most likely orchestrated by Alinsky disciples Obama and Clinton from the dark recesses of their shadow government or deep state. Remember the deceiver always has the advantage and can create or manufacture fake crises to hide the real, in this case to cover not only Biden's corruption while vice president but also the real source of the democratic-sponsored Russian-Ukrainian interference in the 2016 elections to support Hillary Clinton. It is also the most desperate and dangerous act of political deceit by the Democrats who are playing with fire along with a psychotic minority of radical left-wing Socialists to oust a democratically elected president who sixty-three million Americans voted for and many more support today.

The democrat's actions represent treason of the first order. This is also desperation beyond the pale by a Democrat Party and Democrats who know they can't win in 2020 but will do whatever it takes to sabotage the president and reclaim the White House. As a result, Pelosi and Schiff both seem to be suffering from psychopathologies or mental illness, perhaps a combination of high anxiety and narcissism, and Pelosi a case of psychosis and dementia. They and their coconspirators represent a clear and present danger to the security of the president of the United States, public safety, and our Constitutional rights and rule of law. They are all fanning the flames of hate and violence. All we're missing now is for Alinsky disciple Obama and his army of Bolsheviks, those with politically subversive and radical views, and antifa anarchists and communists to crawl out of their spider holes and hit the streets.

Pelosi is so self-absorbed and out of touch with reality that I believe she may actually have desires to move into the White House before the 2020 elections. While we are all still in the midst of this pandemic, with the president and his administration working tirelessly to deal with and end the crisis, the witch is already stirring up her toxic cauldron of lies and deceit with her toad, Adam Schiff, to launch yet another investigation to attempt to discredit the president and his administration's response to the coronavirus, which would also include Vice President Pence. Remember, as Speaker, she is second in the line of succession behind the Vice President to the presidency. This fact should scare the hell out of anyone, even the most ambivalent observer. You can be sure that this committee or panel will be given sweeping authority and will be just as partisan and painfully phony as her impeachment inquiry and investigation. It will also be as she and the Democrats intend an unnecessary distraction and hindrance to all attempting to get through the pandemic.

Pelosi, Schumer, and all entrenched self-serving career politicians like them have demonstrated and proven that they can't be trusted and constantly place their own and their special interests ahead of the common good. The tables need to be turned on the side of justice, and *the time to throw down the gauntlet is long past due.* The Republicans need to initiate an investigation of their own to publicly put Pelosi, Schiff, and Schumer on the firing line to expose their unscrupulous and deliberate attempts to hinder and undermine the president's efforts and all those tirelessly working to mitigate and eliminate the impact of the pandemic. Their malfeasance and misconduct during *a declared national emergency pose a direct threat to the health and welfare of the general public and justifies expulsion or censure.*

Has God abandoned us? No, God will never abandon us; only we can abandon God. With God, all things are possible. It is up to us to do God's will, to make the right choices, to do what's right, and to make sure that the democrats' totally partisan impeachment by the Democrat-controlled House will fail to serve the selfish intentions of the Democrats and will ultimately contribute to their defeat in the 2020 elections.

"I am the vine; you are the branches. Whoever remains in me and I in him will bear much fruit, because without me you can do nothing" (John 15: 5).

God knows that many have abandoned his ways and his flock, and that reason doesn't always rule the day. His only begotten Son subjected himself to the jealousy and hate of false witnesses to die on the cross in expiation of our sins and those of all humanity. Just as the Pharisees and scribes of his day crucified Jesus Christ, the Pharisees and scribes of our day bear false witness and attempt to "crucify" all those who might oppose them and their heretical godless secularism. Is it any wonder then that any president who dares to oppose them can be impeached for anything that the opposition might dream up or manufacture? All that was needed was the phony anti-Trump whistleblower along with a desperate demonic speaker of the House, with Alinsky disciples Hillary Clinton and Barack Obama acting behind the scenes as puppeteers to marshal a simple majority vote in the Democrat-controlled House to impeach. In this case, the unbridled hate and desperation by Democrats to do anything—whatever the cost or consequences to sabotage the president and his certain victory in 2020 with the support of the corrupt media propaganda machine that churns out lies, misinformation, and fake news daily on all matters about the president—provides an environment for the ideal kangaroo court of public passion and political deception and demagoguery to carry the day. By the way, for those uninformed, impeachment is pretty much standard operating procedures for obstructionist and subversive Democrats who have threatened or brought impeachment proceedings against five of the last six republican presidents.

Since President Eisenhower left office in 1961, President Ford is the only republican president the Democrats have not threatened to impeach. I think this says a lot more about the Democrats than it does about any of the presidents they have threatened to impeach. God is going to leave it up to us to do what is right and just and protect the president and prevent the princesses and princes of darkness from hijacking the presidency and our democratic republic.

> Be imitators of God as beloved children, and live in love as Christ loved us and handed himself over for us as a sacrificial offering to God for a fragrant aroma… Be sure of this, that no immoral or impure or greedy person, that is an idolater, has any inheritance in the kingdom of Christ and

of God. Let no one deceive you with empty arguments, for because of these things the wrath of God is coming upon the disobedient. So, do not be associated with them. For you were once in darkness, but now you are light in the Lord. Live as children of light. (Ephesians 4:32–5:8)

The left-wing media has long since abandoned the standards and ethics of journalism and is precisely why they are seen as purveyors of fake news and partisan liberal propaganda. As I've pointed out on several occasions, in any deception, the media provides the deceiver(s), the tyrants, the dictators, their primary conduit for propagating the lies, false narratives, and propaganda to prop up the deception. The media in this case is the enemy of the people, and I applauded President Trump when he first accused the mainstream left-wing media of promoting fake news, because that is precisely what they promote—hide and obscure the real, the truth, and show the fake.

I'm wrapping this chapter up with a prayer and psalm for our president and vice president, who are men of the light, men for the culture of life, disciples of Christ, and men of faith and conviction dedicated to do what is right for America and all Americans. The President has demonstrated and proven this throughout his presidency and has acted on and delivered on most of his campaign promises driving his opposition, the career and entrenched establishment politicians in the cesspool of Washington politics, insane. Regardless of whether you like his style or not, his penchant for telling it like it is and his bold-faced and sometimes shocking degree of honesty are exactly what America and Americans have needed to renew our faith and hope for the future.

Blessed the man who follows not the counsel of the wicked, nor walks in the way of sinners, nor sits in the company of the insolent, but delights in the Law of the Lord, and meditates on his Law day and night. He is like a tree planted near running water, that yields its fruit in due season, and whose leaves never fade. Whatever he does prospers. Not so the wicked, not so! They are like chaff which the wind drives away. For the Lord watches over the way of the Just, but the way of the wicked vanishes. (Psalm 1)

The truth will prevail, and the Democrats will suffer a well-deserved trouncing in the 2020 presidential and congressional elections. God's will be done. May God bless us all and protect us from contempt.

# ABOUT THE AUTHOR

Capt. John Pulsinelli, USN (ret), is a career intelligence officer with forty-six years' experience. He has served with the Office of Naval Intelligence, Defense Intelligence Agency, and Central Intelligence Agency. He served in Vietnam as a naval intelligence liaison officer and naval advisor in the Mekong Delta. In his many command and leadership assignments during his navy and civilian careers, he has served in the Far East and Europe and has been recognized for his analytic and operational acumen with numerous military and civilian awards. He was twice the recipient of the Defense Intelligence Exceptional Civilian Service Award, the highest award bestowed on a civilian intelligence officer.

He served as the senior intelligence representative to the Supreme Allied Commander Europe during Operations Desert Shield and Desert Storm (first Gulf War), a senior intelligence advisor to the Office of the Secretary of Defense, as National and Deputy National Intelligence officer for Warning (CIA headquarters), and Deputy Defense Intelligence officer for Global Trends and Projections (the Pentagon).

He spent his last thirteen years as an intelligence educator/consultant with CIA, teaching and training officers throughout the IC in deception planning and analysis, warning systems and analysis, and targeting. John has a bachelor's degree in political science from Purdue University and is a member of Pi Sigma Alpha, National Political Science Honorary. He has a master's degree in international relations from Purdue University and a master's degree in national security studies from Georgetown University. He also has a Master of Science degree in public policy from Salve Regina University. He is a graduate of both the US Naval War College, Newport, Rhode Island, and the NATO Defense College, Rome, Italy.

CPSIA information can be obtained
at www.ICGtesting.com
Printed in the USA
FSHW011450061020
74489FS